Comments from readers of this book...

"This book is truly fantastic (I rarely write reviews but thought this was the exception). All of the other books that I've seen for Excel spend too much time on explanation and not enough on practice. I don't have a lot of free time, so being able to learn quickly without a lot of extraneous reading has been invaluable. I'm a physician, so didn't have to use Excel until I started doing administrative work (I was completely new to the Excel program). I now can produce charts with beautiful graphics and trend data (everyone on my team is amazed -- even the data analysts)! Thank you again for such an amazing book."
– *A reader from the USA.*

"We first bought this book after upgrading to Excel 2010 and now get a copy for every new trainee accountant. It is structured in a bite size 'lesson' format that makes it easy to pick up and put down during the day. I describe it as a 'basic to intermediate' guide but even advanced users of Excel have been able to pick up tricks and tips."
– *A reader from the UK*

"The book is well laid out. It walks you through all the ins and outs of Excel and can have you producing professional looking spread sheets in no time at all. I very much recommend it."
– *A reader from Canada*

"Mike Smart continues to pave the way for excellence in teaching Microsoft Excel. His approach is well anchored in behavioural principles and consistently results in students learning more, faster. I would highly recommend the book and approach to all those interested in mastering the software and moving on to using it productively."
– *A reader from New York, USA*

"When asked if I could use Excel, I was one of those people who would always say, 'Sure, I use it every day.' Well, after using this book, I found out I really wasn't using Excel. I can now do things with Excel, that a couple of weeks ago, I didn't even know this program could do."
– *A reader from the USA*

"Mike Smart is the best teacher I've ever known. He is concise and precise, showing everything you need to know about this wonderful spread sheet. Even though English is not my mother tongue, I can understand every single word of it."
– *A reader from the USA*

"I bought this book because I consider myself a basic user of Excel and wanted to expand and improve my skills. I can honestly say that this is the best book I have ever bought and has helped me so much. Each section takes about an hour to complete and with only seven sections, this book can be completed very quickly. The layout is easy to follow and has some great tips, and various examples which are very easily downloadable from the website. I always thought I was fairly good on Excel but this book has taught me some stuff I never knew you could even do."
– *A reader from the UK*

"No one can present Excel training any better and more clearly than Mike Smart. I have tried many other books without the success in learning I had with this one. Excellent book."
– *A reader from Houston, Texas, USA*

"The book is well laid out. It walks you through all the ins and outs of Excel and can have you producing professional looking spread sheets in no time at all. I very much recommend it."
– *A reader from Canada.*

"This book has taught me so much about Excel that I did not know. I highly recommend this book. I was done with the entire book in 3 days."
– *A reader from the USA.*

"I purchased the book in the hopes of solidifying my basic skills for Excel 2010 and to hopefully learn a few new things. I was not disappointed. The book is VERY well written and the pictures are very informative in guiding you through the learning process. Whether you are a first time user of Excel or have been using it for some time, this training manual will help you."
– *A reader from Pasadena, Texas, USA.*

"Both my wife and I have been amazed by Mike's method and have confidence with Excel 2010. From total new user to confidence. Just buy the stuff and move forward."
– *A reader from Canada*

"This is the best study guide for learning or updating you Excel skills. I've attended two day training camps, used other books, audio tutorials and nothing can compare to this book. I highly recommend it. This book is the most comprehensive Microsoft Excel Learning program on the market."
- *A reader from the USA*

"The book lets you set your own pace as you proceed through the sessions dealing with different areas that build upon previous areas. Each session is made up of lessons that are laid out on two pages facing one another that make understanding the covered material very easy. Each lesson has an exercise that confirms your understanding. Great method of teaching!"
- *A reader from the USA*

"The Smart method is an excellent tutorial for both the neophyte and the experienced user of Excel 2010. Great online reference material. Well laid out, full of informational tips and tidbits, designed specifically to progressively build the necessary skills required to create a good, solid, workable spread sheet in this version of Excel."
- *A reader from the USA*

"Thorough. Great for the learner who needs to see it, not just read about it or listen to what should be done. I am much better and more confident in my work.
- *A reader from the USA"*

Who Is This Book For?

If you need good Excel skills for your work, or want to add Excel skills to your CV, you've found the right book.

If you've never used Excel 2010 before, this book will give you all of the skills you need to be thoroughly competent. By the end of the book your Excel skills will be better than most office workers with many years of experience.

This book is for Excel 2010 users who:

- Need to acquire essential Excel skills quickly.

- Have never used Excel before, or who have only basic Excel skills.

- Want to learn Excel skills from first principles.

- Are moving to Excel 2010 from an earlier version.

Use of this book as courseware

This book is also the official courseware for The Smart Method's Excel 2010 Essential Skills course.

Smart Method courses have been taken by a varied cross-section of the world's leading companies. We've had fantastic feedback from the vast number of professionals we've empowered with Excel skills.

This book is also suitable for use by other training organizations, teachers, schools and colleges to provide structured, objective-led, and highly effective classroom courses.

Learn Excel 2010 Essential Skills with The Smart Method

Mike Smart

Published by:

The Smart Method® Ltd
Burleigh Manor
Peel Road
Douglas, IOM
Great Britain
IM1 5EP

Tel: +44 (0)845 458 3282 Fax: +44 (0)845 458 3281

E-mail: info@ExcelCentral.com
Web: www.ExcelCentral.com (this book's dedicated web site)

FIRST EDITION

International Standard Book Number (ISBN10): 0-9554599-7-4
International Standard Book Number (ISBN13): 978-0-9554599-7-9

The Smart Method® is a registered trade mark of The Smart Method Ltd.

2 4 6 8 10 9 7 5 3

Contents

Session Two: Doing Useful Work with Excel   63

Session Three: Taking Your Skills to the Next Level   107

Session Four: Making Your Worksheets Look Professional   149

Session Five: Charts and Graphics   201

Session Six: Working With Multiple Worksheets and Workbooks 249

Session Seven: Printing Your Work 271

Index 303

Introduction

Welcome to *Learn Excel 2010 Essential Skills With The Smart Method®*. This book has been designed to enable students to master Excel 2010 by self-study. The book is equally useful as courseware in order to deliver courses using The Smart Method® teaching system.

Smart Method publications are continually evolving as we discover better ways of explaining or teaching the concepts presented.

Feedback

At The Smart Method® we love feedback – both positive and negative. If you have any suggestions for improvements to future versions of this book, or if you find content or typographical errors, the author would always love to hear from you via e-mail to:

feedback@ExcelCentral.com

Future editions will always incorporate your feedback so that there are never any known errors at time of publication.

If you have any difficulty understanding or completing a lesson, or if you feel that anything could have been more clearly explained, we'd also love to hear from you. We've made hundreds of detail improvements to our books based upon reader's feedback and continue to chase the impossible goal of 100% perfection!

Downloading the sample files

In order to use this book it is sometimes necessary to download sample files from the Internet. The sample files are available from:

http://www.ExcelCentral.com

Type the above URL into your web browser and you'll see the link to the sample files at the top of the home page.

Problem resolution

If you encounter any problem downloading or using the sample files please send an e-mail to:

feedback@ExcelCentral.com

We'll do everything possible to quickly resolve the problem.

Typographical Conventions Used In This Book

This guide consistently uses typographical conventions to differentiate parts of the text.

When you see this	Here's what it means
Click *Line Color* on the left-hand bar and then click *No line*.	Italics are used to refer to text that appears in a worksheet cell, an Excel dialog, on the Ribbon, or elsewhere within the Excel application. Italics may sometimes also be used for emphasis or distinction.
Click Home→Font→Underline.	Click on the Ribbon's *Home* tab and then look for the *Font* group. Click the *Underline* button within this group (that's the left-hand side of the button, not the drop-down arrow next to it). Don't worry if this doesn't make sense yet. We cover the Ribbon in depth in session one.
Click Home→Font→ Underline Drop Down→Double Underline.	Click on the Ribbon's *Home* tab and then look for the *Font* group. Click the drop-down arrow next to the Underline button (that's the right-hand side of the button) within this group and then choose *Double Underline* from the drop-down list.
Click: File→Options→ Advanced→General→ Edit Custom Lists→Import	This is a more involved example. 1. Click the File tab on the Ribbon, and then click the *Options* button towards the bottom of the left-hand pane. The *Excel Options* dialog appears. 2. Choose the *Advanced* list item in the left-hand pane and scroll down to the *General* group in the right-hand pane. 3. Click the *Edit Custom Lists…* button. Yet another new dialog pops up. 4. Click the *Import* button.
Type **European Sales** into the cell.	Whenever you are supposed to actually type something on the keyboard it is shown in bold faced text.
Press <Ctrl> + <Z>.	You should hold down the **Ctrl** key and then press the **Z** key.

Σ AutoSum ▾

When a lesson tells you to click a button, an image of the relevant button will often be shown either in the page margin or within the text itself.

note

In Excel 2007/2010 there are a possible 16,585 columns and 1,048,476 rows. This is a great improvement on earlier versions.

If you want to read through the book as quickly as possible, you don't have to read notes.

Notes usually expand a little on the information given in the lesson text.

important

Do not click the *Delete* button at this point as to do so would erase the entire table.

Whenever something can easily go wrong, or when the subject text is particularly important, you will see the *important* sidebar.

You should always read important sidebars.

tip

Moving between tabs using the keyboard

You can also use the <Ctrl>+<PgUp> and <Ctrl>+<PgDn> keyboard shortcuts to cycle through all of the tabs in your workbook.

Tips add to the lesson text by showing you shortcuts or time-saving techniques relevant to the lesson.

The bold text at the top of the tip box enables you to establish whether the tip is appropriate to your needs without reading all of the text.

In this example you may not be interested in keyboard shortcuts so do not need to read further.

anecdote

I ran an Excel course for a small company in London a couple of years ago...

Sometimes I add an anecdote gathered over the years from my Excel classes or from other areas of life.

If you simply want to learn Excel as quickly as possible you can ignore my anecdotes.

trivia

The feature that Excel uses to help you out with function calls first made an appearance in Visual Basic 5 back in 1996 and had the wonderful name: *IntelliSense*. The Excel...

Sometimes I indulge myself by adding a little piece of trivia in the context of the skill being taught.

Just like my anecdotes you can ignore these if you want to. They won't help you to learn Excel any better!

The World's Fastest Cars

When there is a sample file (or files) to accompany a lesson, the file name will be shown in a folder icon. You can download the lesson or file from: *www.ExcelCentral.com*. Detailed instructions are given in: *Lesson 1-4: Download the sample files and open/navigate a workbook.*

Putting The Smart Method to Work

Excel version and service pack

This edition was written using the original release version of *Microsoft Excel* running under the *Microsoft Windows 7 Service Pack 1* operating system. You'll discover how to confirm which versions your computer is running in: *Lesson 1-1: Start Excel and check your program version.*

If you are using an earlier or later operating system (for example Windows XP or Windows Vista) this book will be equally relevant, but you may notice small differences in the appearance of some of the screen grabs in the book. This will only occur when describing an operating system (rather than an Excel) feature.

This book is written purely for Excel 2010 and, due to huge changes in this version, will not be useful for earlier versions (97, 2000, 2002 and 2003). If you are using Excel 2007 you should either upgrade to Excel 2010 or purchase the earlier version of this book: *Learn Excel 2007 Essential Skills with The Smart Method.*

Sessions and lessons

The book is arranged into Sessions and Lessons. In a *Smart Method* course a Session would generally last for between sixty and ninety minutes. Each session would represent a continuous period of interactive instruction followed by a coffee break of ten or fifteen minutes.

When you use this book for self-instruction I'd recommend that you do the same. You'll learn better if you lock yourself away, switch off your telephone and complete the whole session without interruption. The memory process is associative, and we've ensured that each lesson within each session is very closely coupled (contextually) with the others. By learning the whole session in one sitting, you'll store all of that information in the same part of your memory and should find it easier to recall later.

The experience of being able to remember all of the words of a song as soon as somebody has got you "started" with the first line is an example of the memory's associative system of data storage.

We'd also highly recommend that you take a break between sessions and spend it relaxing rather than catching up on your e-mails. This gives your brain a little idle time to do some data sorting and storage!

Read the book from beginning to end

Many books consist of disassociated self-contained chapters, often all written by different authors. This approach works well for pure reference books (such as encyclopedias). The problem with this approach is that there's no concept of building knowledge upon assumed prior knowledge, so the text is either confusing or unduly verbose as instructions for the same skill are repeated in many parts of the book.

This book is more effective as a learning tool because it takes a holistic approach. You will learn Excel in the same way you would be taught during one of our *Smart Method* courses.

In our classroom courses it's often the case that a delegate turns up late. One golden rule is that we can't begin until everybody is present, as each hands-on lesson builds upon skills taught in the previous lesson.

I strongly recommend that you read the book from beginning to end in the order that it is written. Because of the unique presentational style, you'll hardly waste any time reading about things that you already know and even the most advanced Excel user will find some nugget of extremely useful information in every session.

How this book avoids wasting your time

> Nobody has things just as he would like them. The thing to do is to make a success with what material I have.
>
> *Dr. Frank Crane (1861–1928), American clergyman and journalist*

The only material available to me in teaching you Excel from a book is the written word and sample files. I'd rather have you sitting next to me in a classroom, but Frank Crane would have told me to stop complaining and use the tools I have in the most effective way.

Over the years I have read many hundreds of computer text books and most of my time was wasted. The big problem with most books is that I have to wade through thousands of words just to learn one important technique. If I don't read everything I might miss that one essential insight.

This book utilizes some of the tried and tested techniques developed after teaching vast numbers of people to learn Excel during many years of delivering *Smart Method* classroom courses.

As you'll see in this section, many presentational methods are used to help you to avoid reading about things you already know how to do, or things that are of little interest to you.

Why our classroom courses work so well

In *Smart Method* classroom courses we have a 100% success rate training delegates to *Essential Skills* level in one day (the subject matter of this book) and to *Expert* level in a further single day (the subject matter of our follow-on *Expert Skills* book).

One of the reasons we can teach so much in a single day is that we don't waste time teaching skills that the delegates already know. Class sizes are small (six maximum) and the instructor stands behind the delegates monitoring their screens. The instructor will say "Open the sample file *Sales* that you'll find in the *Samples* folder on the C drive". If everybody does this no time is wasted explaining how. If anybody has difficulty, more information is given until all delegates demonstrate success.

Another key to learning effectively is to only teach the best way to accomplish a task. For example, you can save a workbook by clicking the *Save* button on the *Quick Access Toolbar* or you can press the **<Ctrl>+<S>** keys on the keyboard. Because clicking the *Save* button is the easiest, fastest and most intuitive method we only teach this in the classroom. In the book we do mention the alternatives, but only in a sidebar.

How this book mimics our classroom technique

Here's a lesson step:

Note You can also use the **<Ctrl>+<S>** keyboard shortcut to save your work.	1 Save the workbook. When you are editing a workbook the changes you make are only held in the computer's memory. If there is a power cut or your computer crashes, you will lose any work that has been done since the last save. For this reason you should get into the habit of regularly saving your work. Click the *Save button* on the *Quick Access Toolbar* at the top left of the screen.

If you already know how to save a workbook read only the line: *Save the workbook* and just do it. Don't waste your time reading anything else.

Read the smaller print only when you don't already know how to do something.

If you're in a hurry to learn only the essentials, as fast as possible, don't bother with the sidebars either unless they are labeled **important**.

Read the sidebars only when you want to know everything and have the time and interest.

Avoiding repetition

2	Create a new worksheet and name it *January*.
	This was covered in: *Lesson 1-5: Save a workbook.*

A goal of this book (and our classroom courses) is not to waste your time by explaining any skill twice.

In a classroom course, a delegate will sometimes forget something that has already been covered earlier in the day. The instructor must then try to get the student to remember and drop little hints reminding them about how they completed the task earlier.

This isn't possible in a book, so I've made extensive use of cross references in the text pointing you back to the lesson in which the relevant skill was learned. The cross references also help when you use this book as a reference work but have forgotten the more basic skills needed to complete each step.

Use of American English

American English (rather than British English) spelling has been used throughout. This is because the Excel help system and screen elements all use American English spelling, making the use of British English confusing.

Examples of differences are the British English spelling: *Colour* and *Dialogue* as opposed to the American English spelling: *Color* and *Dialog*.

Because this book is used all over the world much care has been taken to avoid any country-specific terminology. In most of the English speaking world, apart from North America, the symbol # is referred to as the **hash sign**. I use the term *hash* throughout this book.

First page of a session

1/ The first page begins with a quotation, often from an era before the age of the computer, that is particularly pertinent to the session material. As well as being fun, this helps us to remember that all of the real-world problems we solve with technology have been around for a long time.

3/ The session objectives *formally* state the precise skills that you will learn in the session.

At the end of the session you should re-visit the objectives and not progress to the next session until you can honestly agree that you have achieved them.

In a *Smart Method* course we never progress to the next session until all delegates are completely confident that they have achieved the previous session's objectives.

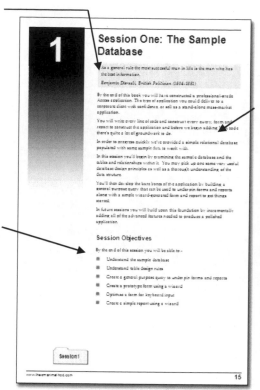

2/ In the next few paragraphs we *informally* summarise why the session is important and the benefits that you will get from completing it.

This is important because without motivation adults do not learn. For adults, learning is a means to an end and not an end in itself.

The aim of the introduction is to motivate your retention of the skills that will be taught in the following session by allowing you to preview the relevance of the material that will be presented. This may subconsciously put your brain into "must remember this" mode—assuming, of course, that the introduction convinces you that the skills will be useful to you!

Every lesson is presented on two facing pages

> Pray this day, on one side of one sheet of paper, explain how the Royal Navy is prepared to meet the coming conflict.
> *Winston Churchill, Letter to the Admiralty, Sep 1, 1939*

Winston Churchill was well aware of the power of brevity. The discipline of condensing thoughts into one side of a single sheet of A4 paper resulted in the efficient transfer of information.

A tenet of our teaching system is that every lesson is presented on *two* facing sheets of A4. We've had to double Churchill's rule as they didn't have to contend with screen grabs in 1939!

If we can't teach an essential concept in two pages of A4 we know that the subject matter needs to be broken into two smaller lessons.

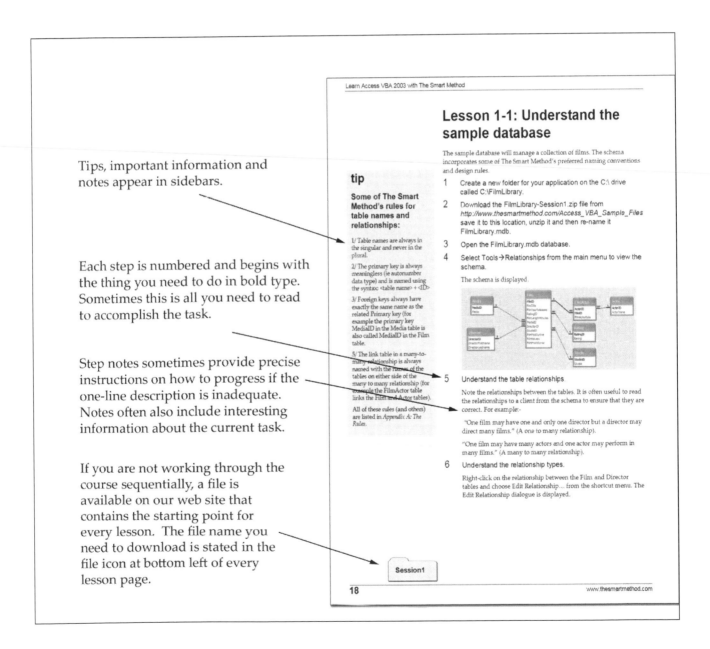

Tips, important information and notes appear in sidebars.

Each step is numbered and begins with the thing you need to do in bold type. Sometimes this is all you need to read to accomplish the task.

Step notes sometimes provide precise instructions on how to progress if the one-line description is inadequate. Notes often also include interesting information about the current task.

If you are not working through the course sequentially, a file is available on our web site that contains the starting point for every lesson. The file name you need to download is stated in the file icon at bottom left of every lesson page.

Learning by participation

> Tell me, and I will forget. Show me, and I may remember. Involve me, and I will understand.
>
> *Confucius (551-479 BC)*

Confucius would probably have agreed that the best way to teach IT skills is hands-on (actively) and not hands-off (passively). This is another of the principal tenets of The Smart Method® teaching system. Research has backed up the assertion that you will learn more material, learn more quickly, and understand more of what you learn, if you learn using active, rather than passive methods.

For this reason pure theory pages are kept to an absolute minimum with most theory woven into the hands-on sessions either within the text or in sidebars. This echoes the teaching method in Smart Method courses, where snippets of pertinent theory are woven into the lessons themselves so that interest and attention is maintained by hands-on involvement, but all necessary theory is still covered.

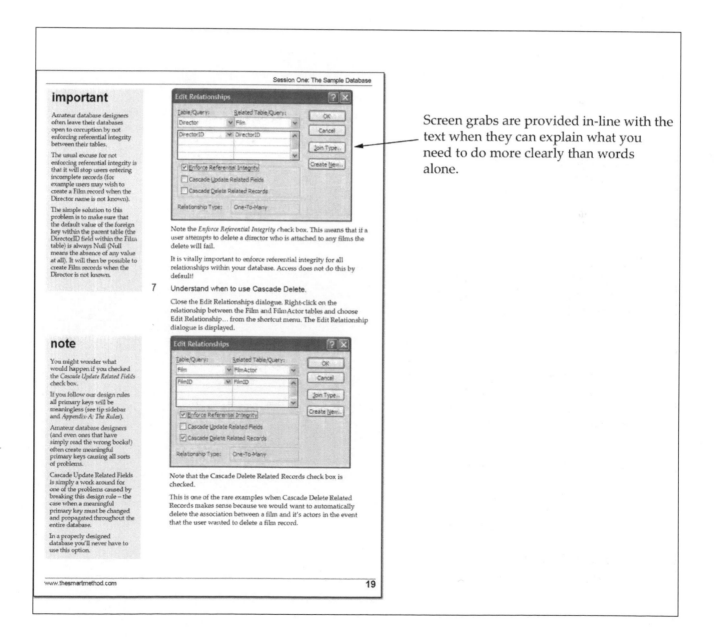

Screen grabs are provided in-line with the text when they can explain what you need to do more clearly than words alone.

Session One: Basic Skills

> A bad beginning makes a bad ending.
>
> *Euripides, Aegeus (484 BC - 406 BC).*

Even if you are a seasoned Excel user, I urge you to take Euripides' advice and complete this session. You'll fly through it if you already know most of the skills covered.

In my classes I often teach professionals who have used Excel for over ten years and they *always* get some nugget of fantastically useful information from this session.

In this session I teach you the absolute basics you need before you can start to do useful work with Excel 2010.

I don't assume that you have any previous exposure to Excel (in any version) so I have to include some very basic skills.

If you're moving to Excel 2010 from Excel 2003 or earlier this session will de-mystify Microsoft's new fluent user interface (Ribbon).

Session Objectives

By the end of this session you will be able to:

- Start Excel and check your program version
- Maximize, minimize, re-size, move and close the Excel window
- Understand the Application and Workbook windows
- Download the sample files and open/navigate a workbook
- Save a workbook
- Understand common file formats
- Pin a workbook and understand file organization
- View, move, add, rename, delete and navigate worksheet tabs
- Use the Versions feature to recover an unsaved Draft file
- Use the Versions feature to recover an earlier version of a workbook
- Use the Ribbon
- Understand Ribbon components
- Customize the Quick Access Toolbar and preview the printout
- Use the Mini Toolbar, Key Tips and keyboard shortcuts
- Understand views
- Use full screen view
- Use the help system

Lesson 1-1: Start Excel and check your program version

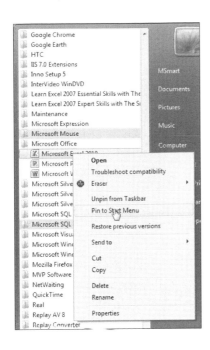

If you are using Windows XP, Windows Vista or Windows 8 (in desktop mode) the procedure is almost the same as described here using Windows 7. You should easily be able to figure out the differences between the earlier (or later) versions and Windows 7.

1 Click the *Windows Start Button* at the bottom left of your screen.

2 Click the *All Programs* item at the bottom of the pop-up menu.

3 Scroll down the list and click on the *Microsoft Office* item.

4 Pin *Microsoft Excel 2010* to the start menu.

You'll be using Excel a lot so it makes sense to pin it to the start menu. This will make it appear at the top of the list in future so you'll be able to start Excel with just two clicks.

To pin to the start menu, point to *Microsoft Excel 2010* in the list, right-click your mouse and then choose *Pin to Start Menu* from the shortcut menu.

5 Left-click Microsoft Excel 2010 to start the application.

Excel starts and is displayed on the screen:

6 Check the program version.

1. Click the *File* button ![File] at the top left of the screen.

   The Backstage View is displayed. Backstage View is a major new Excel 2010 feature and allows you to do a huge number of common tasks from one simple window.

2. Click the Help button ![Help] towards the bottom-left pane of the Backstage View window.

3. You'll see the Excel version number on the right-hand side of the dialog along with a link pointing to additional version information. In this example the Excel version is:

   About Microsoft Excel

   Version: 14.0.6112.5000 (32-bit)

   Additional Version and Copyright Information

   You may have a later version number than the one shown.

important

Service Packs

When a new product like Excel 2010 is first released it often has many bugs (as do all computer programs of any size).

Microsoft is very pro-active at fixing bugs that are found and always release these fixes free of charge as a service pack.

Service packs normally only fix bugs found in the original program, but Microsoft sometimes take things a little further by including new, or at least enhanced, features with their service packs.

I had many emails from readers of my earlier Excel 2007 books suggesting that some of the examples didn't work for them. In almost every case the problem was that they were using an out-of-date version of the application or the operating system. After updating the problems vanished.

For this reason it is important that you make sure your software is up to date.

note

What is the 64-bit version of Excel 2010?

Until recently all computers used 32-bit microprocessors. This type of microprocessor cannot easily work with more than about 4 Gigabytes of memory.

64-bit microprocessors can typically work with around 4 Petabytes of memory. If you've never heard of a Petabyte that's because it is enormous! A Petabyte is actually a million Gigabytes. It is currently believed that this is more memory than you could ever need (but we used to say that about 4 Gigabytes too)!

While 64-bit microprocessors have been around for a long time, it was only with the release of Windows 7 (available in both 32-bit and 64-bit versions) that 64-bit operating systems became widely used. It is estimated that nearly half of the Windows 7 computers in the world are now running the 64-bit version (myself included).

The problem with 64-bit computers is that most of the software in the world is 32-bit. In Windows 7 64-bit edition this isn't a problem, because it can run both 32 and 64 bit software.

Office 2010 is the first Office release that is available in both a 32-bit and a 64-bit version.

For most users, (even those with 64-bit Windows 7 or 8), Microsoft still recommend the use of their 32-bit Office version.

The 64-bit version is specifically recommended for Excel expert users who need to work with Excel spread sheets that are larger than 2 Gigabytes.

While the 64-bit version of Excel is still a rarity, there's no reason to believe that there will be any issues in using it to work with this book.

A very small number of users may find that they have the 64-bit rather than the 32-bit version of Excel 2010 (see sidebar).

4. Click on the *Additional Version and Copyright Information* link.

5. A dialog appears showing more information about your Excel version. In this example the Excel version is:

About Microsoft Excel
Microsoft® Excel® 2010 (14.0.6117.5003) SP1 MSO (14.0.6112.5000)

The important part is *SP1* denoting that you have service pack one installed. If this says *SP2, SP3* or an even larger number this is also fine. It simply means that Microsoft have fixed even more bugs in their product since this book was written (see sidebar facing page). If you do not see any reference to *SPn* you have an early, un-patched version of Excel 2010 and you should update it (the update is free) via the Internet.

7   Check the Operating System version.

Click the *System Info* button at the bottom of the *About Microsoft Excel* dialog (still displayed from the last step). The Operating System (OS) Name and Version will then be visible at the top right of the dialog:

Windows 7

Item	Value
OS Name	Microsoft Windows 7 Professional
Version	6.1.7601 Service Pack 1 Build 7601

Windows Vista

Item	Value
OS Name	Microsoft® Windows Vista™ Ultimate
Version	6.0.6001 Service Pack 1 Build 6001

Windows XP

Item	Value
OS Name	Microsoft Windows XP Professional
Version	5.1.2600 Service Pack 2 Build 2600

It doesn't matter if you have Vista running a later service pack than SP1, Windows XP running a later service pack than SP2 or Windows 7 running a later service pack than SP1.

If you're running Windows 7, Vista or Windows XP, any edition will suffice (it doesn't have to be the Ultimate or Professional edition). All current versions of Windows 8 (even without any service pack) are also reliable.

8   Click the close button on the top right corner of each dialog to return to the Excel screen.

Lesson 1-2: Maximize, minimize, re-size, move and close the Excel window

The great successful men of the world have used their imaginations, they think ahead and create their mental picture, and then go to work materializing that picture in all its details, filling in here, adding a little there, altering this a bit and that bit, but steadily building, steadily building.

Robert Collier, American motivational author, (1885-1950)

Now that Excel is open you are confronted with a dazzling array of buttons, switches and other artifacts.

For now let's explore the big picture by looking at how the Excel window can be sized and moved. The details will come later.

1 Understand the Maximize, Minimize and Restore Down buttons

At the top right corner of the Excel window you'll see three buttons.

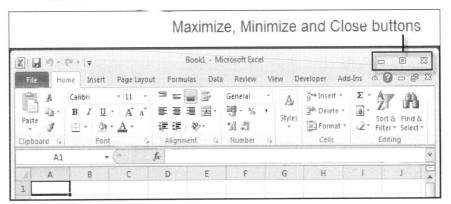

The buttons that you see will depend upon how the Excel window was left last time the application closed down. Normally the Excel screen is Maximized to fill the screeen and you'll see:

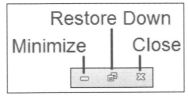

But if you had reduced the size of the Excel window so that it didn't fill the screen you'll see this instead:

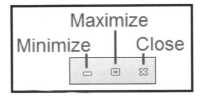

Try clicking the *Maximize, Minimize* and *Restore Down* buttons but be careful to click the group of three buttons at the very top of the

window and not the similar group beneath (we'll be visiting those in the next lesson).

- *Maximize* makes the Excel window completely fill the screen.
- *Minimize* reduces Excel to a button on the bottom task bar.

Click this button again to restore the window to its previous size.

- *Restore Down* makes the Excel window smaller allowing you to re-size the window.

2   Re-size the window

After clicking the *Restore Down* button you are able to re-size the window. Hover over either the side of the window, or a corner of the window, with your mouse cursor. The cursor shape will change to a double-headed arrow.

 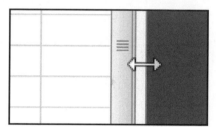

When you see either cursor shape, hold down the left mouse button and move the mouse (this is called *click and drag*) to re-size the window.

Clicking and dragging a corner allows you to change both the height and width of the window.

Clicking an edge allows you to change only one dimension.

3   Move the window.

Click and drag the Title Bar (the bar at the very top of the window) to move the Excel Application window around the screen.

4   Close Excel

There are two common ways to close down Excel and three lesser used methods (see sidebar). Most people will use one of the following methods:

Click on the *Close button* [×] at the top right of the Excel application window.

OR

Click on the *File button* [File] at the top left of the screen and then click on the *Exit* button [× Exit] at the bottom leftt of the dialog.

Lesson 1-3: Understand the Application and Workbook windows

Excel can be thought of as a frame (the Application window) containing one or more Workbook windows. Most of the time you will work with one Application window containing one Workbook window.

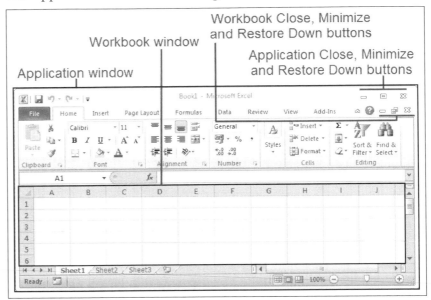

The screen grab above shows the normal way of working. The Workbook window is maximized within the Application window.

If the Workbook (that's the lower group of three buttons) *Restore Down* button is clicked the workbook window floats within the frame provided by the Application window.

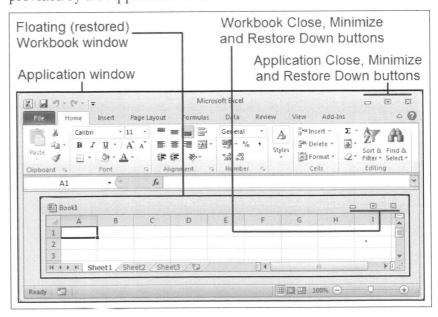

1   Close Excel down and re-start it again.

note

What's the point of having a floating workbook window?

At this stage in your journey of discovery, none at all.

You need to know how to maximize, minimize and restore down the workbook window because you might do it by accident and need to fix things up again.

In: *Lesson 2-2: Create a new workbook and view two workbooks at the same time,* you'll see how Excel is able to display more than one Workbook window within the Application window. This allows you to view two workbooks at the same time.

2   Click the Workbook's *Restore Down* button (that's the one in the lower group of three buttons).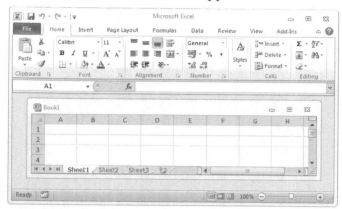

The workbook floats within the Application window:

Notice that the workbook's *Maximize, Minimize* and *Restore Down* buttons have now moved to the top right corner of the floating window.

3   Click the Workbook's *Maximize* button.

The workbook completely fills the Application window:

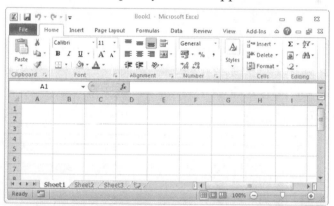

4   Understand the two close buttons.

You've probably noticed that there are two close buttons on screen. One for the Application window, and one for the Workbook window. How these buttons work is quite quirky.

Application close button

- Closes both the application and workbook windows when only one workbook is open, or no workbooks are open.
- Closes only the active workbook (that's the one that is currently on display), when more than one workbook is open.

Workbook close button

- Closes the workbook but always leave the application window open.

The Wealth of Nations

Lesson 1-4: Download the sample files and open/navigate a workbook

Excel uses the analogy of a book that has many pages. In Excel terminology we use the term: *Workbook* for the book and *Worksheet* for each of the pages. We'll be learning more about worksheets later in this session in: *Lesson 1-8: View, move, add, rename, delete and navigate worksheet tabs.*

1   Download the sample files (if you haven't already done so).

1.   Open your web browser and type in the URL:

   www.ExcelCentral.com

2.   Click the *Sample Files* link on the top left of the home page.

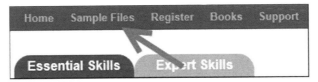

3.   Download the sample files for Excel 2010 Essential Skills.

   Note that we strongly recommend that you click the *Recommended Option* button to download the sample files as a self-extracting .EXE file. This avoids the *Protected View* issue discussed on the facing page sidebar.

2   Open the sample workbook: *The Wealth of Nations*.

1.   Open Excel and then click on the *File* button ![File] at the top left of the screen.

2.   Click: *Open* from the list on the left-hand side of the screen. Navigate to the folder containing the sample files and double click *The Wealth of Nations* to open the sample workbook.

   If you prefer to use the keyboard, another way to open a workbook is to hold down the **<Ctrl>** key and then press the **<O>** key.

3   Go to Cell ZZ3 using the Name box.

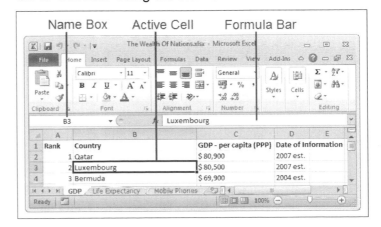

note

Protected View potential problem when downloading sample files

Protected view is a brand new security feature for Excel 2010. It is designed to protect you from potential viruses by treating all files downloaded from the Internet as being suspicious.

Any workbooks that are downloaded from the Internet, or are sent by e-mail attachment, will open in Protected View by default.

The user then has to click an *Enable Editing* button to use the file as normal:

Enable Editing

While some users may find it useful to be reminded about the origin of their files, others may find this feature annoying.

To avoid seeing this message whenever you open a sample file we recommend that you download using the recommended option:

Download Sample Files (Recommended Option)

This downloads the entire sample file set as a digitally signed self-extracting executable file.

We also offer an alternative method to download:

Download Sample Files (Zip file Option)

This has been provided because some companies (or anti-virus products) block the download of executable files.

If you download using the zip file option, you'll have to click the *Enable Editing* button every time you open a sample file.

Excel uses the letter of the column and the number of the row to identify cells. This is called the *cell address*. In the above example the cell address of the active cell is B3.

In Excel 2010 there are a little over a million rows and a little over sixteen thousand columns. You may wonder how it is possible to name all of these columns with only 26 letters in the alphabet.

When Excel runs out of letters it starts using two: X,Y,Z and then AA, AB, AC etc. But even two letters is not enough. When Excel reaches column ZZ it starts using three letters: ZX, ZY, ZZ and then AAA, AAB, AAC etc.

The currently selected cell is called the *Active Cell* and has a black line around it. The Active Cell's address is always displayed in the *Name Box* and its contents are displayed in the *Formula Bar*.

We can also use the Name Box to move to a specific cell.

To see this in action, type **ZZ3** into the *Name Box* and then press the **<Enter>** key. You are teleported to cell ZZ3:

ZZ3			fx				
	ZS	ZT	ZU	ZV	ZW	ZX	ZY	ZZ
1								
2								
3								
4								

4   Return to Cell A1 by pressing <Ctrl>+<Home>.

5   Go to the end of the worksheet by pressing <Ctrl>+<End>.

6   Use the Scroll Bars.

There are two scroll bars for Excel's workbook window.

The vertical scroll bar runs from top to bottom of the worksheet window and allows you to quickly move up and down the worksheet.

The horizontal scroll bar is at the bottom right hand side of the workbook window and allows you to move to the left and right in wide worksheets.

Here's how the scroll bars work:

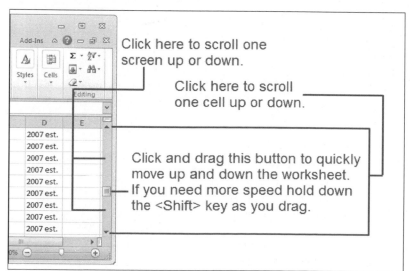

Lesson 1-5: Save a workbook

note

You can also use the **<Ctrl>+<S>** keyboard shortcut to save your work.

1 Open *The Wealth of Nations* from your sample files folder (if it isn't already open).

2 Save the workbook.

When you are editing a workbook, the changes you make are only held in the computer's memory. If there is a power cut or your computer crashes you will lose any work that has been done since the last save.

For this reason you should get into the habit of regularly saving your work.

Even though we haven't changed this worksheet, let's save it now by clicking the *Save* button on the *Quick Access Toolbar* at the top left of the screen.

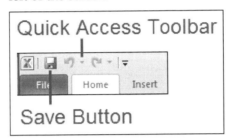

3 Save the workbook with a different name.

note

You can also use the **<F12>** key to instantly display the *Save As* dialog.

1. Click the *File* button. [File]

2. Click: *Save As* [Save As] in the left-hand list. If you are using Windows 7 the following dialog will appear. For Windows Vista and XP users it may be slightly different but you should easily be able to figure out the differences:

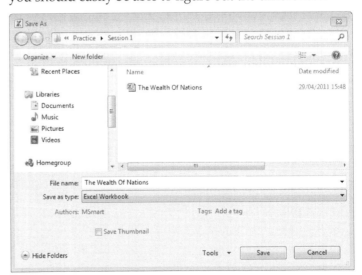

3. Click the drop-down arrow to the right of the *Save as type* drop-down list.

| File name: | The Wealth Of Nations | |
| Save as type: | Excel Workbook | |

The Wealth of Nations

4. A list appears showing a large number of different file types:

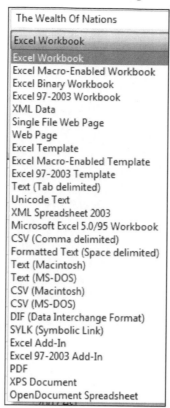

Most of the time you'll want to use the default format: *Excel Workbook* but there may be times when you'll need to save in one of the other formats.

You'll learn all about the most important formats (and when you should use them) in the next lesson: *Lesson 1-6: Understand common file* formats. For now we'll stay with the default: *Excel Workbook* format.

5. Click inside the *File name* box.

6. Type: **The Wealth of Nations Copy**.

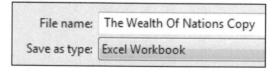

7. Click the *Save* button.

Notice that the name of the workbook in the title bar (at the top of the window) has now changed indicating that you are now viewing the new workbook that you have just saved.

Lesson 1-6: Understand common file formats

Excel Workbook
Excel Workbook
Excel Macro-Enabled Workbook
Excel Binary Workbook
Excel 97-2003 Workbook
XML Data
Single File Web Page
Web Page
Excel Template
Excel Macro-Enabled Template
Excel 97-2003 Template
Text (Tab delimited)
Unicode Text
XML Spreadsheet 2003
Microsoft Excel 5.0/95 Workbook
CSV (Comma delimited)
Formatted Text (Space delimited)
Text (Macintosh)
Text (MS-DOS)
CSV (Macintosh)
CSV (MS-DOS)
DIF (Data Interchange Format)
SYLK (Symbolic Link)
Excel Add-In
Excel 97-2003 Add-In
PDF
XPS Document
OpenDocument Spreadsheet

The Wealth of Nations

1   View the file formats supported by Excel.

1.   Click the *File button.* [File]

2.   Click *Save As* [Save As] in the left-hand list.

The *Save As* dialog appears.

3.   Click the drop-down arrow to the right of the *Save as type* list.

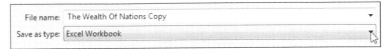

4.   A list appears showing all of the different file formats supported by Excel (see sidebar).

2   Understand the most important file formats.

Excel Workbook (the Open XML format)

Until very recently every program stored its information on the hard disk in a completely different way. These incompatible formats are called *binary formats*. This made it very difficult to write applications that could be used together.

All of this has changed with the new file format: *Office Open XML* that was first introduced in Excel 2007.

Microsoft have published exactly how this format works and given it away free to the world's developer community. This allows other programs to easily work with Excel workbook files. For example, Apple's iPhone already supports Office Open XML Email attachments.

Unfortunately the future has to co-exist with the past and there are a lot of people in the world using pre 2007 versions of Office (97, 2000, 2002 and 2003). If you save your files in the new Open XML format only people running Office 2007/2010 will be able to read them (but see the sidebar on the facing page for a potential solution to this problem).

Excel Macro Enabled Workbook

The Excel Macro Enabled Workbook is simply a workbook that has program code (called Macro code) embedded within it. Macros are beyond the scope of this book but are covered in the *Excel Expert Skills* book in this series.

Macro programming (also called VBA programming) is a vast subject of its own and is not useful to the vast majority of Excel users. The Smart Method® run comprehensive Excel VBA courses but they are usually only taken by scientists and engineers who need to add very advanced functionality to Excel.

Versions of Excel before Excel 2007 could potentially allow a workbook to infect your machine with a macro virus because all Excel files were capable of carrying macros. By separating the formats it is easier to avoid opening potentially infected files.

Excel 97-2003 Workbook

This is the old binary format that allows users with earlier versions of Excel to read your workbooks. Some features won't work in earlier versions and if you've used those in your workbook Excel will display a warning when you save telling you which features will be lost.

Excel Binary Workbook

An oddity in Excel 2007/2010 is a binary: *Excel Binary Workbook*. This is a binary alternative to Open XML but it can't be read by earlier versions of Excel. The only advantage of this format is that it loads and saves more quickly than Open XML.

PDF

If you need to send a worksheet to a user who does not own a copy of Excel you can save it in PDF (Portable Document Format). This format was invented by Adobe and is also sometimes called *Adobe Acrobat* or simply *Acrobat*.

Adobe provides a free reader program for PDF files and most users will already have this installed upon their computers. If you send a user a PDF file they will be able to read and print (but not change) the worksheet.

Other formats

As you can see, there are several other less commonly used formats supported by Excel 2010 but the above formats are the only ones you'll normally encounter.

The most important thing to remember is that, unless there's a good reason to use a different format, you should always save documents in the default *Excel Workbook* format.

note

How users of earlier office versions can read your OpenXML files

Microsoft has a free download: The Microsoft Office Compatibility Pack.

If users of Excel XP (2002) or 2003 install this they will be able to read and save Word, Excel and PowerPoint 2007/2010 files in the new OpenXML format.

If the user has Office 97 or Office 2000 they are out of luck. You'll have to save your files in the old 97-2003 format if you need to share them.

The Smart Method® still runs a dwindling number of Excel 2000 courses (mainly for clients in the banking and finance sector). These users have no solution to read an Open XML workbook other than to upgrade.

Of course, as the years pass this will become less of an issue.

Lesson 1-7: Pin a workbook and understand file organization

1   Close down and restart Excel.

2   Pin a workbook to the *Recent Workbooks* list.

    1.   Click the *File* button **File** at the top left of the screen.

    2.   Click the *Recent* button **Recent** in the left-hand list.

    3.   On the right hand side of the dialog is a list of all recently opened workbooks beginning with the most recent (probably the *Wealth of Nations Copy* workbook saved in: *Lesson 1-5: Save a workbook.*

    4.   Note that there is a pin icon 📌 next to each workbook name.

    5.   When you hover the mouse cursor over the pin a tooltip is displayed saying: *Pin this item to the list.*

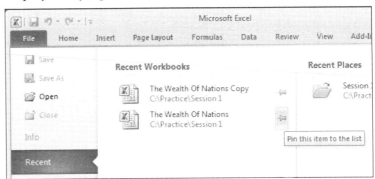

    6.   This can be a great time saver as it enables any workbook that you use a lot to always be at the top of the *Recent Workbooks* list. You won't have to waste time looking for it on the hard drive.

    7.   Click the pin icon. The item moves to the top of the list and the pin icon changes from unpinned 📌 to pinned. 📌

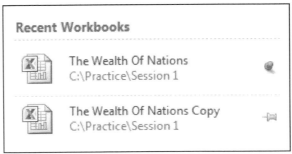

    8.   Click on *The Wealth of Nations* to open the workbook.

3   Understand file organization.

By default Excel saves all workbooks into your documents folder along with other Office documents (such as Word and PowerPoint files). This clearly is going to cause problems when you have a few hundred files.

Better to organize yourself from the start by setting up an orderly filing system.

I create a folder called *Excel* beneath the *Documents* folder (Windows Vista and Windows 7) or the *MyDocuments* folder (Windows XP). In this folder I create subfolders to store my work. You can see a screen grab of my Excel folder in the sidebar (of course, your needs will be different to mine).

Folders
- ◢ 📁 Excel
  - 📁 Accommodation
  - ▷ 📁 Accounts
  - 📁 Bank Reconciliations
  - 📁 Bank Statements
  - 📁 Book Publishing
  - ▷ 📁 Budgets
  - ▷ 📁 Business and employment
  - 📁 Cars and motorcycles
  - 📁 Credit Cards
  - ▷ 📁 Currency
  - 📁 Diet
  - 📁 Inflation Figures RPI RPIX
  - 📁 Insurance
  - 📁 Miscellaneous
  - ▷ 📁 Personal
  - 📁 Recipes
  - 📁 Stationery Orders
  - ▷ 📁 Taxes
  - ▷ 📁 Training
  - ▷ 📁 Travel
  - 📁 Tutorials
  - 📁 VBA Examples
  - 📁 Web Sites

4 Set the default file location.

If you take my advice and create an Excel folder you will waste a mouse click every time you open a file because Excel will take you to the *Documents* folder by default.

Here's how to reset the default file location to your new Excel folder:

1. Click the *File button* [File] at the top left of the screen.

2. Click the *Options* button [Options] towards the bottom of the left-hand list.

   The *Excel Options* dialog appears.

3. Choose the *Save* category from the left hand side of the dialog.

4. Change the default file location.

   You have to actually type in the default file location. Microsoft seem to have forgotten to add a browse button!

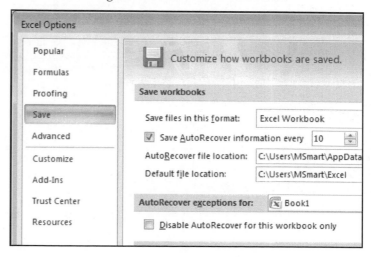

When you click File→Open in future you'll automatically be taken to your Excel folder ready to choose a category.

During the remainder of the book I'll explain the above sequence of choices like this:

Click: File→Options→Save, and then change the default file location.

This will save a lot of time and forests!

tip

Learning more about file organization

Microsoft have some great ideas about good file organization. You can read their recommendations at:

www.microsoft.com/atwork/manageinfo/files.mspx

note

Changing the default number of worksheets created in new workbooks

When you open a new workbook, three worksheets are automatically created called *Sheet1*, *Sheet2* and *Sheet3*.

Some users may prefer only one worksheet to be created.

Other users may prefer more than three worksheets to be created.

You can change the default number of worksheets created using this method:

1. Click:

File→Options→General→
When creating new workbooks
→Include this many sheets:

2. Enter the number of sheets required:

Lesson 1-8: View, move, add, rename, delete and navigate worksheet tabs

When you save an Excel file onto your hard disk, you are saving a single workbook containing one or more worksheets.

You can add as many worksheets as you like to a workbook.

There are two types of worksheet. Regular worksheets contain cells. Chart sheets, as you would expect, each contain a single chart. We'll be exploring charts in depth in: *Session Five: Charts and Graphics*.

1   Open *The Wealth of Nations* from your sample files folder (if it isn't already open).

2   Move between worksheets.

Look at the tabs on the bottom left corner of your screen. Notice that this sample workbook contains three worksheets: GDP, Life Expectancy and Mobile Phones. Click on each tab in turn to view the different worksheets.

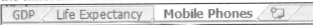

3   Add a new worksheet.

1.   Click the Insert Worksheet tab (the tiny tab next to Mobile Phones). A new tab appears named *Sheet1*.

2.   Double-click the *Sheet1* tab.

3.   Type the word **Population** followed by the **<Enter>** key.

4   Move a worksheet's tab.

1.   Click on the Population tab (you may have to do this twice).

2.   Hold the mouse button down and drag to the left. As you drag you'll notice an icon of a page and a black arrow telling you where the tab will be placed.

3.   Release the mouse button to move the tab to the location of your choice.

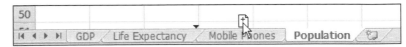

5   Understand the tab scroll buttons

Because this workbook only has four tabs, there's no need to use the tab scroll buttons (in fact, they won't work at all when all tabs are visible).

First
Previous
Next
Last

The Wealth of Nations

When there are more tabs than will fit on the screen the *tab scroll buttons* are used to move between tabs.

6   Move between worksheets using the keyboard.

You can move between worksheets using only the keyboard by pressing the **<Ctrl>+<PgUp>** and **<Ctrl>+<PgDn>** keyboard shortcuts to cycle through all of the tabs in your workbook.

7   Change tab colors.

Even though the colored tab feature was added in Excel 2003, most users have yet to discover that they can color code their tabs. Others will be very impressed if you color code yours!

1.   Right-click on any of the tabs and choose *Tab Color* from the shortcut menu.

2.   Choose any color.

It is best practice to choose a color from the top block of *Theme Colors* rather than one of the *Standard Colors*.

You'll discover why later, in: *Lesson 4-8: Understand themes* and in: *Lesson 4-10: Add color and gradient effects to cells (sidebar)*.

3.   Repeat for the other tabs on the worksheet.

8   Delete a worksheet.

Right click on the Population tab and select *Delete* from the shortcut menu.

9   Delete several worksheets at the same time.

1.   Hold down the **<Ctrl>** key.

2.   Click each tab you want to delete in turn. Don't select them all as it isn't possible to delete every worksheet in a workbook.

3.   Right click any of the selected tabs and select *Delete* from the shortcut menu.

Don't worry about the missing tabs. We're going to close the workbook without saving it so you won't overwrite the original workbook.

10   Close the workbook without saving it.

1.   Click File→Close.

A dialog is displayed:

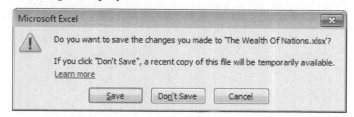

2.   Click *Don't Save* so that you don't over-write the workbook.

Because you haven't saved the workbook it will remain in its original state when you next open it.

Lesson 1-9: Use the Versions feature to recover an unsaved Draft file

note

The new versions feature isn't just for Excel

Microsoft has also included the Versions feature in Word and PowerPoint.

Now that you've learned how to use it in Excel you should be able to figure out the small differences in the way it is implemented in the other Office applications.

important

Version files don't stay around forever

As discussed in this lesson, *Draft* versions of unsaved files are kept for four days.

But what about the regular *Version* backups that Excel makes? Obviously Excel would fill up your hard drive with version files if it didn't have a mechanism for automatically deleting them.

Excel uses two rules when deciding whether version files are still useful.

1/ While you are in the current editing session, version files are **never** deleted (even if you save the current version).

2/ When you close the workbook **all version files are deleted** unless you close without saving. If you close without saving only the last version is retained (assuming that the *Keep the last autosaved version if I close without saving* option remains checked - see lesson).

Excel 2010 introduces a major new feature called *Versions*. The Versions feature is fantastically useful as it finally solves two common problems that are as old as computing itself:

- Your computer crashes, there's a power cut, or you close your work without saving… and then discover that you've lost all of your work since the last save.

- You delete parts of your workbook and then save, only to realize that you deleted something important before saving. Because saving over-writes the old version of the file you find that you've lost the deleted work forever.

Microsoft has finally figured out how to solve both problems. The Versions feature works like this:

1. Every so often Excel saves a backup of your workbook (called a *Version*) for you. The default time interval for these automatic backups is every 10 minutes (but you can change this to any interval). You'll see the Versions feature at work in the next lesson: *Lesson 1-10: Use the Versions feature to recover an earlier version of a workbook.*

2. If you create a brand new workbook and then close it without saving, Excel will still keep the last automatic backup it made. Excel calls this a *Draft* version. Draft versions are automatically deleted after four days. The Draft feature is the subject of this lesson.

You'll need a watch or clock with a seconds hand for this lesson.

1 **Set the AutoSave interval to one minute and check that AutoSave features are enabled.**

1. Click File→Options→Save.

2. Change the *Save AutoRecover information every* box to 1 minute.

3. Make sure that the other options are set in the same way as in this screen grab (the two check boxes will already be checked unless another user has changed them):

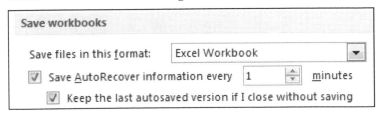

4. Click *OK* and check the time on your clock or watch. The first AutoSave will happen one minute from now!

5. Type the following into cells A1 and A2 , pressing the **<Enter>** key after each line:

note

The versions feature will not protect you from a hard drive failure

Every day, throughout the world, thousands of hard drives roll over and die. Carnegie Melon University conducted a study of 100,000 hard drives in 2007. They found that there's a probability of between 1 in 50 and 1 in 25 of your hard drive failing each year.

In an office of 100 workers that means that between two and four unlucky workers will suffer a hard drive failure every year.

To insure against drive failure you need to back up your data to a different hard drive (or other media).

If your computer is part of an office network the normal solution is to save your files on a shared network drive. The IT department are then responsible for backing this up every night.

For home users (or small companies that only have one computer) you should back up all of your data to an external hard drive (or a memory stick if your files are not very large).

When I write my books it would be a disaster even to lose one day's writing so I save my files onto a special drive called a RAID Array (Redundant Array of Independent Disks). This drive contains two hard drives and automatically writes my data to each drive (this is called mirroring). If one drive fails the other will still have my data.

RAID arrays are now quite cheap to buy so you should consider buying an external RAID drive if you consider a day of your time to be more valuable than the cost of a RAID drive.

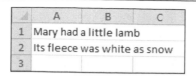

6. Wait for at least one minute. (After one minute Excel will automatically save your workbook).

7. After a little over a minute try to close the workbook. The following dialog will appear:

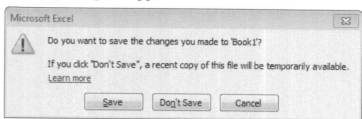

Excel is telling you that it has saved a draft copy of the workbook.

8. Click the *Don't Save* button.

Even though you told Excel not to save there's still a draft copy saved just in case you made a mistake and may need the file later.

2 Recover the draft document.

1. Open Excel.

2. Click File→Recent.

You will see a list of all documents that have been recently worked on.

3. Click: *Recover Unsaved Workbooks*.

4. You'll find this at the bottom right-hand corner of the screen.

5. A dialog appears showing the unsaved document that you were working on:

6. Double-click the document to open it.

The document is now shown on screen (even though you have never saved it).

7. Recover the unsaved file.

Click the *Save As* button in the yellow top information bar.

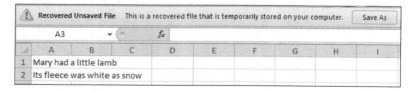

8. Save the file in your samples file folder with the name: **Mary**.

Lesson 1-10: Use the Versions feature to recover an earlier version of a workbook

Excel's ability to automatically backup your document at a chosen time interval was explored in the last lesson: *Lesson 1-9: Use the Versions feature to recover an unsaved Draft file.*

This lesson will show you how to view the automatic backups and to revert to an earlier version if you've messed up the current version.

You can even cut-and-paste sections from older versions of a workbook and paste them into the current version.

You'll need a watch or clock with a seconds hand for this lesson.

1   Open *Mary* from your sample files folder (if it isn't already open).

2   Cause Excel to automatically save a different version of the workbook.

In the last lesson: *Lesson 1-9: Use the Versions feature to recover an unsaved Draft file*, you set time interval for automatic backups to 1 minute. If you are not completing this course sequentially you will need to go back to this lesson and make sure that this setting is set to 1 minute.

Add the following text to the workbook pressing the **<Enter>** key after each line:

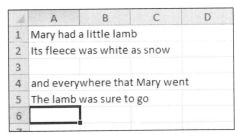

	A	B	C	D
1	Mary had a little lamb			
2	Its fleece was white as snow			
3				
4	and everywhere that Mary went			
5	The lamb was sure to go			
6				

Look at your watch or clock and wait for a little over one minute. Excel should have automatically backed up the workbook.

3   Make sure that Excel AutoSaved the file.

I've noticed that Excel sometimes takes as long as three minutes to AutoSave a file (even when the AutoSave interval is set to one minute). Here's how to check that it performed as it should:

1.   Click the *File button.*

You should see an AutoSave file version alongside the *Manage Versions* button.

Mary

2. If you don't see the AutoSave version, click the *Home* tab, wait another minute and then click the *File* tab again. Don't move on to the next step until it has appeared.

4   Further modify the file and then save it.

1. Add the following text to the workbook pressing the **<Enter>** key after each line:

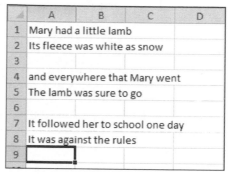

⬚	A	B	C	D
1	Mary had a little lamb			
2	Its fleece was white as snow			
3				
4	and everywhere that Mary went			
5	The lamb was sure to go			
6				
7	It followed her to school one day			
8	It was against the rules			
9				

2. Save the workbook.

5   View the earlier version that Excel automatically saved.

1. Click the *File button.*

2. Double-click the earlier AutoSaved version.

Versions

🗐 Today, 21:04 (autosave)

The earlier version opens in Excel.

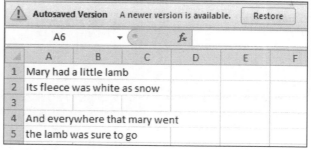

⚠	**Autosaved Version**	A newer version is available.		Restore		
	A6	▼	*fx*			
⬚	A	B	C	D	E	F
1	Mary had a little lamb					
2	Its fleece was white as snow					
3						
4	And everywhere that mary went					
5	the lamb was sure to go					

6   Replace the current version of the workbook with the earlier AutoSaved version.

1. Click the *Restore* button on the top yellow information bar.

Excel warns that you will over-write the current version of the workbook.

Microsoft Excel

⚠ You are about to overwrite the last saved version with the selected version.

OK   Cancel

2. Click OK.

7   Reset the AutoSave interval to 10 minutes.

You learned how to do this in: *Lesson 1-9: Use the Versions feature to recover an unsaved Draft file.*

note

Before Excel 2007/2010, all of Excel's best features were hidden underneath an arcane system of menu navigation. Many users didn't know that half of the features were there at all.

Because only the standard and formatting toolbars were visible on screen, users didn't explore the menu options and, instead, used only a tiny subset of Excel's features.

The Ribbon makes Excel seem overwhelming because all of those features are right in your face.

Hardly anybody in the workplace today understands every one of Excel's features. You'll be doing productive work with Excel by session two of this book while using a tiny subset of the full feature set. By the end of the book you'll be thoroughly competent working with Excel.

important

The Ribbon shows more if you have a wide screen

When I work with Excel I use a 22 inch widescreen monitor running at 1,680*1,050 pixels.

Excel uses the extra screen space to display extended descriptions of each feature on the Ribbon.

For example, the *Styles* pane on the *Home* Ribbon expands to show buttons for nine common cell styles allowing them to be applied with a single click rather than two clicks.

Lesson 1-11: Use the Ribbon

Look what they've done to my song, Ma
Look what they've done to my song
Well it's the only thing I could do half right
And it's turning out all wrong, Ma
Look what they've done to my song

Song lyric by Melanie (M. Safka)

The Ribbon causes huge frustration for seasoned Excel 97 to 2003 users as everything seems to be in the "wrong place". "Look what they've done to Excel" they cry. But it's a better, and an entirely new, way of working.

The sheer breadth of Excel features can seem overwhelming. This book will gently introduce all of the most important features, one at a time. By the end of the book you'll be really comfortable and productive with the Ribbon.

1 **Start Excel and open a new workbook.**

1. Click File→New.

    The *Templates* pane appears in the center of the screen:

2. Double-click the *Blank Workbook* icon to create a new blank workbook.

2 **Use Ribbon tabs.**

Each Ribbon tab has its own toolkit available to you. By far the most important tab is the *Home* tab which has buttons for all of the most common and useful features.

Click each tab in turn and view the buttons. The screen grab below has the *Insert* Tab selected. Don't worry if the buttons seem cryptic at the moment. Most of them will make complete sense by the end of this book. (And if you later go on to complete the *Expert Skills* course, Excel will have no mysteries left at all)!

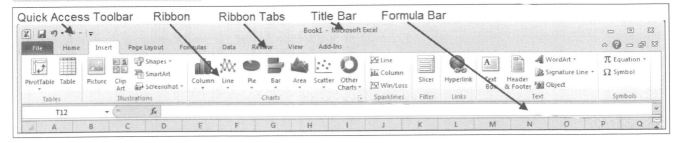

note

Contextual Tabs

Sometimes Excel will show you even more tabs. For example, when you select a picture, a *Picture Tools* tab group will magically appear containing a *Format* tab. This enables you to enhance the picture.

important

If your ribbon doesn't look like the illustrations in this book

Remember that the Ribbon will look different depending upon the size of your screen (see important sidebar on previous page) but all of the features should still be there.

Excel 2010 now includes a new future that allows you to customize the ribbon.

If another user has been playing with this feature they may have rendered Excel unusable!

If you suspect this to be the case you can put things back to normal like this:

1. Right-click the Ribbon.

2. Click *Customize the Ribbon…* from the shortcut menu.

3. Click Customizations→ Reset→ Reset all customizations.

4. Click Yes.

Customizing the Ribbon is covered in depth in the *Expert Skills* book in this series.

3   Type the word **Test** into any blank cell and then press the **<Enter>** key on the keyboard once.

Notice how the Active Cell moves to the cell beneath.

4   Make the cell with the word *Test* into the active cell.

Click once on the word *Test* or use the arrow keys on the keyboard to navigate back to the cell. Be very careful not to double-click otherwise Excel will think that you want to edit the cell.

5   Click the *Home* tab on the Ribbon and focus upon the Font panel (it's the second panel from the left). Try clicking each of the buttons and you will see the word *Test* change to reflect your choices.

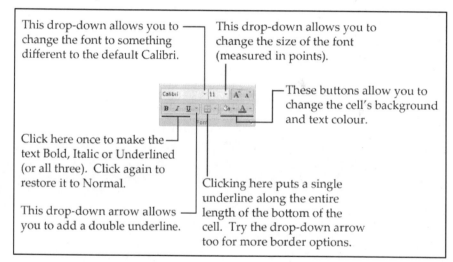

This drop-down allows you to change the font to something different to the default Calibri.

This drop-down allows you to change the size of the font (measured in points).

These buttons allow you to change the cell's background and text colour.

Click here once to make the text Bold, Italic or Underlined (or all three). Click again to restore it to Normal.

This drop-down arrow allows you to add a double underline.

Clicking here puts a single underline along the entire length of the bottom of the cell. Try the drop-down arrow too for more border options.

6   Minimize the Ribbon.

1. Double-click any of the ribbon tabs except the *File* tab (for example the *Home* tab or the *Insert* tab.

2. Notice how the Ribbon is now minimized order to save screen space (though the *Formula Bar* is still visible).

3. Click once on any tab except the *File* tab once more to bring the Ribbon back to full size. Note that the Ribbon has now appeared but the *Formula Bar* has disappeared.

4. Double-click on any tab except the *File* tab to bring back both the Ribbon and the *Formula Bar*.

7   Close Excel.

Click File→Exit.

Lesson 1-12: Understand Ribbon components

> The whole is more than the sum of its parts.
> *Aristotle, Greek critic, philosopher, physicist & zoologist*
> *(384 BC – 322 BC)*

The Ribbon is made up of several different artifacts.

Normal button

Simply executes a command when clicked. The Bold button on the Home tab is a good example.

Menu button

This type of button has a little down-arrow on it. It will display a Menu or Gallery when clicked.

Split button

This is the hardest button to understand because these buttons look almost the same as the *menu or gallery* button. When you hover the mouse cursor over a split button, the icon and drop-down arrow highlight seperately as different "buttons within a button".

A good example is the *underline* button on the Home toolbar.

Clicking the icon part of a split button (the U) will perform the default action of the button (in this case a single underline). Clicking the arrow part of the button will display a menu of further choices (in this case the choice between a single and double underline).

Check box

A little square box that you can click to switch an option on or off.

In this example (from the *Page Layout* Ribbon) you are able to switch the gridlines on and off for the screen display and/or the printout.

Command group

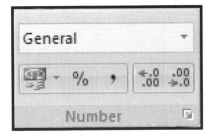

Similar actions are grouped into a cluster. For example, every component relating to numbers is clustered into the Number group.

Dialog launcher

Dialog launchers appear on the bottom right-hand corner of some command groups. Dialogs offer more choice than it is possible for the Ribbon to express graphically. Many of the dialog launchers will present a dialog that is identical to the old dialogs from Excel 2003.

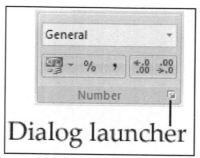

Drop down list

I often shorten this to simply "Drop Down" in this book. A drop down is a simple menu listing several choices.

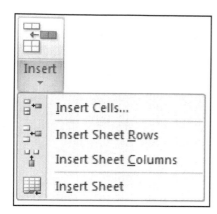

If you see an ellipsis (…) after a drop down list item this means that a dialog will be displayed after you click, offering further choices.

Drop down gallery

This is a little like a drop down list but has graphics to visually demonstrate the effect of each choice.

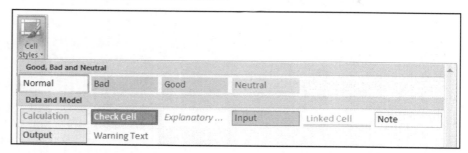

Rich menu

The rich menu is Microsoft's way of trying to coerce you into being brave enough to use a feature that you might not have understood in previous Excel versions. A sort of an "in your face" help system.

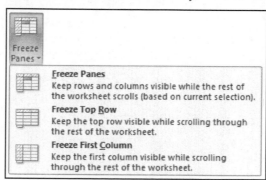

This rich menu can be found at:

View→Window→Freeze Panes

You'll find out what it is used for later in the book in: *Lesson 3-16: Freeze columns and rows.*

note

If you are moving from Excel 2003 you might wonder where all of the toolbars have gone?

In earlier versions of Excel (before 2007) it was possible to create as many of your own custom toolbars as you wanted.

In Excel 2007 and 2010 the new Ribbon based user interface (Microsoft calls this the *Fluent Interface)* has replaced the old Excel 2003 menus/toolbars interface.

But there's still one toolbar (the *Quick Access Toolbar*) that is fully customizable and is the subject of this lesson.

Excel 2010 also has a brand new feature that makes it possible to completely re-design the Ribbon itself. This feature is covered in depth in the *Expert Skills* book in this series.

Lesson 1-13: Customize the Quick Access Toolbar and preview the printout

You can customize the *Quick Access Toolbar* to suit your own special requirements. In this lesson we'll add some useful buttons to *the Quick Access Toolbar* to save a few clicks when accessing common commands.

The *Quick Access Toolbar* is one of the keys to being really productive with Excel 2010. This lesson will introduce you to the main features.

1 Open *The Wealth of Nations* from your sample folder, (if it isn't already open).

2 Preview how the *Life Expectancy* worksheet will look when printed.

1. Click the *Life Expectancy tab* at the bottom of the worksheet.

2. Click File→Print.

Backstage view displays a huge number of print-related features. A preview of how the page will look when printed is displayed on the right-hand side of the screen..

Notice there's a button to the bottom-left of the preview pane that allows you to cycle through each page:

3. Click the *Next Page* and *Previous Page* buttons to move through the print preview.

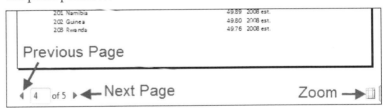

4. Use the *Zoom* button to magnify the page for a clearer view.

5. Click the *Home* tab on the Ribbon to exit *Backstage View* and return to the workbook.

3 Add a Print Preview button to the Quick Access Toolbar.

The quick *Print Preview* offered by the *Backstage View* is a very useful feature and you'll probably use it a lot. Every time you use it, however, it is going to take two clicks of the mouse. Wouldn't it be better if you could show a print preview with just one click?

1. Click the *Customize Quick Access Toolbar button* (see sidebar).

2. Click the *Print Preview and Print* item in the drop-down list.

A new button now appears on the Quick Access Toolbar. You are now able to Print Preview your work with a single click of the mouse.

Customize Quick Access Toolbar Button

The Wealth of Nations

note

Some amazing Excel features cannot be used at all without customizing the Quick Access Toolbar or the Ribbon!

One of my favourite features in Excel 2010 is its ability to read the workbook to me via its *Text to Voice* facility.

When I need to input lots of numbers from a sheet of paper and want to check them I get Excel to read them to me as I tick each off my list. This is much faster and nicer than continuously looking first at the screen, then at the paper, for each entry.

This feature is covered in depth in the *Expert Skills* book in this series.

You can't use this feature at all unless you either add some custom buttons to the Quick Access Toolbar or customize the Ribbon.

tip

The Quick Access Toolbar is one of the keys to being really productive with Excel 2010.

Always try to minimize the number of mouse clicks needed to do common tasks.

If you find yourself forever changing tabs to use a button, change two clicks into one by adding the button to the Quick Access Toolbar.

All of those extra clicks add up to a lot of time over the weeks and years.

4   Add a Font Color button to the Quick Access Toolbar.

The *More Commands...* option is available when you click the *Customize Quick Access Toolbar* button. This enables you to add any command in Excel to the toolbar. But there's an easier way!

1. Click the *Home tab* on the Ribbon (if it isn't already selected).

2. Right-click on the *Font Color* button  in the *Font Group*.

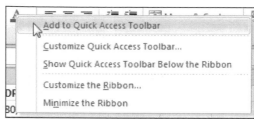

3. Click *Add to Quick Access Toolbar*.

A *Font Color* button is added to the Quick Access Toolbar.

5   Remove a button from the Quick Access Toolbar.

1. Right-click on the *Font Color* button you've just added to the Quick Access Toolbar.

2. Click *Remove from Quick Access Toolbar* on the shortcut menu.

6   Add separators to make heavily customized Quick Access toolbars more readable.

1. When you add many items to the Quick Access toolbar it is a good idea to use separators to split icons into logical groups.

2. Click the Customize Quick Access Toolbar button.

3. Click *More Commands...* on the shortcut menu.

4. Click the `<Separator>` item at the top of the *Commands* list.

5. Click the Add>> button.

6. Use the up and down buttons to move the separator to the required location.

7. Click the OK button.

Here's a screen grab of my own Quick Access Toolbar. I've added buttons for all of the features I use most often.

This means that I can always access these features with a single click of the mouse:

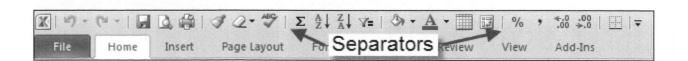

Lesson 1-14: Use the Mini Toolbar, Key Tips and keyboard shortcuts

note

Keyboard shortcuts are one of the secrets of maximizing productivity with Excel

Many years ago I took my mouse and stuck it to the back of my monitor with sticky tape.

For a whole day I struggled to work without it.

The first few hours weren't much fun but after that my work became faster and faster. It became a challenge to figure out how to do things without the mouse.

You will be far more productive if you can get into the same habit.

These days, there are some things that you simply need the mouse for, and some things that are genuinely faster (or easier) with the mouse. For most common tasks, however, there are keyboard shortcuts and (since the Excel 2007 release) things have become a lot easier with the new Key Tips feature.

The Wealth of Nations

1 Open the *Wealth of Nations* sample worksheet (if it isn't already open).

2 Select cell B2 (Qatar) on the GDP worksheet.

   1. Click on the *GDP* tab.

   2. Click on cell B2 (Qatar).

     Make sure that you only click once otherwise Excel will think that you are trying to edit the cell.

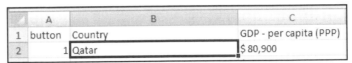

3 Make cell B2 (Qatar) bold, italicized and underlined.

   1. Click Home→Font→Bold.

   2. Click Home→Font→Italic.

   3. Click Home→Font→Underline.

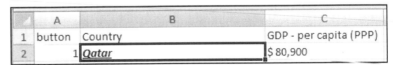

4 Display Key Tips.

Hold down the **<Alt>** key on the keyboard.

Notice how Key Tips are now displayed on the Ribbon and the Quick Access Toolbar:

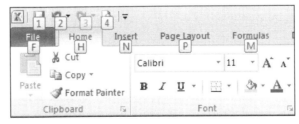

5 Use the Key Tips to show a print preview using only the keyboard.

The key tips reveal the key you need to press to simulate clicking any of the Ribbon and Quick Access Toolbar icons.

Hold down the **<Alt>** key and press the relevant number to show a print preview (in the above example this is 4).

NB: Your toolbar, and the number you need to press, may look different to the screen grab above. Note that the print preview button will not be on the Quick Access Toolbar unless you added it during: *Lesson 1-13: Customize the Quick Access Toolbar and preview the printout.*

6 Click the Home tab to leave the Backstage View and return to the worksheet.

7 Use the mouse to select the text *Qatar* in cell B2.

1. Double-click the cell containing the text.

2. You'll see the cursor flashing in the cell.

3. Position the cursor just after the word Qatar and hold down the left mouse button.

4. Drag the mouse across the complete word until it is highlighted like this:

5. Release the mouse button.

8 Observe the *Mini Toolbar*.

1. Hover the mouse cursor over the selected text and move it slightly upwards. You should see a "ghost" image of the Mini Toolbar just above the cell:

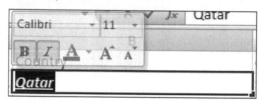

2. Move the mouse cursor up and over the Mini Toolbar. The Mini toolbar will then light up and become solid and more visible.

9 Use the Mini Toolbar to restore the text to non-bold and non-italic.

Click on the Bold **B** and Italic *I* buttons to remove the bold and italic attributes from the text.

Qatar

10 Show a bigger Mini Toolbar with a right-click.

Right-click on *Bermuda* (Cell B4). Notice that, as well as the shortcut menu (see sidebar), you now get an even better Mini Toolbar with a few extra buttons.

11 Remove the underline from Qatar using a shortcut key.

1. Click on Qatar again (cell B2).

2. Press the **<Ctrl>+<U>** keys on the keyboard to remove the underline.

But how can you remember cryptic keyboard shortcuts like <Ctrl>+<U>? Fortunately you don't have to. Hover the mouse over the underline button **U** (on the Home tab of the Ribbon) and you'll see the keyboard shortcut listed in the tooltip.

Lesson 1-15: Understand views

Views provide different ways to look at your worksheet.

Excel 2010 has three main views. They are:-

View	Icon	What it is used for
Normal		This is the view you've been using until now. It's the view most users use all of the time when they are working with Excel.
Page Layout		This is a fantastic new view introduced in Excel 2007. It allows you to see (almost) exactly what the printout will look like. Unlike running a Print Preview you are able to edit cells just as you can in Normal view.
Page Break Preview		A page break is when the printer advances onto a new sheet of paper. We'll use this view in: *Lesson 7-5: Insert, delete and preview page breaks* to make sure that the page breaks in the right place.

1   Open the *Wealth of Nations* sample worksheet (if it isn't already open).

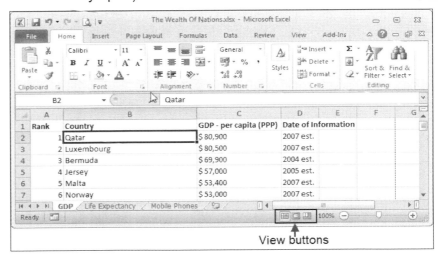

You can change views in two ways:

1. By clicking one of the View buttons at the bottom of the window (see above).

2. By clicking one of the buttons in the *Workbook Views* group on the Ribbon's *View* tab (see below).

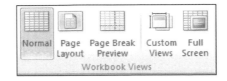

The Wealth of Nations

2 Click on the GDP tab and then select *Page Layout* view.

	A	B	C
21	20	British Virgin Islands	$ 38,500
22	21	Austria	$ 38,400
23	22	Canada	$ 38,400
24	23	Gibraltar	$ 38,200
25	24	Denmark	$ 37,400
26	25	United Arab Emirates	$ 37,300

The worksheet is displayed in *Page Layout* view. You are able to see (almost) exactly what will be printed. Headers, footers and margins are all shown.

You are able to edit the worksheet.

You may wonder why we don't use *Page Layout* view as the default when editing worksheets. While some users may prefer to do this, most will want to see the maximum amount of data possible on screen and so will prefer the *Normal* view.

3 Select *Page Break Preview* view.

The worksheet is displayed in *Page Break Preview* view (you may also see a help dialog first).

This view shows each page with a watermark to indicate which sheet of paper it will be printed on:

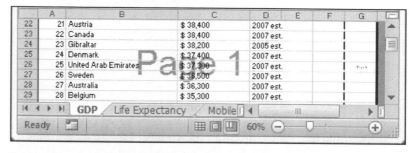

It also shows the break between each page as a dotted line:

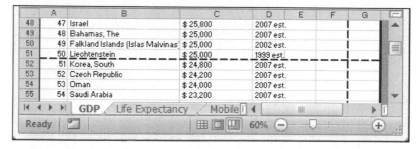

It is possible to click and drag the dotted line to change the place where the page breaks.

This will be covered in depth in: *Lesson 7-6: Adjust page breaks using Page Break Preview*.

Lesson 1-16: Use full screen view

1   Open the *Wealth of Nations* from your sample files folder (if it isn't already open) and click the *Life Expectancy* tab.

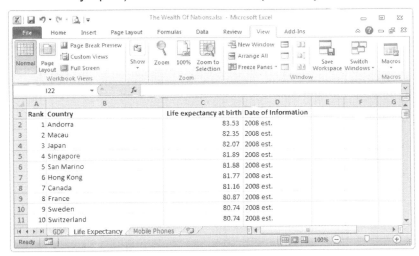

Notice that the Ribbon, Formula Bar and Status Bar are all taking up space that could be used to display information. In the example above only the first ten rows are visible.

1   Double-click on any of the Ribbon tabs to hide the Ribbon.

You learned to do this in: *Lesson 1-11: Use the Ribbon.*

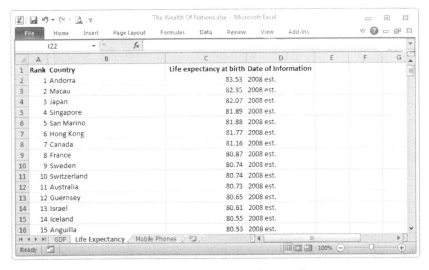

With the Ribbon hidden things are a little better. Sixteen rows are now visible. Perhaps you may need to view even more. This is what *Full Screen View* is for.

2   Click View→Workbook Views→Full Screen.

The Wealth of Nations

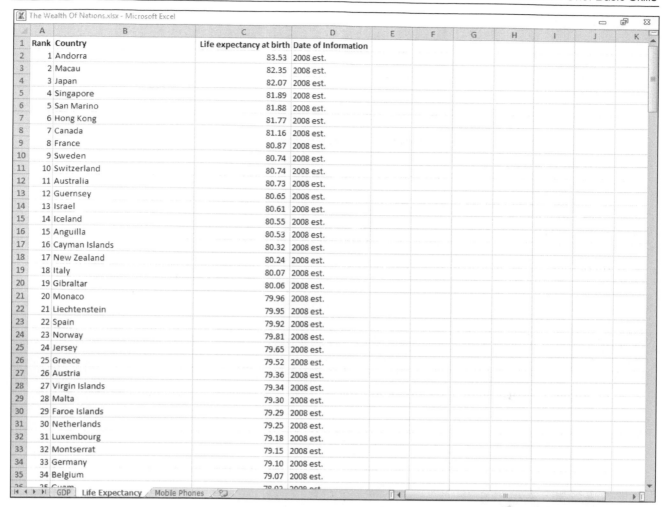

	A	B	C	D	E	F	G	H	I	J	K
1	Rank	Country	Life expectancy at birth	Date of Information							
2	1	Andorra	83.53	2008 est.							
3	2	Macau	82.35	2008 est.							
4	3	Japan	82.07	2008 est.							
5	4	Singapore	81.89	2008 est.							
6	5	San Marino	81.88	2008 est.							
7	6	Hong Kong	81.77	2008 est.							
8	7	Canada	81.16	2008 est.							
9	8	France	80.87	2008 est.							
10	9	Sweden	80.74	2008 est.							
11	10	Switzerland	80.74	2008 est.							
12	11	Australia	80.73	2008 est.							
13	12	Guernsey	80.65	2008 est.							
14	13	Israel	80.61	2008 est.							
15	14	Iceland	80.55	2008 est.							
16	15	Anguilla	80.53	2008 est.							
17	16	Cayman Islands	80.32	2008 est.							
18	17	New Zealand	80.24	2008 est.							
19	18	Italy	80.07	2008 est.							
20	19	Gibraltar	80.06	2008 est.							
21	20	Monaco	79.96	2008 est.							
22	21	Liechtenstein	79.95	2008 est.							
23	22	Spain	79.92	2008 est.							
24	23	Norway	79.81	2008 est.							
25	24	Jersey	79.65	2008 est.							
26	25	Greece	79.52	2008 est.							
27	26	Austria	79.36	2008 est.							
28	27	Virgin Islands	79.34	2008 est.							
29	28	Malta	79.30	2008 est.							
30	29	Faroe Islands	79.29	2008 est.							
31	30	Netherlands	79.25	2008 est.							
32	31	Luxembourg	79.18	2008 est.							
33	32	Montserrat	79.15	2008 est.							
34	33	Germany	79.10	2008 est.							
35	34	Belgium	79.07	2008 est.							

GDP | Life Expectancy | Mobile Phones

Note that the Quick Access Toolbar, the Ribbon, the Formula Bar and the Status Bar have all vanished. On the above example shown at 1,024*768 screen resolution 35 rows are visible.

On my own 22 inch monitor running at 1,680*1,050 pixels in portrait mode I can view 81 rows of information on one screen.

3 Switch back to *Normal* view.

To return to *Normal* view either:

Press the **<Esc>** key on the keyboard.

OR

Right click in any cell and then click *Close Full Screen*.

4 Double-click on any of the Ribbon tabs to bring back the Ribbon.

You learned to do this in: *Lesson 1-11: Use the Ribbon.*

Lesson 1-17: Use the help system

1   Click the Help button 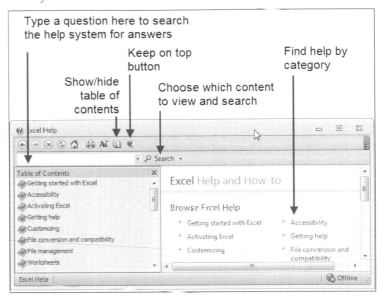 at the top right of your screen.

> If you are connected to the Internet click the: *Show me offline help from my computer* link when the Help system starts.
>
> If your screen doesn't look like the grab below, click the *show/hide table of contents* button.

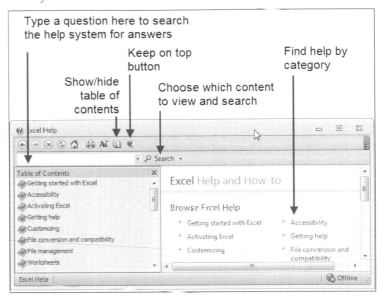

Type a question here to search the help system for answers

Keep on top button

Find help by category

Show/hide table of contents

Choose which content to view and search

Tip

The *Keep On Top* button

When this button is pinned in like this: 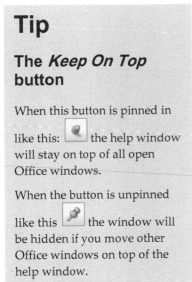 the help window will stay on top of all open Office windows.

When the button is unpinned like this 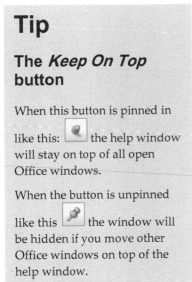 the window will be hidden if you move other Office windows on top of the help window.

Note that this is only the case with Microsoft Office windows and not with windows from other applications.

2   Type **how do I save a file** into the search box followed by the **<Enter>** key.

> The help system provides many potential answers to the question:

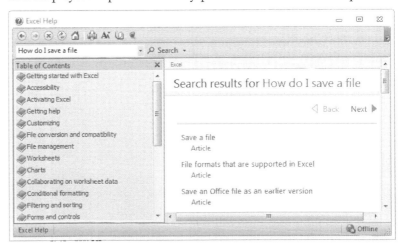

3   Click on the most likely answer to read the help topic.

> Step by step instructions are displayed showing how to save a file.

4   Find help by category.

> Let's do the same thing now using the *Category* pane. The *Category* pane is a little like a web page. You find the answer to your question by navigating a series of hyperlinks.

1. Close down the help system and re-start it.

2. Look at all of the categories and decide which is most relevant. See if you can find a help topic for saving a file by navigating the hyperlinks.

   On my system I got there by clicking: Printing→Save a File. (Perhaps this wasn't the most logical place for Microsoft to have placed it)! By the time you read this book the help system may have been updated and your links may differ.

5   Choosing which content to search.

Excel is a huge application and just one help reference wouldn't be enough. As well as the help files stored on your hard disk you can also search a perpetually updating help resource on-line at Microsoft via the Internet.

Click the drop-down arrow next to the *Search* button at the top of the Help dialog.

The Search drop-down menu appears:

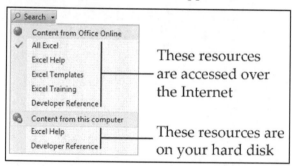

The *Developer Reference* contains topics only of interest to programmers who understand VBA macro code. This is a very advanced subject (the relationship between VBA code and macros is covered in the *Expert Skills* book in this series).

6   Get help directly from the Ribbon.

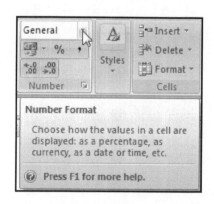

1. Click the *Home tab* on the Ribbon and hover the mouse cursor over the drop down arrow to the right of the word *General* in the *Number* group.

   If you keep the mouse still, after a short delay a screen tip pops up providing a short description of what the drop-down list is for and also advising that you can obtain more help by pressing the <F1> key on your keyboard.

2. Press the <F1> button (at the top left of your keyboard) to obtain help about topics relevant to this control.

7   Obtain help directly from a dialog.

1. Click File→Save As.

   At the top right corner of the *Save As* dialog there is a help button ![icon] (if you are using Windows Vista or Windows 7).

2. Click the icon for detailed help about the *Save As* dialog.

Session 1: Exercise

In this exercise you'll try to remember the name of each of the Excel screen elements. The answers are on the next page so you might want to recap by turning the page for a little revision before you start.

Keep trying until you are able to name each of the screen elements from memory. We'll be using this terminology during the remainder of the book so it's important that you can correctly identify each element.

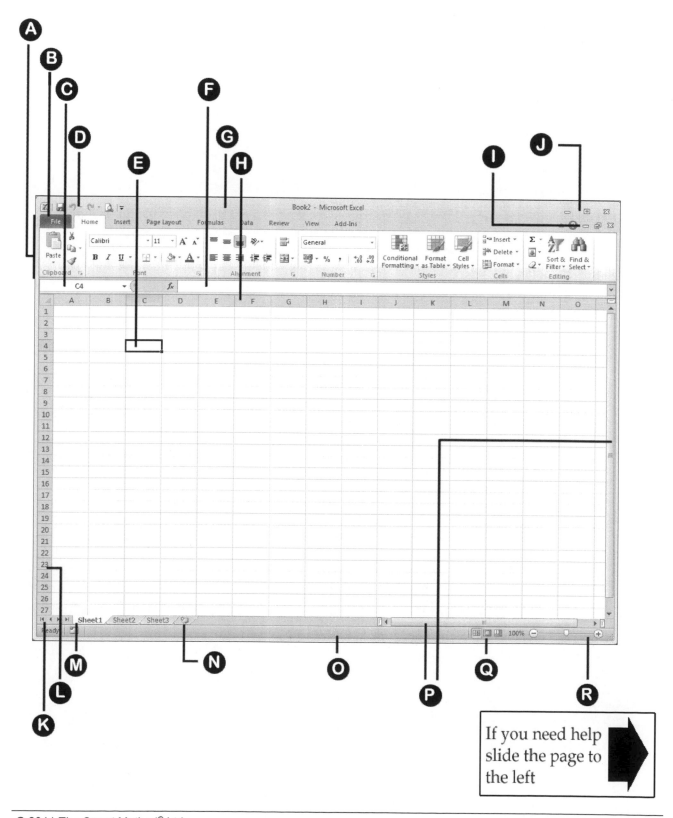

If you need help slide the page to the left

Session 1: Exercise answers

Ribbon

File button (this opens the Backstage View)

Name Box   Formula Bar   Minimize, Maximize
                                        and Close buttons:
Quick Access   *For Excel application*
Toolbar   Title bar   *For this worksheet*
Active Cell   Column Header

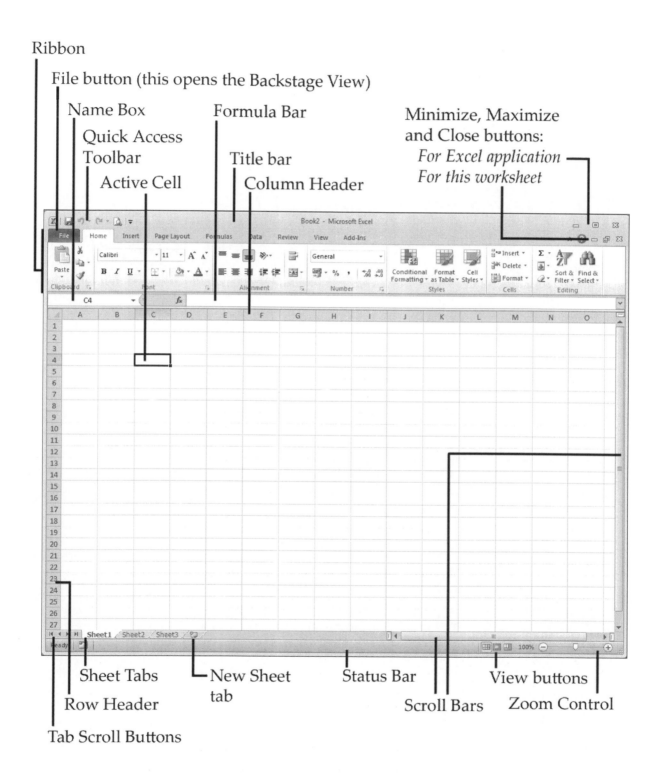

Sheet Tabs   New Sheet   Status Bar   View buttons
                  tab
Row Header   Zoom Control
                                   Scroll Bars

Tab Scroll Buttons

Session Two: Doing Useful Work with Excel

> Only those who have the patience to do simple things perfectly ever acquire the skill to do difficult things easily.
>
> *Unknown author*

Now that you've mastered the basics you are ready to do really useful work with this amazing tool. In this session you will learn to use all of Excel's basic features properly. This will put you way ahead of anybody that hasn't been formally trained in Excel best practice. You'll be doing simple things, but you'll be doing them perfectly!

Even after years of daily use many users are unable to properly use Excel's fundamental features. They often reach their goal, but get there in a very inefficient way simply because they were never taught how to do things correctly. By the end of this session you'll be astonished with how well you are working with Excel. What originally seemed like a baffling array of little colored buttons will suddenly all begin to make sense.

Session Objectives

By the end of this session you will be able to:

- Enter text and numbers into a worksheet
- Create a new workbook and view two workbooks at the same time
- Use AutoSum to quickly calculate totals
- Select a range of cells and understand Smart Tags
- Enter data into a range and copy data across a range
- Select adjacent and non-adjacent rows and columns
- Select non-contiguous cell ranges and view summary information
- Re-size rows and columns
- AutoSelect a range of cells
- Use AutoSum to sum a non-contiguous range
- Use AutoSum to quickly calculate averages
- Create your own formulas
- Create functions using Formula AutoComplete
- Use AutoFill for text and numeric series
- Use AutoFill to adjust formulas
- Use AutoFill Options
- Speed up your AutoFills and create a custom fill series
- Use the zoom control
- Print out a worksheet

Lesson 2-1: Enter text and numbers into a worksheet

Excel beginners tend to reach for the mouse far too often. One of the keys to productivity with Excel is to avoid using the mouse when entering data. In this lesson we'll quickly populate a worksheet without using the mouse at all.

1   Open the Sample file: *First Quarter Sales and Profit.*

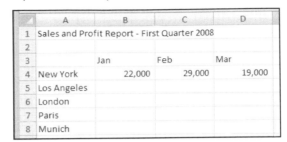

	A	B	C	D
1	Sales and Profit Report - First Quarter 2008			
2				
3		Jan	Feb	Mar
4	New York	22,000	29,000	19,000
5	Los Angeles			
6	London			
7	Paris			
8	Munich			

2   Notice the difference between values and text.

Cells can contain values or text. Values can be numbers, dates or formulas (more on formulas later).

Excel usually does a great job of recognizing when there are values in a cell and when there is text. The giveaway is that text is always (by default) left aligned in the cell and values are right aligned.

Look at the numbers on this worksheet. Notice how they are all right aligned. This lets you know that Excel has correctly recognized them as values and will happily perform mathematical operations using them.

3   Save a value into a cell.

1. Type the value 42000 into cell B5. Notice that the mouse cursor is still flashing in the cell.

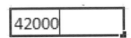

At this stage the value has not been saved into the cell.

If you change your mind, you can still undo the value by pressing the **<ESC>** key at the top left of your keyboard or by clicking the *Cancel button* on the left hand side of the Formula Bar.

2. Decide that you want to keep this value in the cell by either pressing the **<Enter>**, **<Tab>** or an **<Arrow>** key on the keyboard, or by clicking the *Confirm button* on the Formula Bar.

4   Enter a column of data without using the mouse.

When you enter data into a column there's no need to use the mouse. Press the **<Enter>** key after each entry and the active cell moves to the cell beneath. Try this now with the following January sales data:

First Quarter Sales and Profit

The many ways of entering numbers

Negative numbers

-123.56
(123.56)

Currency prefixes

Excel is quite happy for you to prefix a number with a currency symbol. The currency symbol it will accept depends upon how you defined the regional options in your operating system.

$123.56 (works in USA)
£123.56 (works in UK)

See: *Lesson 4-3: Format numbers using built-in number formats* for an easy method of setting $, £ and € currency prefixes whatever your locale.

Commas

12,234,567.78

Fractions

You must leave a space between a number and a fraction for this to work.

6 1/4
(six, space, one, /, four)

The above will appear on the worksheet as 6.25 after you enter it in this way.

0 1/4
(zero, space, one,/,four)

The above will appear on the worksheet as 0.25. The leading zero is needed to prevent Excel from thinking that you are entering a date.

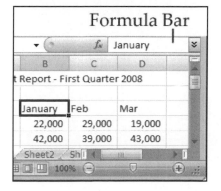

1. Type **18,000** into cell B6.

2. Press the **<Enter>** key to move to cell B7.

3. Do the same to enter the relevant values into the next two cells.

	A	B	C	D
4	New York	22,000	29,000	19,000
5	Los Angeles	42,000		
6	London	18,000		
7	Paris	35,000		
8	Munich	12,000		

5 Enter a row of data without using the mouse.

When you enter a row of data you also don't have to use the mouse.

1. Click in Cell C5.

2. Type **39,000** and then press the **<Tab>** key on your keyboard.

   The <Tab> key is on the left hand side of the keyboard above the <Caps Lock> key. Notice how pressing the <Tab> key saves the value into the cell and then moves one cell to the right.

3. Type **43,000** in cell D5 and press the **<Enter>** key.

   You magically move to cell C6 as Excel assumes you want to begin entering the next row.

6 Complete the table without using the mouse.

By using the **<Tab>** or **<Enter>** key in the right place you should be able to complete the table now without using the mouse:

	A	B	C	D
3		Jan	Feb	Mar
4	New York	22,000	29,000	19,000
5	Los Angeles	42,000	39,000	43,000
6	London	18,000	20,000	22,000
7	Paris	35,000	26,000	31,000
8	Munich	12,000	15,000	13,000

7 Change the text in cell B3 to January.

1. Double-click cell B3. Notice that there is now a flashing cursor in the cell.

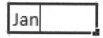

2. Type **uary** on the keyboard to change Jan to January.

3. Press the **<Enter>** key.

8 Change the text in cell B3 back to **Jan** using the formula bar.

Click once in cell B3 and then change the text in the formula bar back to **Jan** (see sidebar).

9 Save your work as *First Quarter Sales and Profit-2.*

tip

Other ways of creating a new workbook

- Use the keyboard shortcut <Ctrl>+<N>.

- Add a button to the Quick Access Toolbar.

See more details of how this is done in: *Lesson 1-13: Customize the Quick Access Toolbar and preview the printout.*

note

What are templates?

The vast majority of users know nothing about templates and simply base every workbook upon the *Blank Workbook* default template supplied by Microsoft.

The *Blank Workbook* template has no information in the worksheet itself, but contains all of the Excel Option settings such as the default font size and type.

Templates can also contain anything that a workbook can contain and are used to store workbook frameworks to give you a flying start when you find that you often create very similar workbook layouts.

If you explore the *New Workbook* dialog a little more you'll see that there are hundreds of pre-built templates provided by Microsoft.

Later in this course, in: *Lesson 3-14: Create a template* you'll learn how to create your own template library to personalize the appearance of your workbooks.

Lesson 2-2: Create a new workbook and view two workbooks at the same time

1   Create a new workbook by opening Excel

The easiest way to create a new workbook is to simply open Excel. Excel helpfully creates a workbook, unimaginatively named Book1. If you already have a workbook open called Book1, the new workbook will be called Book2... and so on.

Open Excel now and see this in action. Notice that *Book1 – Microsoft Excel* is displayed on the Title Bar.

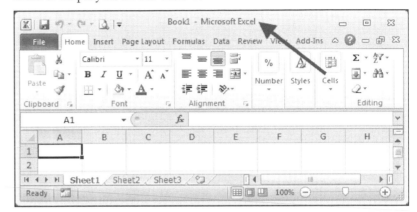

2   Create another new workbook.

You wouldn't want to have to open and close Excel every time you needed a new workbook.

1.   Click the *File* button at the top left of the screen and click the *New* button in the left hand menu.

The *New Workbook* window is displayed in Backstage view:

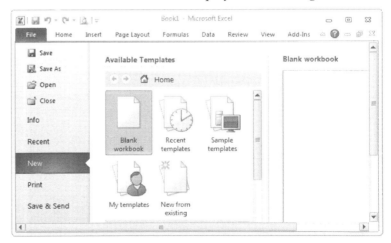

2.   Double-Click the *Blank workbook* template. A new blank workbook called *Book2* is displayed in the workbook window.

You could be forgiven for thinking that nothing has happened but you can see that the Title Bar now says: *Book2 – Microsoft Excel*, showing that you are now looking at a different workbook.

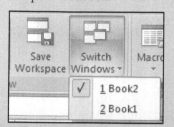

note

Finding a workbook when many are open

An alternative way to quickly find a workbook when many are open is to click:

View→Window→ Switch Windows

This presents you with a list of all open workbooks.

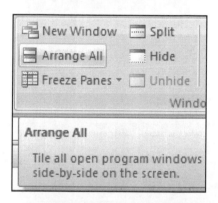

You can also use the <Ctrl>+<Tab> keyboard shortcut to cycle through all open workbooks.

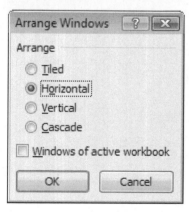

Arrange All

Tile all open program windows side-by-side on the screen.

Arrange Windows

Arrange

○ Tiled
◉ Horizontal
○ Vertical
○ Cascade

☐ Windows of active workbook

OK   Cancel

See the *What are templates* sidebar for more information about templates.

3 **Use the taskbar to move between workbooks.**

You'll see an Excel icon with two right-hand borders at the bottom of the screen. Hover over this icon with your mouse. A menu will pop up showing two workbooks: Book1 and Book2.

Click on each item in the pop-up menu to show each workbook in the worksheet window. The only difference you will see is the Title Bar changing from *Book1* to *Book2* because both workbooks are empty.

See the sidebar for other methods of switching windows.

4 **Show both *Book1* and *Book2* in the worksheet window at the same time.**

1. Click View→Window→Arrange All.

   The *Arrange Windows* dialog is displayed.

2. Choose the *Horizontal* arrangement and click the OK button.

Both workbooks are now shown within the workbook window:

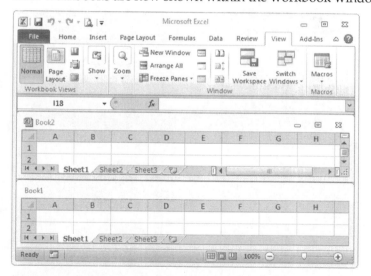

Notice that as you click each workbook window the title bar lights up and the *Close/Minimize/Restore Down* buttons appear, to show that this is the active workbook.

5 **Close Book2 and maximize Book1 to restore the display to a single workbook.**

If you've forgotten how to do this, refer back to: *Lesson 1-3: Understand the Application and Workbook windows.*

Lesson 2-3: Use AutoSum to quickly calculate totals

Excel's AutoSum feature is a really useful and fast way to add the values in a range of cells together.

1   Open *First Quarter Sales and Profit-2* from your sample files folder (if it isn't already open).

2   In cell A9 Type the word **Total** followed by the **<Tab>** key.

The cursor moves to the right and is now in cell B9:

	A	B	C	D
7	Paris	35,000	26,000	31,000
8	Munich	12,000	15,000	13,000
9	Total			

3   Click: Home→Editing→ Σ (this is the AutoSum button).

Autosum Button

Something interesting has happened to the worksheet:

	A	B	C	D
3		Jan	Feb	Mar
4	New York	22,000	29,000	19,000
5	Los Angeles	42,000	39,000	43,000
6	London	18,000	20,000	22,000
7	Paris	35,000	26,000	31,000
8	Munich	12,000	15,000	13,000
9	Total	=SUM(B4:B8)		
10		SUM(**number1**, [number2], ...)		

Excel has placed a marquee around the number range that AutoSum has guessed we want to work with. The pattern of dots that marks the boundary of the marquee is called the *marching ants* (that really is the technical term for them)!

The marching ants surround all of the numbers in the column above, up to the first blank cell or text cell (in this case, up to the word Jan).

=Sum(B4:B8) is your first glimpse of an Excel Formula. Formulas always begin with an equals sign. This formula is using the SUM function to compute the Sum (or total) of the values in cells B4 to B8.

tip

Entering an AutoSum using only the keyboard

You can also execute an AutoSum using the keyboard shortcut:

<Alt>+<=>

4 Press the **<Enter>** key or click the AutoSum button Σ once more to display the total January sales:

	A	B	C	D
3		Jan	Feb	Mar
4	New York	22,000	29,000	19,000
5	Los Angeles	42,000	39,000	43,000
6	London	18,000	20,000	22,000
7	Paris	35,000	26,000	31,000
8	Munich	12,000	15,000	13,000
9	Total	129,000		

5 Type the word **Total** in cell E3 and press the **<Enter>** key once.

The cursor moves down one row and is now in cell E4.

	B	C	D	E
3	Jan	Feb	Mar	Total
4	22,000	29,000	19,000	
5	42,000	39,000	43,000	

6 Use AutoSum to calculate sales for New York.

1. Click Home→Editing→AutoSum. Σ

This time AutoSum correctly guesses that you want to sum the values to the left of cell E4:

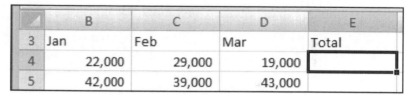

	B	C	D	E
3	Jan	Feb	Mar	Total
4	22,000	29,000	19,000	=SUM(B4:D4)
5	42,000	39,000	SUM(**number1**, [number2], ...)	
6	18,000	20,000	22,000	

2. Press the **<Enter>** key, or click the AutoSum button once more.

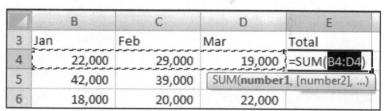
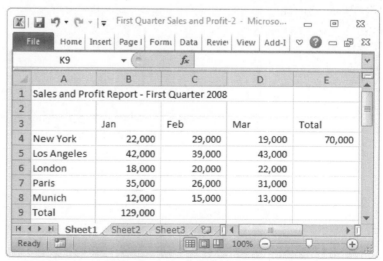

	A	B	C	D	E
1	Sales and Profit Report - First Quarter 2008				
2					
3		Jan	Feb	Mar	Total
4	New York	22,000	29,000	19,000	70,000
5	Los Angeles	42,000	39,000	43,000	
6	London	18,000	20,000	22,000	
7	Paris	35,000	26,000	31,000	
8	Munich	12,000	15,000	13,000	
9	Total	129,000			

7 Save your work as *First Quarter Sales and Profit-3*.

Lesson 2-4: Select a range of cells and understand Smart Tags

Sometimes you don't want to add all of the values in a column. You only want to add a selection of cells that you define yourself.

This lesson shows you how to do this with a different AutoSum technique.

1   Open *First Quarter Sales and Profit-3* from your sample files folder (if it isn't already open).

2   Observe the formula behind the value in cell B9.

Click on cell B9 or move to it with the arrow keys on your keyboard.

Look at the *formula bar* at the top of the screen. Notice that the cell displays the *value* of a calculation and the formula bar shows the *formula* used to calculate the value:

	B9	▼		*fx*	=SUM(B4:B8)
	A	B		C	D
8	Munich	12,000		15,000	13,000
9	Total	129,000			
10			Value	Formula	
11					

3   Delete the contents of cell B9.

The easiest way to delete the contents of a cell is to press the **<Delete>** key on your keyboard but you can also right-click the cell and then click *Clear Contents* from the shortcut menu.

4   Change the word *Total* in cell A9 to *USA Sales* and press the **<Tab>** key once.

You don't have to delete the word *Total* before typing *USA Sales*. When you click once in a cell (be careful not to double-click) and immediately begin to type, the existing cell contents are replaced.

The cursor moves to cell B9.

8	Munich	12,000
9	USA Sales	
10		

5   Select cells B4:B5 with your mouse.

When the mouse cursor hovers over a cell there are three possible cursor shapes:

First Quarter Sales and Profit-3

note

Selecting cells with the keyboard

To select cells with the keyboard hold down the **<Shift>** key and then use the **<Arrow>** keys to select the range needed.

note

Selecting a large range of cells with the <Shift>-click technique

If you need to select a very large range of cells it is sometimes useful to use this technique:

1. Click the cell in the top left corner of the required range.

2. If necessary, use the scroll bars to make the bottom right corner of the required range visible.

3. Hold down the **<Shift>** key.

4. Click in the bottom right corner of the required range.

Cursor	What it does
1.6 (white cross)	The white cross (Select) cursor appears when you hover over the center of the active cell. You can then click and drag to select a range of cells.
1.6 (black cross)	The black cross (AutoFill) cursor appears when you hover over the bottom right-hand corner of the active cell. We'll be covering AutoFill later in this session.
1.6 (four headed arrow)	The four headed arrow (Move) cursor appears when you hover over one of the black edges of the cell (but not the bottom right corner).

Beginners often have difficulty selecting cells and end up moving them or AutoFilling them by mistake.

Position the mouse at the center of cell B4 so that you see the White Cross (select) cursor. When you see the white cross, hold down the left mouse button and drag down to cell B5. You have now selected cells B4 and B5 (in Excel speak we say that you have selected the *range* B4:B5).

	A	B
3		Jan
4	New York	22,000
5	Los Angeles	22,000

6 Click the AutoSum button. **Σ**

USA sales are shown in cell B9. Notice the small green triangle at the top left of B9. This is Excel's way of saying: "I think you may have made a mistake".

9	USA Sales		64,000

Select cell B9 and you will see an Exclamation Mark icon. This is called a *Smart Tag*.

7 Hover the mouse cursor over the Smart Tag.

A tip box pops up telling you what Excel thinks you may have done wrong (see below). Of course, in this case, everything is fine. The Smart Tag thinks that perhaps we didn't want just the USA sales – but the Smart Tag is mistaken!

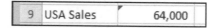

USA Sale ⚠ ▾ 64,000

The formula in this cell refers to a range that has additional numbers adjacent to it.

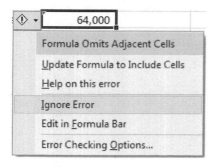

⚠ ▾ 64,000

Formula Omits Adjacent Cells
Update Formula to Include Cells
Help on this error
Ignore Error
Edit in Formula Bar
Error Checking Options...

8 Examine the remedial actions suggested by the Smart Tag.

Click the drop-down arrow next to the exclamation mark icon. A list of possible remedial actions is displayed. In this case you can choose *Ignore Error* to remove the green triangle from the corner of the cell.

9 Save your work as *First Quarter Sales and Profit-4.*

Lesson 2-5: Enter data into a range and copy data across a range

Now that you have mastered the technique of selecting cells, you can use it to speed up data entry.

When you select a range of cells prior to entering data, Excel knows that all data entered belongs in that range. Several key combinations are then available to greatly speed up data entry.

1   Open a new workbook and save it as *Data Range Test*.

2   Select cells B2:D4.

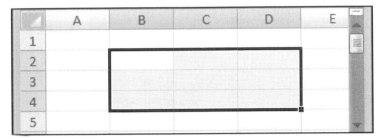

3   Type **London.**

The text appears in Cell B2, the top left cell in the range selected.

4   Press the **<Enter>** Key.

The cursor moves to cell B3 as it normally would.

5   Type **Paris** followed by the **<Enter>** key.

The cursor moves to cell B4 as it normally would.

6   Type **New York** followed by the **<Enter>** key.

This time something new happens. The cursor doesn't move to cell B5 as you might expect but jumps to cell C2.

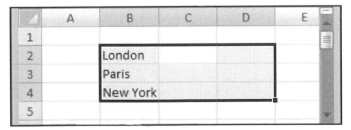

7   Type **150,000** followed by the **<Enter>** key.

The value appears in C2 and Excel moves down the column again to cell C3.

8   Press the **\<Enter\>** key without entering a value to leave C3 blank.

Excel moves down the column to cell C4.

9   Type **225,000** followed by the **\<Enter\>** key.

The cursor jumps to cell D2.

10   Press **\<Shift\>+\<Enter\>** twice to change your mind about leaving Paris blank.

1.   Press **\<Shift\>+\<Enter\>** to move backwards to New York sales.

2.   Press **\<Shift\>+\<Enter\>** a second time and you are back to the Paris cell.

◢	A	B	C	D	E
1					
2		London	150,000		
3		Paris			
4		New York	225,000		
5					

11   Type **180,000** followed by the **\<Tab\>** key.

\<Tab\> moves you across the range, to cell D3.

◢	A	B	C	D	E
1					
2		London	150,000		
3		Paris	180,000		
4		New York	225,000		
5					

You can now appreciate how to use this technique of \<Enter\>, \<Tab\>, \<Shift\>+\<Tab\> and \<Shift\>+\<Enter\> to save a lot of time when entering a whole table of data.

12   Select cells D2:D4.

13   Type **50%** but don't press the \<Enter\> or \<Tab\> keys.

The challenge this time is to place the same value into cells D3 and D4 without having to type the value two more times.

14   Press **\<Ctrl\>+\<Enter\>**.

The value is replicated into all of the other cells in the range.

◢	A	B	C	D	E
1					
2		London	150,000	50%	
3		Paris	180,000	50%	
4		New York	225,000	50%	
5					

Lesson 2-6: Select adjacent and non-adjacent rows and columns

1   Open *First Quarter Sales and Profit-4* from your sample files folder (if it isn't already open).

2   Select all of column A.

Hover the mouse cursor over the letter **A** at the top of the column. The button lights up and the mouse cursor changes to a black down arrow:

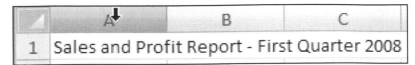

Click to select the entire column. The column becomes slightly shaded and a black line surrounds all of the cells.

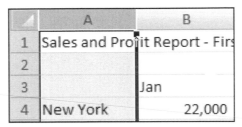

3   Click: Home→Font→Bold to bold face the column.

Because the whole column was selected, all of the values become bold faced.

4   Click: Home→Font→Bold once more to change the type in column A back to normal.

5   Select all of row 4.

To select a row, hover the mouse cursor over the number on the left hand side of the row. The button lights up and the mouse cursor changes to a black arrow pointing across the row:

3		Jan	
➡	New York		22,000
5	Los Angeles		42,000

Click to select the row.

6   Select columns B and C.

Hover over the letter at the top of column B until you see the black down arrow. When you see the arrow, click and drag to the right to select both columns.

First Quarter Sales and Profit-4

	A	B	C	D
1	Sales and Profit Report - First Quarter 2008			
2				
3		Jan	Feb	Mar
4	New York	22,000	29,000	19,000

7   Select rows 6 and 7.

Hover over the number at the left of row 6 until you see the black arrow pointing across the row. When you see the arrow, click and drag down to row 7 to select both rows.

5	Los Angeles	42,000	39,000
6	London	18,000	20,000
→7	Paris	35,000	26,000
2R	Munich	12,000	15,000

8   Select columns A, B, C, D and E.

Sometimes you will need to select a large number of adjacent columns or rows. You could drag across them but it is often easier to use the following technique:

1.   Select Column A.

2.   Hold down the **<Shift>** key.

3.   Select Column E.

Columns A to E are selected.

	A	B	C	D	E
1	Sales and Profit Report - First Quarter 2008				
2					

9   Select rows 4 and 6.

Perhaps you need to perform an operation on two non-adjacent rows. To select rows 4 and 6 you need to:

1.   Select row 4.

2.   Hold down the **<Ctrl>** key on the keyboard.

3.   Select Row 6.

		Jan	Feb	Mar
3		Jan	Feb	Mar
4	New York	22,000	29,000	19,000
5	Los Angeles	42,000	39,000	43,000
6	London	18,000	20,000	22,000
7	Paris	35,000	26,000	31,000

Lesson 2-7: Select non-contiguous cell ranges and view summary information

Non-contiguous is a very impressive word! It simply means a range of cells that is split across two blocks of cells in different parts of the worksheet.

Non-contiguous ranges can be selected using both the mouse and keyboard. The keyboard method may seem a little involved at first but you'll find it much faster once you have the hang of it.

1   Open *First Quarter Sales and Profit-4* from your sample files folder (if it isn't already open).

2   Select the contiguous range B4:D8 with the keyboard.

When you need to select a contiguous range with the keyboard here's how it's done:

1. Use the arrow keys on the keyboard to navigate to cell B4.

2. Hold down the **<Shift>** key on the keyboard

3. Still holding the **<Shift>** key down, use the arrow keys on the keyboard to navigate to cell D8

The contiguous range B4:D8 is selected.

	A	B	C	D	E
1	Sales and Profit Report - First Quarter 2008				
2					
3		Jan	Feb	Mar	Total
4	New York	22,000	29,000	19,000	70,000
5	Los Angeles	42,000	39,000	43,000	
6	London	18,000	20,000	22,000	
7	Paris	35,000	26,000	31,000	
8	Munich	12,000	15,000	13,000	
9	USA Sales	64,000			

3   Select the non-contiguous range B4:B8,D4:D8 using the mouse.

1. Select the range B4:B8.

2. Hold down the **<Ctrl>** key and select the range D4:D8.

The non-contiguous range **B4:B8,D4:D8** is selected:

	A	B	C	D	E
1	Sales and Profit Report - First Quarter 2008				
2					
3		Jan	Feb	Mar	Total
4	New York	22,000	29,000	19,000	70,000
5	Los Angeles	42,000	39,000	43,000	
6	London	18,000	20,000	22,000	
7	Paris	35,000	26,000	31,000	
8	Munich	12,000	15,000	13,000	
9	USA Sales	64,000			

First Quarter Sales and Profit-4

4 Select the same non-contiguous range with the keyboard.

This is a little more involved than using the simple **<Shift>+<Arrow keys>** method used earlier.

Here's how it's done:

1. Use the arrow keys on the keyboard to navigate to cell B4
2. Press the **<F8>** key (it is on the very top row of your keyboard)
3. Use the arrow keys to navigate to cell B8
4. Press **<Shift>+<F8>**
5. Use the arrow keys to navigate to cell D4
6. Press **<F8>**
7. Use the arrow keys to navigate to cell D8
8. Press **<Shift>+<F8>** one last time

The non-contiguous range B4:B8,D4:D8 is selected:

	A	B	C	D	E
1	Sales and Profit Report - First Quarter 2008				
2					
3		Jan	Feb	Mar	Total
4	New York	22,000	29,000	19,000	70,000
5	Los Angeles	42,000	39,000	43,000	
6	London	18,000	20,000	22,000	
7	Paris	35,000	26,000	31,000	
8	Munich	12,000	15,000	13,000	
9	USA Sales	64,000			

5 Obtain a total sales figures for January and March using the status bar.

The status bar contains summary information for the currently selected range.

Look at the bottom right of your screen. You can see the average sales and total sales (sum of sales) for January and March:

Average: 25,700   Count: 10   Sum: 257,000

6 View the Maximum and Minimum sales for January and March using the status bar.

Right-click the status bar and click *Maximum* and *Minimum* on the pop-up menu (see sidebar).

The status bar now also displays Maximum and Minimum values.

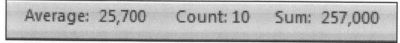

Average: 25,700   Count: 10   Min: 12,000   Max: 43,000   Sum: 257,000

7 Close the workbook without saving.

Lesson 2-8: AutoSelect a range of cells

When data is arranged in a block (as it is in the Sales and Profit Report) it is referred to as a *Range* (in early versions of Excel it used to be called a database or list).

You will often want to select a row or column of cells within a range, or even the entire range.

You can select ranges by using any of the techniques covered so far but this could be very time consuming if the range encompassed thousands of rows and columns.

In this lesson you'll learn how to select range rows, range columns and entire ranges with a few clicks of the mouse.

1   Open *Sales Report* from your sample files folder.

This report contains a range of cells. The range is the block of cells from A3 to E19.

	A	B	C	D	E
1	Weekly Sales Report				
2					
3	Invoice No	Date	Customer	Country	Total
4	10918	10 March 2008	Bottom-Dollar Markets	Canada	1,700.81
5	10917	10 March 2008	Romero y tomillo	Spain	429.92
6	10926	10 March 2008	Ana Trujillo Emparedados y helados	Mexico	604.42
7	10929	11 March 2008	Frankenversand	Germany	1,380.33
8	10934	11 March 2008	Lehmanns Marktstand	Germany	587.50
9	10939	11 March 2008	Magazzini Alimentari Riuniti	Italy	749.05
10	10939	11 March 2008	Magazzini Alimentari Riuniti	Italy	- 749.05
11	10925	12 March 2008	Hanari Carnes	Brazil	558.29
12	10944	12 March 2008	Bottom-Dollar Markets	Canada	1,204.75
13	10923	12 March 2008	La maison d'Asie	France	879.83
14	10937	13 March 2008	Cactus Comidas para llevar	Argentina	757.64
15	10947	13 March 2008	B's Beverages	UK	258.50
16	10933	13 March 2008	Island Trading	UK	1,081.71
17	10938	14 March 2008	QUICK-Stop	Germany	3,209.95
18	10949	14 March 2008	Bottom-Dollar Markets	Canada	5,195.85
19	10945	14 March 2008	Morgenstern Gesundkost	Germany	287.88
20					↖Range
21	This report excludes sales to Asia and South Africa.				

2   Select all cells within the range to the right of cell A7.

1. Click in cell A7 to make it the active cell.

2. Hover over the right hand border of cell A7 until you see the four headed arrow cursor shape.

7	10929 11
8	10934 11

3. When you see this cursor shape hold down the **<Shift>** key and double-click.

All cells to the right of A7, but within the range, are selected.

7	10929 11 March 2008 Frankenversand	Germany	1,380.33

Sales Report

note

Other ways to AutoSelect a range

Using the keyboard

Here's how you would select the entire range in the Weekly Sales Report (excluding the header row) using the keyboard method.

Make cell A4 the active cell by navigating to it with the **<Arrow>** keys.

1. Press: **<Ctrl>+<Shift>+ <DownArrow>**

    Cells A4:A19 are selected.

2. Press: **<Ctrl>+<Shift>+ <RightArrow>**

    The entire range (excluding the header row) is selected.

Using shortcut keys

The shortcut keys method is the fastest way to select the entire range *including* the header row.

1. Click anywhere inside the range.

2. Press: **<Ctrl>+<A>**

    The entire range (including the header row) is selected.

From the Ribbon

The Ribbon method isn't as powerful as the other methods but does provide a way to select the current range (described as the *region* in the dialog).

Make sure that the active cell is within the range.

1. Click:

    Home→Editing→ Find & Select→ GoTo Special...

    The *GoTo Special* dialog is displayed.

2. Click the *Current Region* option button and then click the OK button.

The entire range (including the header row) is selected.

3 Select all cells within the range except the header row.

1. Click in cell A4 to make it the active cell.

2. Hover over the right hand border of cell A4 until you see the four headed arrow cursor shape.

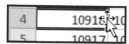

3. When you see this cursor shape hold down the **<Shift>** key and double-click.

    All cells to the right of cell A4, but within the range, are selected.

4. Hover over the bottom border of the selected range until you see the four headed arrow cursor shape.

	Customer
1arch 2008	Bottom-Dollar Markets
1arch 2008	Romero y tomillo

5. When you see this cursor shape hold down the **<Shift>** key and double-click.

The entire range (except the header row) is selected.

	A	B	C	D	E
1	Weekly Sales Report				
2					
3	Invoice No	Date	Customer	Country	Total
4	10918	10 March 2008	Bottom-Dollar Markets	Canada	1,700.81
5	10917	10 March 2008	Romero y tomillo	Spain	479.92
6	10926	10 March 2008	Ana Trujillo Emparedados y helados	Mexico	604.42
7	10929	11 March 2008	Frankenversand	Germany	1,380.33
8	10934	11 March 2008	Lehmanns Marktstand	Germany	587.50
9	10939	11 March 2008	Magazzini Alimentari Riuniti	Italy	749.05
10	10939	11 March 2008	Magazzini Alimentari Riuniti	Italy	- 749.05
11	10925	12 March 2008	Hanari Carnes	Brazil	558.29
12	10944	12 March 2008	Bottom-Dollar Markets	Canada	1,204.75
13	10923	12 March 2008	La maison d'Asie	France	879.83
14	10937	13 March 2008	Cactus Comidas para llevar	Argentina	757.64
15	10947	13 March 2008	B's Beverages	UK	258.50
16	10933	13 March 2008	Island Trading	UK	1,081.71
17	10938	14 March 2008	QUICK-Stop	Germany	3,209.95
18	10949	14 March 2008	Bottom-Dollar Markets	Canada	5,195.85
19	10945	14 March 2008	Morgenstern Gesundkost	Germany	287.88
20					
21	This report excludes sales to Asia and South Africa.				

You can also use this technique to select cells to the left of the active cell or above the active cell.

4 Close the workbook without saving.

Lesson 2-9: Re-size rows and columns

1   Open *First Quarter Sales and Profit-4* from your sample files folder (if it isn't already open).

Notice that columns B, C, D and E are far too wide for their contents. It would be useful to make them narrower to keep the worksheet compact.

2   Re-size column B so that it is just wide enough to contain the January sales figures.

Hover over the line separating the letters B and C until you see the re-size cursor shape:

When you see this shape, keep the mouse still and click and drag to the left. Column B will re-size as you drag. Make it narrower so that the values just fit in the column. Notice that the column width in points and pixels are displayed as you drag (one point = 1/72 inch).

A1		▼	Width: 8.86 (67 pixels)	Profit Re
	A	B	C	D
1	Sales and Profit Report - First Quarter 2008			
2				
3		Jan	Feb	Mar
4	New York	22,000	29,000	19,000

3   Re-size column B so that it is too narrow to contain the January sales figures.

Notice that when the column isn't wide enough to contain the contents, hash signs are shown instead of values (if you're used to hashes being called **pound signs** or **number signs** see the sidebar).

	A	B	C	D
1	Sales and Profit Report - First Quarter 2008			
2				
3		Jan	Feb	Mar
4	New York	#####	29,000	19,000

4   Automatically re-size column B so that it is a perfect fit for the widest cell in the column.

Hover over the line separating the letters B and C until you see the re-size cursor shape:

When you see this shape, double-click to automatically re-size column B.

note

Why are you calling the pound sign a hash?

You like potato and I like potahto,
You like tomato and I like tomahto;
Potato, potahto, tomato, tomahto!
Let's call the whole thing off!

Song lyric by George Gershwin,
American Composer (1898-1937)

In the USA and Canada the hash symbol is called the **pound sign** or the **number sign**.

In different USA/Canada regions the single symbol has different names because it can be used to denote a number (as in contestant #5) or as a weight (as in 3# of butter).

Throughout this book I will refer to the # as a hash because that is the term used in most other English speaking countries.

First Quarter Sales and Profit-4

note

Other ways to re-size rows and columns

You can also re-size rows and columns using the Ribbon.

Click Home→Cells→Format.

A drop-down menu appears.

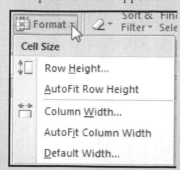

You can use the *Row Height* and *Column Width* settings to set the row or column to a specific number of points (a point is 1/72 of an inch).

You can also use the *AutoFit Row Height* and *AutoFit Column Width* options to automatically size the row or column (you achieved this more efficiently with a double-click in the lesson).

Default Width... often confuses as it doesn't appear to work. This is because it re-sets all columns to default width *except those that have already been re-sized.*

note

Making several columns or rows the same size

Sometimes you will want to make several columns exactly the same width.

To do this, select the multiple columns and then click and drag the intersection of any of the selected columns. This will make each of the columns exactly the same width.

5 Automatically re-size every column in the worksheet in one operation.

1. Select every cell in the workbook by clicking the *select all* button in the top left corner of the worksheet (you can also do this by clicking in any blank cell and then pressing <Ctrl>+<A>).

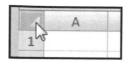

2. Hover over the intersection of any two columns until you see the re-size cursor shape ⊞ and then double-click.

Every column is now perfectly sized.

Notice that Auto-resize has done its job rather too well. Column A is now wide enough to accommodate all of the text in cell A1.

	A	B	C
1	Sales and Profit Report - First Quarter 2008		

6 Automatically re-size column A so that it is only wide enough to contain the longest city name (Los Angeles).

	A	B	C	D	E
1	Sales and Profit Report - First Quarter 2008				
2					
3		Jan	Feb	Mar	Total
4	New York	22,000	29,000	19,000	70,000
5	Los Angeles	42,000	39,000	43,000	

1. Select cells A4:A9.

2. Click: Home→Cells→Format→AutoFit Column Width.

This time the column is automatically sized so that it is wide enough to contain all of the text in the selected cells.

Notice that the text has spilled over from cell A1 into the adjoining columns B, C, D and E. This always happens when a cell contains text and the adjacent cells are empty.

7 Manually size row 3 so that it is about twice as tall as the other rows.

Do this in exactly the same way you re-sized the column but, this time, hover between the intersection of rows 3 and 4 until you see the re-size cursor shape, and then click and drag downwards.

1	Sales and Profit Report - First Quarter 2008		
2 Height: 30.00 (40 pixels)			
	Jan	Feb	Mar
3 New York	22,000	29,000	19,000
4 Los Angeles	42,000	39,000	43,000

8 Auto-resize row 3 so that it is the same size as the other rows again.

Lesson 2-10: Use AutoSum to sum a non-contiguous range

In: *Lesson 2-7: Select non-contiguous cell ranges and view summary information*, you learned how to view the sum of January and March sales using the status bar. But how can you put that value onto the worksheet?

Now that you have the hang of selecting non-contiguous ranges you can use this in conjunction with your AutoSum skills to create a formula that will calculate the total of a non-contiguous range.

1   Open *First Quarter Sales and Profit*-4 from your sample files folder (if it isn't already open).

2   Enter the text **Jan/Mar Sales** in cell A10 and press the <Tab> key.

The active cell moves to cell B10.

3   Re-size column A so that it is wide enough to contain the text.

   1. Hover over the line separating the letters A and B until you see the re-size cursor shape:

   2. When you see this shape, keep the mouse still and click and drag to the right. Column A will re-size as you drag. Make it wider so that the words *Jan/Mar Sales* comfortably fit in the column:

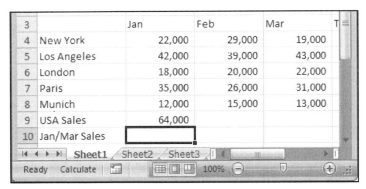

4   Click Home→Editing→ Σ (the AutoSum button).

An AutoSum appears in cell B10 but it isn't anything like what we want yet. It guesses that we simply want to repeat the value in the USA Sales cell.

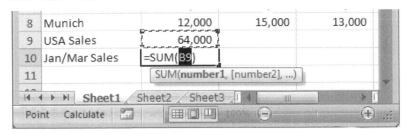

5   Select the range B4:B8 with the mouse.

First Quarter Sales and Profit-4

---

6   Hold down the **<Ctrl>** key and select the range D4:D8 with the mouse.

Notice that the non-contiguous range **B4:B8,D4:D8** is shown in the AutoSum's formula:

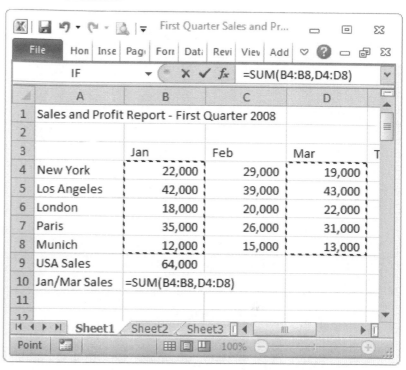

7   Press the **<Enter>** key or click the AutoSum button  again to view the sales for January and March in cell B10.

8   Save your work as *First Quarter Sales and Profit-5*.

Lesson 2-11: Use AutoSum to quickly calculate averages

Excel's *AutoSum* feature isn't only restricted to addition. It is also able to compute averages and maximum/minimum values.

In this lesson we'll use AutoSum to calculate the average sales for each month.

1   Open *First Quarter Sales and Profit 5* from your sample files folder (If it isn't already open).

2   Delete cells E3:E4.

Select cells E3 and E4 and press the **<Delete>** key on your keyboard.

3   Type the word *Average* in cell E3 and press the **<Enter>** key.

The cursor moves to cell E4:

	C	D	E
3	Feb	Mar	Average
4	29,000	19,000	

Click
Here

4   Use AutoSum to create a formula that will show the Average New York sales.

1.   Click: Home→Editing→AutoSum →Drop down arrow (see sidebar).

A drop down menu is displayed showing all of the different ways in which AutoSum can operate upon a range of cells:

2.   Click *Average*.

3.   Excel generates an Average function and inserts the cell range B4:D4. This is exactly what we want:

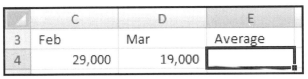

4.   Press the **<Enter>** key or click the AutoSum button 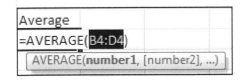 again to see the average sales for New York:

3		Jan	Feb	Mar	Average
4	New York	22,000	29,000	19,000	23,333

5   Type the word **Maximum** in Cell F3 and then press the **<Enter>** key.

6   Use AutoSum to create a formula in cell F4 that will show the Maximum New York Sales for this period.

First Quarter Sales and Profit-5

1. Place an AutoSum in cell F4 but this time, choose Max from the drop-down menu.

    This time we have a small problem. AutoSum is including the average value (23,333) in the calculation.

Jan	Feb	Mar	Average	Maximum
22,000	29,000	19,000	23,333	=MAX(B4:E4)

2. Select cells B4:D4 with the mouse

    The marquee corrects and the average value in cell E4 is no longer included.

New York	22,000	29,000	19,000	23,333	=MAX(B4:D4)

    Notice that the Max function is now working with the range B4:D4.

3. Press the **<Enter>** key or click the AutoSum button Σ once more to see the maximum sales the New York office managed during the first quarter of the year:

3		Jan	Feb	Mar	Average	Maximum
4	New York	22,000	29,000	19,000	23,333	29,000

7 Change the words *USA Sales* in cell A9 back to *Sales* and press the **<Tab>** key.

8 Press the **<F2>** key on the keyboard (or double-click cell B9) to bring back the marquee (shown as a blue box).

9 Adjust the marquee using click and drag so that all offices are included in the Sales total.

Notice that there is a small blue spot on each corner of the range. These are called sizing handles.

1. Hover the mouse cursor over the bottom right (or bottom left) sizing handle until the cursor shape changes to a double headed arrow. It is really important that you see the double headed arrow and not the four headed arrow or white cross.

4	New York	22,000
5	Los Angeles	42,000
6	London	18,000

2. When you see the double headed arrow click and drag with the mouse down to cell B8.

3. Release the mouse button.

4. Press the **<Enter>** key or click the AutoSum button again.

7	Paris	35,000
8	Munich	12,000
9	Sales	129,000

10 Save your work as *First Quarter Sales and Profit-6*.

Lesson 2-12: Create your own formulas

The AutoSum tool is very useful for quickly inserting Sum(), Average(), Count(), Max() and Min() formulas into cells. Many Excel users never get any further with their formulas than this.

In this session we'll create our own formulas without the use of AutoSum. You'll be amazed at how easy it is.

1   Open *First Quarter Sales and Profit*-6 from your sample files folder (if it isn't already open).

2   Select cells A10:B10 and press the **<Delete>** key once.

The previous contents of cells A10:B10 are removed.

3   Type the word **Costs** into cell A11 and **Profit** into cell A12.

4   Type the value 83,000 into cell B11 and press the **<Enter>** key to move down to cell B12.

11	Costs	83,000	
12	Profit		

5   Enter a formula into cell B12 to compute the profit made in January.

   1.   Type: **= B9-B11** into cell B12.

   2.   Press the **<Enter>** key.

The profit for January is displayed:

9	Sales	129,000
10		
11	Costs	83,000
12	Profit	46,000

6   Enter the formula again using a better technique.

The method that you have just used to enter the formula works just fine but it isn't the best method. Sooner or later you will make a mistake. For example you could easily type **=B8-B11** resulting in an incorrect answer.

To eliminate such errors you should always select cell references visually rather than simply type them in. You can visually select cells using either the mouse or the keyboard. First we'll use the mouse method.

   1.   Click in cell B12 and press the **<Delete>** key on the keyboard to clear the old formula.

   2.   Press the equals **<=>** key on the keyboard.

   3.   Click once on the value 129,000 in cell B9.

First Quarter Sales and Profit-6

4. Press the minus <-> key on the keyboard.

5. Click once on the value 83,000 in cell B11.

6. Press the <Enter> key on the keyboard.

If you followed the above steps carefully you will see that you have created the same formula but with a much lower possibility of making a mistake.

7 Enter the formula again using the visual keyboard technique.

The very best Excel experts hardly use the mouse at all. You waste valuable seconds every time you reach for the mouse.

Here's the expert technique of visual selection via keyboard:

1. Use the arrow keys to navigate to cell B12 and then press the <Delete> key on the keyboard to clear the old formula.

2. Press the <=> key on the keyboard.

3. Press the <Up Arrow> key three times to move to cell B9.

4. Press the <-> key on the keyboard.

5. Press the <Up Arrow> key once to move to cell B11.

6. Press the <Enter> key on the keyboard.

8 Enter a formula that uses the multiplication operator.

This employer is very generous and pays the staff ten percent of all profits as an incentive bonus.

In cell A13 type the words **10% Bonus** and then press the **<Tab>** key on the keyboard to move to cell B13.

9 Enter a formula that uses the multiplication operator.

The multiplication operator is not an X as you might expect but an asterisk (*). The other Excel operators are shown in the sidebar.

You need to press **<Shift>+<8>** to enter an asterisk. If you are using a full size keyboard with a numeric keypad at the right-hand side you can also use the numeric keypad's <X> key.

Whichever key you use you'll still see an asterisk in the formula.

Use either the *mouse click* technique or the *visual keyboard* technique to enter the formula shown below into cell B13 and then press the **<Enter>** key to see how much bonus was earned:

11	Costs	83,000
12	Profit	46,000
13	10% Bonus	=B12*.1

11	Costs	83,000
12	Profit	46,000
13	10% Bonus	4,600

10 Save your work as *First Quarter Sales and Profit-7*.

important

The Excel Operators

	Name	Example
+	Addition	1+2
-	Subtraction	7-5
*	Multiplication	6*3
/	Division	15/5
%	Percent	25%
^	Exponentiation	4^2

Lesson 2-13: Create functions using Formula AutoComplete

1   Open *First Quarter Sales and Profit*-7 from your sample files folder (if it isn't already open).

2   Type the words **USA Sales** into cell A15 and **European Sales** into cell A16.

Notice that the text *European Sales* spills over into column B because column A isn't wide enough to contain it.

3   Re-size column A so that it is wide enough for the words *European Sales* to fit within the column.

You learned how to do this in: *Lesson 2-9: Re-size rows and columns.*

	A	B
15	USA Sales	
16	European Sales	

4   Click into cell B15 and type **=S** into the cell.

Something amazing happens:

15	USA Sales	=S
16	European Sales	*fx* SEARCH
17		*fx* SECOND
18		*fx* SERIESSUM
19		*fx* SIGN

A list drops down showing every function in the Excel function library beginning with S. This feature was introduced in Excel 2007 and is called *Formula AutoComplete* (if AutoComplete didn't display as expected see the sidebar).

You've already encountered the Sum(), Average() and Max() functions courtesy of AutoSum.

You may be pleased (or dismayed) to know that there are over 300 functions in the Excel function library. The good news is that most untrained Excel users only ever get to understand Sum() and Average()!

When you typed **=S** Excel listed all functions beginning with S.

5   Continue typing: **=SU**.

Notice that the list now only shows functions beginning with SU and look... there's the *SUM()* function we need three down in the list.

You could simply click on it with the mouse but let's behave like an Excel pro and do it with the keyboard.

6   Press the **<Down Arrow>** key twice to move the cursor over the SUM function.

The Sum function now has a tip telling you what the function does:

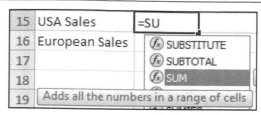

7 Display detailed information about the SUM() function.

The tip tells you a little about the SUM() function but to get the full story press the **<F1>** key while SUM is still highlighted in the dropdown list:

The Excel help system opens showing detailed help for the SUM() function.

Read the help text if you are interested and then close the help window.

Notice that Excel has now left you with only *=SU* in the cell. Complete the formula by typing **M(**

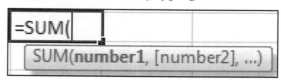

Notice that a little box has appeared beneath the function call. This is the *Syntax* (see sidebar for more information).

8 Select the cells that you need to sum (cells B4:B5) with the mouse or keyboard.

If you want to be a real pro you should select them with the keyboard. To do this:

1. Press the **<Up Arrow>** key repeatedly until you reach cell B4.

2. Hold down the **<Shift>** key and press the **<Down Arrow>** key once to select cells B4:B5.

9 Type a closing bracket to complete the formula and then press the **<Enter>** key.

The total USA sales are displayed in cell B15.

10 Use the same technique to create a SUM() function in cell B16 to show the total European sales (cells B6:B8).

1. Click in cell B16.

2. Type **= SU**.

3. Press the **<Down Arrow>** key twice to move the cursor over the SUM function.

4. Press the **<Tab>** key to automatically enter the SUM function into cell B16.

5. Select the range B6:B8.

6. Type the closing bracket followed by the **<Enter>** key. The formula should now be: **=SUM(B6:B8).**

11 Save your work as *First Quarter Sales and Profit 8.*

note

The syntax box

The Syntax box tells you what arguments (sometimes called parameters) the function needs. The first argument has no square brackets meaning that you can't leave it out. The argument in square brackets is optional.

For such a simple function as SUM() the syntax box is hardly needed but later we'll discover functions that require several arguments and then the syntax box will be invaluable.

Lesson 2-14: Use AutoFill for text and numeric series

1 Open *First Quarter Sales and Profit-8* from your sample files folder (if it isn't already open).

2 Delete the text **Feb** and **Mar** from cells C3:D3.

Select cells C3:D3 and then press the **<Delete>** key on your keyboard.

3 Make B3 the active cell.

Notice that there is a black border around the cell and a black spot on the bottom right-hand corner. This is the AutoFill handle. If you don't see it, refer to the sidebar.

4 Hover over the AutoFill handle with your mouse until the cursor shape changes to a black cross.

Many of my students have great difficulty with this when they try it for the first time.

- You don't want the four-headed arrow: ✛ – that would move the cell.

- You don't want the white cross: ⬦ – that would select the cell.

- You want the black cross: ✚ – the AutoFill cursor.

5 When the black cross cursor is visible, hold down the mouse button and drag your mouse to the right to AutoFill the other months: **Feb** and **Mar**.

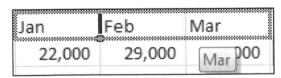

Notice the tip that appears as you drag, previewing the month that will appear in each cell.

6 In cell A18 type **Monday** and AutoFill down to cell A24 to show the days of the week.

(If you are not using an English language version of Excel you will need to type **Monday** in your own language).

7 In cell B18 type the number **1** and in cell B19 type the number **2**.

First Quarter Sales and Profit-8

8   Select cells B18 and B19.

9   AutoFill down to B24 to create sequential numbers:

18	Monday	1
19	Tuesday	2
20	Wednesday	3
21	Thursday	4

10   In cell C18 type **9** and in cell C19 type **18**.

11   Select cells C18 and C19.

12   AutoFill down to B24 to create the nine times table.

18	Monday	1	9
19	Tuesday	2	18
20	Wednesday	3	27

13   Use AutoFill to create sequential dates.

1.   Type 01-Jan-08 into cell D18.

2.   Type 02-Jan-08 into cell D19.

3.   Select Cells D18:D19.

4.   AutoFill down to D24 to create sequential dates.

14   Use AutoFill to quickly copy values.

Sometimes you will want to duplicate the value from one cell into many others to the right of, left of, beneath, or above the active cell.

When a cell containing text is the active cell and it isn't defined as a *fill series* (the built-in fill series are days of the week and months of the year), AutoFill will simply duplicate the contents of the cell:

Type the text **Adjusted** into cell E18 and then AutoFill it down as far as cell E24.

The same text is now shown in each of the cells:

18	Monday	1	9	01-Jan-08	Adjusted
19	Tuesday	2	18	02-Jan-08	Adjusted
20	Wednesday	3	27	03-Jan-08	Adjusted
21	Thursday	4	36	04-Jan-08	Adjusted
22	Friday	5	45	05-Jan-08	Adjusted
23	Saturday	6	54	06-Jan-08	Adjusted
24	Sunday	7	63	07-Jan-08	Adjusted

15   Save your work as *First Quarter Sales and Profit-9*.

Lesson 2-15: Use AutoFill to adjust formulas

AutoFill can save you a lot of time when extending or copying text and number ranges. But the story's not over yet.

AutoFill's ability to copy and adjust formulas is one of the most powerful tools in Excel's impressive armory.

1   Open *First Quarter Sales and Profit 9* from your sample files folder (If it isn't already open).

2   Consider the formula in cell B9.

Click onto cell B9 and view the formula displayed in the formula bar (the formula bar is at the top right of the screen grab below).

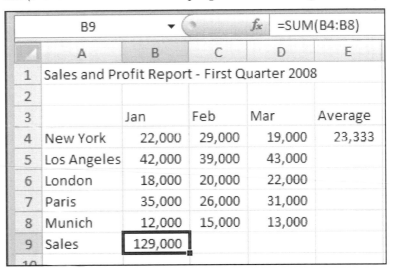

The formula is **=SUM(B4:B8)**. AutoSum created it for us in: *Lesson 2-3: Use AutoSum to quickly calculate totals.* The formula uses the SUM() function to add together the values in the range B4:B8.

Think about the formula that would work in cell C9 (the total sales for February). It would be: **=SUM(C4:C8)**. Similarly the formula that would work in cell D9 (the total sales for March) would be **=SUM(D4:D8)**.

As we move to the right all that is needed is to increment the letter for each cell reference in the formula and we'll get the right answer every time.

Now AutoFill is very clever and realizes this. When we AutoFill a cell containing a formula to the right, AutoFill increments the letters in each cell reference.

Most of the time that is exactly what we want.

Later, in *Lesson 3-12: Understand absolute and relative cell references,* we'll learn how to fine-tune the way in which AutoFill adjusts cell references. This will allow you to implement some more advanced AutoFill techniques.

3   AutoFill cell B9 to the right as far as cell D9.

First Quarter Sales and Profit-9

You may see a row of hashes in Cell C9. This is because the value is too wide to fit in the cell. If this is the case, AutoFit the column using the skills learned in: *Lesson 2-9: Re-size rows and columns.*

The correct answers for Feb and Mar sales are shown on the worksheet. Click on the Feb total cell (C9) and look at the formula in the formula bar.

| C9 | | f_x | =SUM(C4:C8) |

	A	B	C	D	E
3		Jan	Feb	Mar	Average
4	New York	22,000	29,000	19,000	23,333
5	Los Angeles	42,000	39,000	43,000	
6	London	18,000	20,000	22,000	
7	Paris	35,000	26,000	31,000	
8	Munich	12,000	15,000	13,000	
9	Sales	129,000	129,000	128,000	
10					

You can see that AutoFill has done its work perfectly, creating a sum of the values in cells C4:C8. Our five branches have sold exactly the same amount in both January and February, but a little less in March.

4 Consider the formula in cell E4.

Click onto cell E4 and view the formula displayed in the formula bar.

| E4 | | f_x | =AVERAGE(B4:D4) |

	A	B	C	D	E
3		Jan	Feb	Mar	Average
4	New York	22,000	29,000	19,000	23,333
5	Los Angeles	42,000	39,000	43,000	
6	London	18,000	20,000	22,000	

The formula is **=AVERAGE(B4:D4)**. AutoSum created it for us in: *Lesson 2-11: Use AutoSum to quickly calculate averages.*

Think about the formula that would work in cell E5 (the average sales for Los Angeles). It would be: **=Average(B5:D5)**. Similarly the formula that would work in cell E6 (the total sales for London) would be **=Average(B6:D6)**.

As we move downward all that is needed is to increment the number for each cell reference in the formula. This is exactly what AutoFill will do.

5 AutoFill cell E4 down to E8 to see the Average sales for each branch.

6 AutoFill cell F4 down to F8 to view the maximum sales for each branch.

7 Save your work as *First Quarter Sales and Profit-10.*

E	F
Average	Maximum
23,333	29,000
41,333	43,000
20,000	22,000
30,667	35,000
13,333	15,000

Lesson 2-16: Use AutoFill options

Sometimes AutoFill begins to misbehave and actually gets in the way of efficient work by wrongly anticipating what you need.

1 Open *First Quarter Sales and Profit-10* from your sample files folder (If it isn't already open).

2 In cell F18 type the date **1-Jan-09**.

3 AutoFill down as far as cell F24.

The cells are populated with sequential dates:

	A	B	C	D	E	F
18	Monday	1	9	01-Jan-08	Adjusted	01-Jan-09
19	Tuesday	2	18	02-Jan-08	Adjusted	02-Jan-09
20	Wednesday	3	27	03-Jan-08	Adjusted	03-Jan-09
21	Thursday	4	36	04-Jan-08	Adjusted	04-Jan-09
22	Friday	5	45	05-Jan-08	Adjusted	05-Jan-09
23	Saturday	6	54	06-Jan-08	Adjusted	06-Jan-09
24	Sunday	7	63	07-Jan-08	Adjusted	07-Jan-09

4 In cell G18 type the date **31-Mar-09**.

5 AutoFill down as far as cell G24.

At some time you'll need to add transaction dates to a worksheet and will have four or five entries with the same date.

AutoFill is perfect for eliminating the need to re-type the date for each transaction, but its insistence upon incrementing the date every time could be very frustrating.

Fortunately we can change the default behavior.

6 Click the Auto Fill Options Smart Tag ⊞ at the bottom right corner of the filled cells.

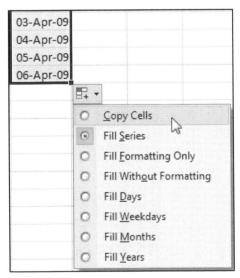

First Quarter Sales and Profit-10

7   Click *Copy Cells* to tell AutoFill not to increment the date.

The purpose of the *Fill Formatting* options will be clear later in the course when you have completed: *Session Four: Making Your Worksheets Look Professional.*

Here's what the other options will do:

Copy Cells	Fill Series	Fill Days	Fill Weekdays	Fill Months	Fill Years
This is what we just did. The first cell is copied to the other cells.	The default for dates that include the day. The date increments by one day at a time.	The date increments by one day at a time.	Because 3rd April 2009 is a Friday the weekend days are omitted and the series jumps from 3rd April to 6th April.	Normally this would show the same day number for each month. In this example, there are only 30 days in two of the months so 30th is shown instead of 31st.	The same calendar day is shown for each subsequent year.
31-Mar-09	31-Mar-09	31-Mar-09	31-Mar-09	31-Mar-09	31-Mar-09
31-Mar-09	01-Apr-09	01-Apr-09	01-Apr-09	30-Apr-09	31-Mar-10
31-Mar-09	02-Apr-09	02-Apr-09	02-Apr-09	31-May-09	31-Mar-11
31-Mar-09	03-Apr-09	03-Apr-09	03-Apr-09	30-Jun-09	31-Mar-12
31-Mar-09	04-Apr-09	04-Apr-09	06-Apr-09	31-Jul-09	31-Mar-13
31-Mar-09	05-Apr-09	05-Apr-09	07-Apr-09	31-Aug-09	31-Mar-14
31-Mar-09	06-Apr-09	06-Apr-09	08-Apr-09	30-Sep-09	31-Mar-15

8   Access fill options using right-click AutoFill.

1. Click on cell F18 to make it the active cell.

2. AutoFill down to cell F24, but this time, hold down the right mouse button.

    When you release the mouse button you are presented with the AutoFill options (see sidebar).

    This method is preferred to the Smart Tag method because it is faster (one click instead of two)!

9   Change back to Fill Series or Fill Days.

In this example *Fill Series* and *Fill Days* produce exactly the same result.

10   Save your work as *First Quarter Sales and Profit-11.*

Lesson 2-17: Speed up your AutoFills and create a custom fill series

In this lesson we're going to learn some advanced AutoFill techniques that will massively speed up your efficient use of the AutoFill feature.

1   Open *First Quarter Sales and Profit*-11 (if it isn't already open).

2   Delete the contents of cells G18:G24.

3   Type **31-Mar-09** into cell G18.

	A	B	C	D	E	F	G
17							
18	Monday	1	9	01-Jan-08	Adjusted	01-Jan-09	31-Mar-09
19	Tuesday	2	18	02-Jan-08	Adjusted	02-Jan-09	
20	Wednesday	3	27	03-Jan-08	Adjusted	03-Jan-09	
21	Thursday	4	36	04-Jan-08	Adjusted	04-Jan-09	
22	Friday	5	45	05-Jan-08	Adjusted	05-Jan-09	
23	Saturday	6	54	06-Jan-08	Adjusted	06-Jan-09	
24	Sunday	7	63	07-Jan-08	Adjusted	07-Jan-09	

4   Double click the AutoFill handle to automatically fill cells G19:G24.

This is a real master tip!

Hover over the AutoFill handle (the black spot at the bottom right hand corner of cell G18). When you are sure that you have the correct black cross cursor shape, double click to automatically fill down.

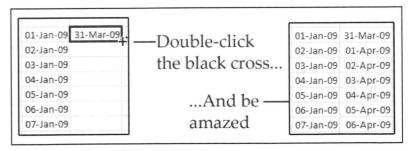

5   Use AutoFill to copy a cell value.

1.   Delete all of the dates from cells G19:G24 leaving only the date 31-Mar-09 in cell G18.

2.   Click in cell G18 to make it the active cell.

3.   Hold down the **<Ctrl>** key and AutoFill cell G18 down as far as cell G24 by dragging the AutoFill handle down with the mouse.

4.   Release the mouse button.

Because you held the <Ctrl> key down AutoFill simply copied the cell instead of creating a series of values.

First Quarter Sales and Profit-11

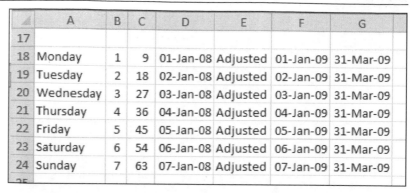

	A	B	C	D	E	F	G
17							
18	Monday	1	9	01-Jan-08	Adjusted	01-Jan-09	31-Mar-09
19	Tuesday	2	18	02-Jan-08	Adjusted	02-Jan-09	31-Mar-09
20	Wednesday	3	27	03-Jan-08	Adjusted	03-Jan-09	31-Mar-09
21	Thursday	4	36	04-Jan-08	Adjusted	04-Jan-09	31-Mar-09
22	Friday	5	45	05-Jan-08	Adjusted	05-Jan-09	31-Mar-09
23	Saturday	6	54	06-Jan-08	Adjusted	06-Jan-09	31-Mar-09
24	Sunday	7	63	07-Jan-08	Adjusted	07-Jan-09	31-Mar-09

This is even faster than using the right-click method when you want to prevent the date incrementing.

6   Create a custom list.

1.   Click File→Options→Advanced.

2.   Scroll down to the *General* category and click the gray *Edit Custom Lists...* button.

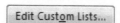

The *Custom Lists* dialog appears.

3.   Click in the *List entries* window and add four custom list entries: **North, South, East** and **West.**

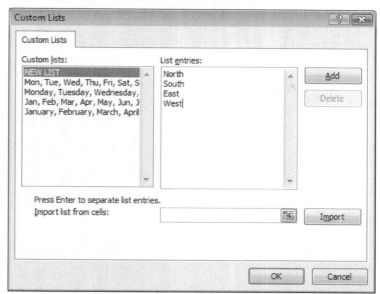

4.   Click the OK button and OK again to close the dialogs.

7   Use a custom list.

Type **North** in any cell and AutoFill down.

As you AutoFill the custom list entries appear in the worksheet (see sidebar).

North
South
East
West
North
South
East
West

8   Delete the North, South, East, West... cells from the worksheet.

9   Save your work as *First Quarter Sales and Profit-12.*

Lesson 2-18: Use the zoom control

Zooming is used to magnify or reduce the worksheet. If you have a lot of rows in a worksheet and have good eyes you might want to zoom out sometimes to see more of the worksheet on one screen.

1   Open *First Quarter Sales and Profit-12* from your sample files folder (if it isn't already open).

2   Zoom in and out of a worksheet using the mouse wheel.

The fastest way to zoom a worksheet is by using the mouse.

Most mice these days have a wheel in the middle of the buttons. To zoom using this wheel hold down the **<Ctrl>** key on the keyboard and roll the wheel to zoom in and out.

3   Zoom in and out of a worksheet using the zoom control.

The zoom control is at the bottom right of your screen,

Click and drag on the zoom control slider to zoom in and out of your worksheet. You can also zoom by clicking the plus and minus buttons on either side of the Zoom control.

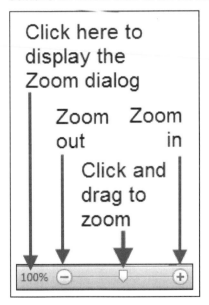

4   Select cells A3:D9.

	A	B	C	D	E
2					
3		Jan			Average
4	New York	22,000	29,000	19,000	23,333
5	Los Angeles	42,000	39,000	43,000	41,333
6	London	18,000	20,000	22,000	20,000
7	Paris	35,000	26,000	31,000	30,667
8	Munich	12,000	15,000	13,000	13,333
9	Sales	129,000	129,000	128,000	
10					

First Quarter Sales and Profit-12

We're going to use the *Zoom* dialog to make this selection completely fill the screen.

5   Double-click the left hand side of the zoom bar.

The *Zoom* dialog is displayed.

6   Select the *Fit Selection* option button and click the OK button.

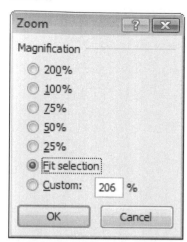

The worksheet is zoomed so that the selected cells completely fill the screen.

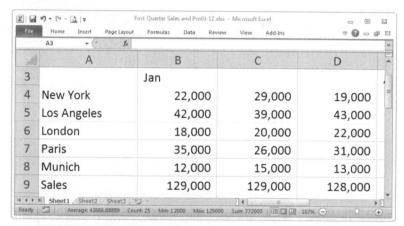

7   Zoom back to 100% using the Ribbon.

You'll probably find the zoom bar to be the quickest and most convenient way to zoom, but the *View* Ribbon also has a *Zoom* group containing three buttons:

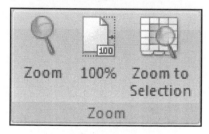

Use the 100% button to restore the screen to normal.

Lesson 2-19: Print out a worksheet

We aren't going to explore every option for preparing and printing a worksheet in this lesson. Printing is such a huge subject that we devote a whole session to it in: *Session Seven: Printing Your Work.*

This lesson only aims to teach you the bare minimum skills you need to put your work onto paper.

1   Open First *Quarter Sales and Profit-12* from your sample files folder (if it isn't already open).

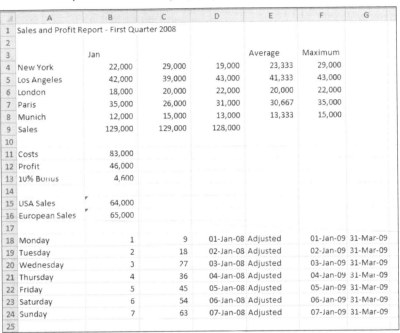

2   Click File→Print.

Backstage View appears offering many preview and print options:

Send the worksheet to the printer   Select Printer   Preview of how the page will look when printed

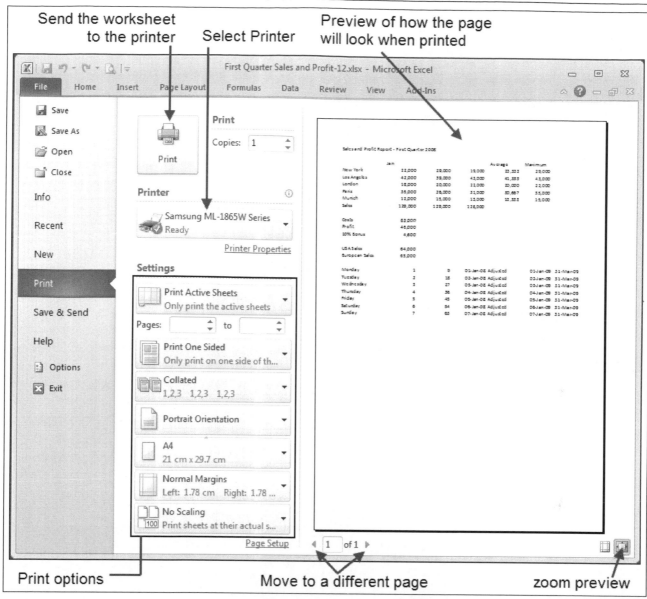

Print options   Move to a different page   zoom preview

3   Click on the zoom button to see the zoom feature working.

Each time you click on the button the page zooms in and out.

4   Print the worksheet.

Click the *Print* button:

The page is printed on the selected printer.

Session 2: Exercise

1   Open a new blank workbook.

2   Use AutoFill to put the three months Jan, Feb, and Mar into cells A4:A6.

3   Using only the keyboard add the following data:

	A	B	C	D	E
1	Profit Analysis				
2					
3		London	Paris	New York	Average
4	Jan	2,500	3,100	2,300	
5	Feb	2,200	2,700	2,600	
6	Mar	2,100	2,600	2,800	
7	Total				

4   Use AutoSum to compute London's total profit for Jan/Feb/Mar in cell B7.

5   Use AutoSum to compute the average January profit in cell E4.

6   Use AutoFill to extend the London total in cell B7, to the Paris and New York totals in cells C7 and D7.

7   Use AutoFill to extend the January average profit in cell E4, to the February and March average profits in cells E5 and E6.

8   Select all of Column A and all of Column E (at the same time) and bold face the values in them.

9   Select row 3 and row 7 (at the same time) and bold face the values in them.

	A	B	C	D	E
1	**Profit Analysis**				
2					
3		**London**	**Paris**	**New York**	**Average**
4	**Jan**	2,500	3,100	2,300	**2,633**
5	**Feb**	2,200	2,700	2,600	**2,500**
6	**Mar**	2,100	2,600	2,800	**2,500**
7	**Total**	**6,800**	**8,400**	**7,700**	

10   Select cells B4:B6 and cells D4:D6 at the same time and then read the total London and New York sales figure for Jan, Feb and March from the summary information displayed on the status bar.

11   Select cells B4:D6 and zoom the selection so that these cells fill the screen.

12   Save your work as *Exercise2-End*.

> If you need help slide the page to the left ➡

Session 2: Exercise answers

These are the four questions that students find the most difficult to remember:

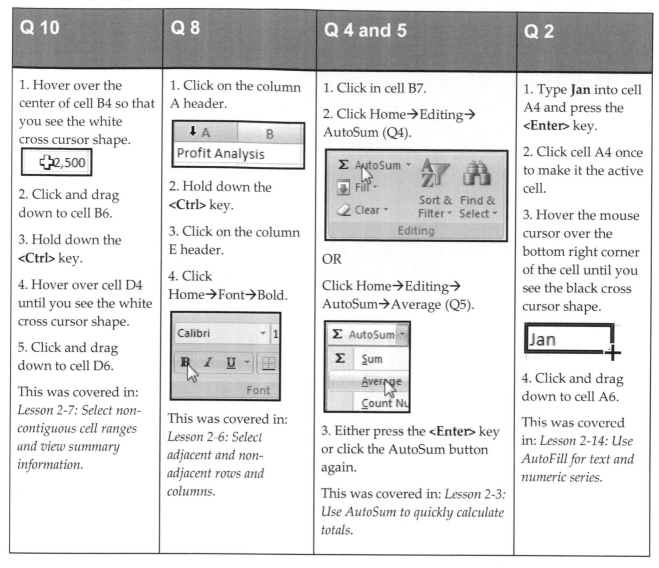

Q 10	Q 8	Q 4 and 5	Q 2
1. Hover over the center of cell B4 so that you see the white cross cursor shape. ⊕2,500 2. Click and drag down to cell B6. 3. Hold down the **<Ctrl>** key. 4. Hover over cell D4 until you see the white cross cursor shape. 5. Click and drag down to cell D6. This was covered in: *Lesson 2-7: Select non-contiguous cell ranges and view summary information.*	1. Click on the column A header. ↓ A | B Profit Analysis 2. Hold down the **<Ctrl>** key. 3. Click on the column E header. 4. Click Home→Font→Bold. Calibri ▾ 1 **B** *I* U̲ ▾ Font This was covered in: *Lesson 2-6: Select adjacent and non-adjacent rows and columns.*	1. Click in cell B7. 2. Click Home→Editing→ AutoSum (Q4). Σ AutoSum ▾ ▣ Fill ▾ ⌫ Clear ▾ Sort & Find & Filter ▾ Select ▾ Editing OR Click Home→Editing→ AutoSum→Average (Q5). Σ AutoSum ▾ Σ Sum Average Count Nu 3. Either press the **<Enter>** key or click the AutoSum button again. This was covered in: *Lesson 2-3: Use AutoSum to quickly calculate totals.*	1. Type **Jan** into cell A4 and press the **<Enter>** key. 2. Click cell A4 once to make it the active cell. 3. Hover the mouse cursor over the bottom right corner of the cell until you see the black cross cursor shape. Jan 4. Click and drag down to cell A6. This was covered in: *Lesson 2-14: Use AutoFill for text and numeric series.*

If you have difficulty with the other questions, here are the lessons that cover the relevant skills:

1 Refer to: Lesson 2-2: Create a new workbook and view two workbooks at the same time.

3 Refer to: Lesson 2-1: Enter text and numbers into a worksheet.

6 Refer to: Lesson 2-15: Use AutoFill to adjust formulas.

7 Refer to: Lesson 2-15: Use AutoFill to adjust formulas.

9 Refer to: Lesson 2-6: Select adjacent and non-adjacent rows and columns.

11 Refer to: Lesson 2-18: Use the zoom control.

12 Refer to: Lesson 1-5: Save a workbook.

Session Three: Taking Your Skills to the Next Level

> One only gets to the top rung of the ladder by steadily climbing up one at a time, and suddenly all sorts of powers, all sorts of abilities which you thought never belonged to you – suddenly become within your own possibility.
>
> *Margaret Thatcher,*
> *Prime Minister of the United Kingdom from 1979-1990*

After mastering all of the techniques covered in session two, you're already able to do useful work with the world's most powerful business tool, but of course, you're only on the first rung of a very long ladder.

While you are now able to do the simple things well, there are a few more insights you need to really get Excel working.

Most of the skills covered in this session will take your powers beyond those of casual Excel users.

Session Objectives

By the end of this session you will be able to:

- Insert and delete rows and columns
- Use AutoComplete and fill data from adjacent cells
- Cut, copy and paste
- Cut, copy and paste using drag and drop
- Use Paste Values
- Increase/decrease decimal places displayed
- Transpose a range
- Use the multiple item clipboard
- Use Undo and Redo
- Insert, View and Print cell comments
- Understand absolute, relative and mixed cell references
- Create a template
- Use a template
- Freeze columns and rows
- Split the window into multiple panes
- Check spelling

Lesson 3-1: Insert and delete rows and columns

1 Open *The World's Fastest Cars* from your sample files folder.

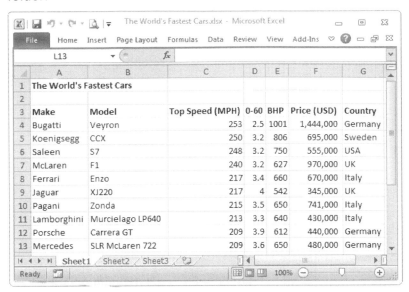

A worksheet opens showing some of the fastest cars in the world.

Until September 2007 the Bugatti Veyron was the fastest car in the world. Shelby has now stolen the crown with their SSC Ultimate Aero. There will probably be an even faster car by the time you read this book! We need to insert a row above row 4 to add the new car to the list.

2 Insert a blank row above row 4.

Right-click the row header button ⟦4⟧ and click *Insert* from the shortcut menu.

3 Add the following data to the new row:

3	Make	Model	Top Speed (MPH)	0-60	BHP	Price (USD)	Country
4	Shelby	SSC Ultimate Aero	257	2.7	1183	654,400	USA

4 If the text is bold faced restore it to normal.

This was covered in: *Lesson 1-14: Use the Mini Toolbar, Key Tips and keyboard shortcuts.*

5 Add a column to the left of column A.

Adding columns is just like adding rows. Right-click on the column header ⟦ A ⟧ and then click *Insert* from the short cut menu.

A blank column appears on the left hand side of the worksheet:

The World's Fastest Cars

◢	A	B	C	D	E
1		The World's Fastest Cars			
2					
3		Make	Model	Top Speed (MPH)	0-60
4		Shelby	SSC Ultimate Aero	257	2.7
5		Bugatti	Veyron	253	2.5
6		Koenigsegg	CCX	250	3.2

6   Delete the newly-inserted Column A.

Deleting is just like adding. Right-click on the column header

![A] but, this time, select *Delete* from the shortcut menu.

7   Insert four rows above row 3.

Nearly every Excel user does this by inserting a single row four times until they learn the correct technique.

1. Select the four rows 3:6 by clicking and dragging across the row header buttons.

2. Right-click anywhere in the selected area.

3. Click *Insert* from the shortcut menu.

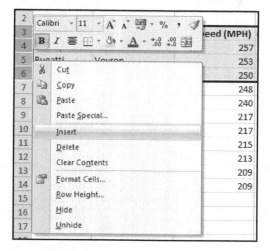

Four blank rows are inserted.

1	The World's Fastest Cars						
2							
3							
4							
5							
6							
7	Make	Model	Top Speed (MPH)	0-60	BHP	Price (USD)	Country
8	Shelby	SSC Ultimate Aero	257	2.7	1183	654,400	USA
9	Bugatti	Veyron	253	2.5	1001	1,444,000	Germany

8   Delete the newly-inserted four rows.

1. Select the four rows you want to delete (by dragging the mouse over row headers 3,4,5 and 6).

2. Right-click anywhere in the selected area.

3. Click *Delete* from the shortcut menu.

9   Save your work as: *The World's Fastest Cars-2.*

Lesson 3-2: Use AutoComplete and fill data from adjacent cells

1   Open *The World's Fastest Cars-2* from your sample files folder (if it isn't already open).

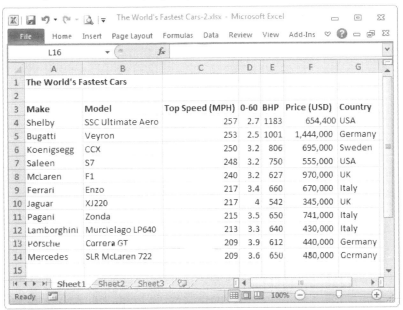

2   Type the letter **F** into cell A15.

Notice that Excel guesses that you want to type *Ferrari* into the cell. This is because the word Ferrari appears above it in the column.

If this doesn't happen somebody has switched AutoComplete off. See the sidebar to find out how to switch it back on.

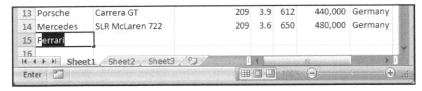

3   Press the **<Tab>** key to accept the guess.

4   Enter **599 GTB** for the model and **205** for the top speed.

14	Mercedes	SLR McLaren 722		209	3.6	650
15	Ferrari	599GTB		205		
16						

5   Use the *Fill* command to enter **3.6** into cell D15.

The Ferrari has the same 0-60 time as the McLaren SLR. Instead of typing **3.6** into the cell we can use the *Fill* command.

1. Click in cell D15.

2. Click Home→Editing→Fill→Down.

The World's Fastest Cars-2

Notice that the Fill down hotkey combination of <Ctrl>+<D> is also revealed. This is an even faster way to fill down than using the mouse.

Notice that there are also *Right, Up* and *Left* options. These can be used to copy values to adjacent cells in any direction.

6   Enter **620** for the BHP and **264,034** for the price.

7   Right-click in G15 and choose *Pick from Drop down list...* from the shortcut menu.

All unique countries that currently exist in column G are displayed as a list.

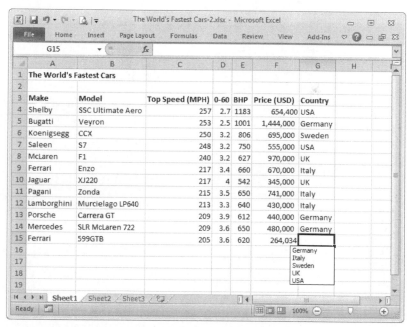

8   Click *Italy* to automatically enter the country.

9   Save your work as *The World's Fastest Cars-3.*

Lesson 3-3: Cut, copy and paste

1   Open *The World's Fastest Cars-3* from your sample files folder (if it isn't already open).

2   Click cell A1 to make it the active cell.

3   Copy the text from cell A1 to the clipboard.

The clipboard is a container for copied text and is common to all of Microsoft Office. When you ask Excel to copy it takes the value in cell A1 (in this case text) and places a copy of it onto the clipboard.

The clipboard is useful because we can later paste the clipboard's contents back into the worksheet (or into any other Office document such as a PowerPoint presentation, Word document or Outlook Email).

There are three ways to copy but these two are the quickest:

EITHER

- Right click and select *Copy* from the shortcut menu.

OR

- Press **<Ctrl>+<C>** on the keyboard.

The third method is to click Home→Clipboard→Copy.

4   Click cell A17 to make it the active cell.

5   Paste the copied text into cell A17.

There are also three ways to paste but these two are the quickest:

EITHER

Right click cell A17 and then select: Paste Options→Paste from the shortcut menu (see sidebar). The other paste options will be covered later in this lesson.

OR

Click cell A17 and then Press **<Ctrl>+<V>** on the keyboard.

The third (and slowest) method is to click:

Home→Clipboard→Paste

The text appears in cell A17.

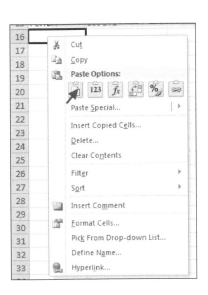

14	Mercedes	SLR McLaren 722		209
15	Ferrari	599GTB		205
16				
17	**The World's Fastest Cars**			
18				

The World's Fastest Cars-3

6   Edit the text to read: The World's Fastest Italian Cars.

This was covered in: *Lesson 2-1: Enter text and numbers into a worksheet.*

7   Select all of row 9 and copy it to the clipboard.

Selecting an entire row was covered in: *Lesson 2-6: Select adjacent and non-adjacent rows and columns.*

8   Select all of row 19 and paste into it.

The contents of row 9 are copied to row 19.

17	The World's Fastest Italian Cars			
18				
19	Ferrari	Enzo	217	3.4

9   Select the range A11:G12.

These cells contain data for two more Italian cars.

10	Jaguar	XJ220	217	4	542	345,000	UK
11	Pagani	Zonda	215	3.5	650	741,000	Italy
12	Lamborghini	Murcielago LP640	213	3.3	640	430,000	Italy
13	Porsche	Carrera GT	209	3.9	612	440,000	Germany

10   Cut the text from A11:G12 to place it onto the clipboard.

There are three ways to cut but these two are the quickest:

EITHER

Right click and select *Cut* from the shortcut menu.

OR

Press **<Ctrl>+<X>**.

The third (and slowest) method is to click Home→Clipboard→Cut.

11   Click in cell A20 to make it the active cell.

12   Paste the cut range into the range beginning in cell A20.

The cut text appears with the top left hand corner in cell A20.

10	Jaguar	XJ220	217	4	542	345,000	UK
11							
12							
13	Porsche	Carrera GT	209	3.9	612	440,000	Germany
14	Mercedes	SLR McLaren 722	209	3.6	650	480,000	Germany
15	Ferrari	599GTB	205	3.6	620	264,034	Italy
16							
17	The World's Fastest Italian Cars						
18							
19	Ferrari	Enzo	217	3.4	660	670,000	Italy
20	Pagani	Zonda	215	3.5	650	741,000	Italy
21	Lamborghini	Murcielago LP640	213	3.3	640	430,000	Italy
22							

13   Save your work as *The World's Fastest Cars-4*.

Lesson 3-4: Cut, copy and paste using drag and drop

1   Open *The World's Fastest Cars-4* from your sample files folder (if it isn't already open).

2   Select cells A20:G21.

3   Hover the mouse cursor over the black border surrounding the range until you see a four-headed arrow.

19	Ferrari	Enzo		217	3.4	660	670,000	Italy
20	Pagani	Zonda		215	3.5	650	741,000	Italy
21	Lamborghini	Murcielago LP640		213	3.3	640	430,000	Italy
22								

It is very important that you see the four headed arrow and not the white cross or AutoFill cursor shape.

If you do not see a four headed arrow somebody may have switched the drag and drop facility off. See sidebar for how to bring it back.

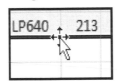

4   Click and drag the cells, dropping them to their previous location (beginning at cell A11).

You'll see a gray outline showing where the cells will be dropped. Move them to the location shown in the screen grab below.

10	Jaguar	XJ220	217	4	542	345,000	UK
11							
12							
13	Porsche	Carrera GT	A11:G12	3.9	612	440,000	Germany

When you release the mouse button the contents of the cells are moved back to A11:G12.

10	Jaguar	XJ220	217	4	542	345,000	UK
11	Pagani	Zonda	215	3.5	650	741,000	Italy
12	Lamborghini	Murcielago LP640	213	3.3	640	430,000	Italy
13	Porsche	Carrera GT	209	3.9	612	440,000	Germany

5   Select cells A11:G12.

6   Hover the mouse cursor over the black border surrounding the range until you see a four-headed arrow.

7   Right-click and drag the rectangle to rows 20 and 21.

When you release the mouse button several options are presented (see sidebar).

8   Click *Copy Here* from the shortcut menu.

---

note

If drag and drop doesn't work somebody has switched it off

It's almost certain that drag and drop will be enabled on any computer that you work on. It is such a useful feature that you'd never want to disable it.

If drag and drop doesn't work for you it's because somebody has switched it off.

Bring it back like this:

1. Click File→Options→Advanced.

2. In the first section (*Editing Options*) check *Enable fill handle and cell drag and drop.*

Move Here
Copy Here
Copy Here as Values Only
Copy Here as Formats Only
Link Here
Create Hyperlink Here
Shift Down and Copy
Shift Right and Copy
Shift Down and Move
Shift Right and Move
Cancel

The World's Fastest Cars-4

This time the contents of the cells are copied rather than moved.

17	The World's Fastest Italian Cars						
18							
19	Ferrari	Enzo	217	3.4	660	670,000	Italy
20	Pagani	Zonda	215	3.5	650	741,000	Italy
21	Lamborghini	Murcielago LP640	213	3.3	640	430,000	Italy

9 Select all of row 15.

Selecting an entire row was covered in: *Lesson 2-6: Select adjacent and non-adjacent rows and columns.*

14	Mercedes	SLR McLaren 722		209	3.6	650	480,000	Germany
15	Ferrari	599 GTB		205	3.6	620	264,034	Italy
16								

10 Using drag and drop, copy the contents of row 15 to row 22.

17	The World's Fastest Italian Cars						
18							
19	Ferrari	Enzo	217	3.4	660	670,000	Italy
20	Pagani	Zonda	215	3.5	650	741,000	Italy
21	Lamborghini	Murcielago LP640	213	3.3	640	430,000	Italy
22	Ferrari	599GTB	205	3.6	620	264,034	Italy

11 Rename Sheet1 to *World Cars* and Sheet2 to *Italian Cars*.

You learned how to re-name tabs in: *Lesson 1-8: View, move, add, rename, delete* and navigate worksheet tabs.

12 Select cells A17:G22 on the *World Cars* worksheet.

13 Cut the cells and paste them into cell A1 of the *Italian Cars* worksheet.

	A	B	C	D	E	F	G
1	The World's Fastest Italian Cars						
2							
3	Ferrari	Enzo	217	3.4	660	670,000	Italy
4	Pagani	Zonda	215	3.5	650	741,000	Italy
5	Lamborgh	Murcielag	213	3.3	640	430,000	Italy
6	Ferrari	599GTB	205	3.6	620	264,034	Italy

World Cars　Italian Cars　Sheet3

note

Other ways of copying cells via drag and drop

Hover over the border of the selected cells with the <Ctrl> key held down. You will see the mouse cursor shape change to a plus sign.

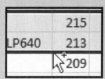

You can now drag and drop (holding the left mouse button down) to copy the cells to a new location.

14 Insert one blank row above row 3 on the *Italian Cars* worksheet.

You learned how to do this in: *Lesson 3-1: Insert and delete rows and columns.*

15 Copy the titles from row 3 of the *World Cars* worksheet to row 3 of the *Italian Cars* worksheet.

1	The World's Fastest Italian Cars						
2							
3	Make	Model		Top Speed (MPH)	0-60	BHP	Price (USD)	Country
4	Ferrari	Enzo		217	3.4	660	670,000	Italy

16 Save your work as *The World's Fastest Cars-5*.

Lesson 3-5: Use Paste Values and increase/decrease decimal places displayed

1   Open *The World's Fastest Cars-5* from your sample files folder (if it isn't already open).

2   Select the *World Cars* worksheet and add a new column to the left of column D.

Right click on the column D header and click *Insert* from the shortcut menu.

3   Rename cell C3 from *Top Speed (MPH)* to *MPH*.

4   Type **KM/H** into cell D3.

5   Re-size column C so that it is just wide enough for the contents.

This skill was covered in: *Lesson 2-9: Re-size rows and columns.*

6   Given that one mile=1.609344 Km, enter a formula into cell D4 to convert MPH into KM/H.

This skill was covered in: *Lesson 2-12: Create your own formulas.*

The correct formula is: **=C4*1.609344.**

The Shelby's speed is now also displayed in Kilometers per hour.

	A	B	C	D	E	F
3	Make	Model	MPH	KM/H	0-60	BHP
4	Shelby	SSC Ultimate Aero	257	413.601408	2.7	1183

7   AutoFill the formula in Cell D4 down to (D15) the bottom of the list.

This skill was covered in: *Lesson 2-15: Use AutoFill to adjust formulas.*

	A	B	C	D	E	F
3	Make	Model	MPH	KM/H	0-60	BHP
4	Shelby	SSC Ultimate Aero	257	413.601408	2.7	1183
5	Bugatti	Veyron	253	407.164032	2.5	1001

The worksheet is giving the right answers but we're not really interested in seeing speeds to six decimal places. It would be nice to simply show whole numbers (also called integers) as we do for Miles per Hour.

8   Use the *Decrease Decimal* button to format the values in column D to display as whole numbers.

1.   Select cells D4:D15.

2.   Click the Home→Number→Decrease Decimal button six times.

The World's Fastest Cars-5

note

Other ways to paste values.

Using the Smart Tag

If you perform a regular *paste* and then suddenly realize that you really wanted to *paste values* you don't need to start again.

Notice that a Smart Tag is displayed at the bottom right corner of the pasted cells.

You can click the Smart Tag to change the paste to *Values*.

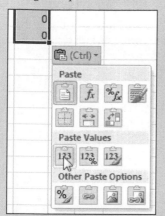

Using the Ribbon

If you click:

Home→Clipboard→Paste

... you'll be presented with the same set of icons. You've only learned about the *Paste* and *Paste Values* options so far but you'll encounter some of the others later in this course:

9   Make column D narrower to make things neater.

This skill was covered in: *Lesson 2-9: Re-size rows and columns.*

	A	B	C	D	E	F
3	Make	Model	MPH	KM/H	0-60	BHP
4	Shelby	SSC Ultimate Aero	257	414	2.7	1183
5	Bugatti	Veyron	253	407	2.5	1001

10 Copy cells D4:D15 and paste into cells D17:D28.

1. Select cells D4:D15.

2. Right-click anywhere in the selected range and then click *Copy* from the shortcut menu.

3. Right-click cell D17 and click: Paste Options→Paste from the shortcut menu.

Paste Options:

4. Unexpectedly, all of the values are pasted as zeros.

	A	B	C	D	E
17				0	
18				0	

5. Click cell D17 and look at the formula displayed in the Formula Bar at the top of the screen:

f_x =C17*1.609344

When you paste a formula Excel will, by default, adjust the formula in exactly the same way it does when you AutoFill.

11 Undo the previous paste.

Click the undo button  on the quick access toolbar.

12 Paste again, this time using Paste Values.

Right-click cell E17 and click: Paste Options→Values from the shortcut menu.

Paste Options:

This time the values within the cells (rather than the formulas used to calculate the values) are pasted.

15	Ferrari	599GTB	205	330	3.6	620
16						
17				413.6		
18				407.2		
19				402.3		

13 Delete the values in cells E17:E28.

Select cells E17:E28 and press the **<Delete>** key.

14 Save your work as *The World's Fastest Cars-6.*

Lesson 3-6: Transpose a range

Paste Values is the most used special pasting option but there's another that is often very useful.

If a worksheet has many columns but few rows it may become impossible to print. In this case you may wish to reverse the arrangement so that the worksheet has many rows but few columns.

Transposing allows you to do this automatically.

1   Open *The World's Fastest Cars-6* from your sample files folder (if it isn't already open).

2   Rename Sheet3 to *Transposed.*

    This skill was covered in: *Lesson 1-8: View, move, add, rename, delete and navigate* worksheet tabs.

3   Select and copy the range A3:H15 on the *World Cars* worksheet.

	A	B	C	D	E	F	G	H
2								
3	Make	Model	MPH	KM/H	0-60	BHP	Price (USD)	Country
4	Shelby	SSC Ultimate Aero	257	414	2.7	1183	654,400	USA
5	Bugatti	Veyron	253	407	2.5	1001	1,444,000	Germany
6	Koenigsegg	CCX	250	402	3.2	806	695,000	Sweden
7	Saleen	S7	248	399	3.2	750	555,000	USA
8	McLaren	F1	240	386	3.2	627	970,000	UK
9	Ferrari	Enzo	217	349	3.4	660	670,000	Italy
10	Jaguar	XJ220	217	349	4	542	345,000	UK
11	Pagani	Zonda	215	346	3.5	650	741,000	Italy
12	Lamborghini	Murcielago LP640	213	343	3.3	640	430,000	Italy
13	Porsche	Carrera GT	209	336	3.9	612	440,000	Germany
14	Mercedes	SLR McLaren 722	209	336	3.6	650	480,000	Germany
15	Ferrari	599 GTB	205	330	3.6	620	264,034	Italy
16								

4   Select cell A3 on the *Transposed* worksheet.

5   Click Home→Clipboard→Paste→Transpose.

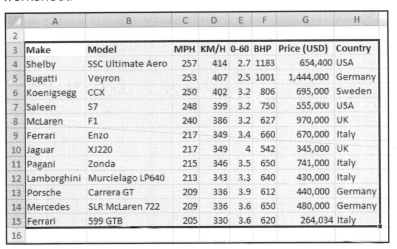

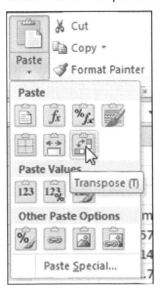

The World's Fastest Cars-6

The cells are copied in a rather interesting way. The columns have now become rows and the rows have become columns.

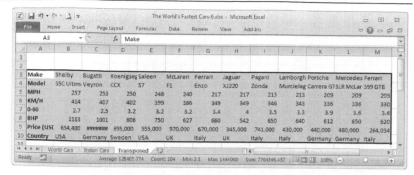

Notice also that the width of the columns has not been maintained. In the case of the (very expensive) Bugatti Veyron there isn't even enough space in the cell to display the price and a row of hashes is displayed instead.

(If you're used to calling the hash (#) a **pound sign** or **number sign** see the sidebar in: *Lesson 2-9: Re-size rows and columns* for an explanation).

6 Automatically size all columns in one operation.

1. Select every cell in the workbook by clicking the *select all* button in the top left corner of the worksheet:

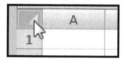

2. Hover the mouse cursor over the intersection of any two columns until you see the *re-size* cursor shape 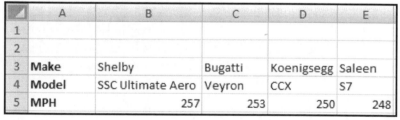 and then double-click.

Every column is perfectly sized.

	A	B	C	D	E
1					
2					
3	**Make**	Shelby	Bugatti	Koenigsegg	Saleen
4	**Model**	SSC Ultimate Aero	Veyron	CCX	S7
5	**MPH**	257	253	250	248

7 Save your work as *The World's Fastest Cars-7*.

Lesson 3-7: Use the Multiple Item Clipboard

When you copy items from any non-Office Windows application, the selected item is copied to the *Windows Clipboard*. You are then able to paste this item into any other Windows application.

While the *Windows Clipboard* can only contain one item, Office has its own clipboard that can contain up to 24 items.

Because all Office applications share the same *Office Clipboard*, it is possible to copy and paste up to 24 items between Excel, PowerPoint, Word, Access, Outlook… and all other Office applications.

In this lesson we'll use the *Office Clipboard* to add content to a new page in the workbook. The new page will contain details of the world's fastest *German* cars.

1   Open *The World's Fastest Cars-7* from your sample files folder (if it isn't already open).

2   Insert a new worksheet and name it *German Cars*.

This skill was covered in: *Lesson 1-8: View, move, add, rename, delete and navigate* worksheet tabs.

3   Click Home→Clipboard→Dialog Launcher.

This is our first experience of a dialog launcher button. The dialog launcher button is situated on the bottom right-hand corner of some dialogs.

The Clipboard task pane is displayed:

4   If any items are shown on the Clipboard click the Clear All button ![Clear All] to remove them.

5   Copy row 3 on the World Cars worksheet to the clipboard.

Right-click the row 3 row header and click *Copy* on the shortcut menu.

The World's Fastest Cars-7

6   Copy row 5 in the World Cars worksheet to the clipboard.

7   Copy row 13 in the World Cars worksheet to the clipboard

8   Copy row 14 in the World Cars worksheet to the clipboard.

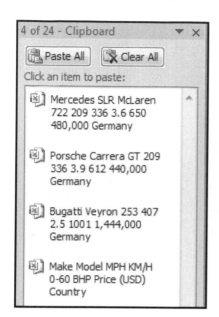

The header row, along with details for the three German cars, is now displayed on the clipboard (see sidebar).

9   Click the *German Cars* tab.

The blank *German Cars* worksheet is displayed.

10 Type **The World's Fastest German Cars** into cell A1 and bold face the text.

11 Click cell A3 to make it the Active Cell.

12 Complete the worksheet with a single click by clicking the Paste All button.

It would be possible to click once upon each of the four items on the Clipboard. Because we want the entire contents of the Clipboard four clicks are saved by using the *Paste All* button.

When you click the *Paste All* button, all of the items on the clipboard are pasted into adjacent rows:

13 Automatically Re-size all of the columns.

This skill was covered in: *Lesson 2-9: Re-size rows and columns.*

14 Close the clipboard.

Click the *Close* button at the top right-hand corner of the clipboard.

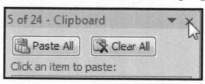

15 Save your work as *The World's Fastest Cars-8.*

Lesson 3-8: Use Undo and Redo

Excel's *Undo* feature is a lifesaver.

It is only possible to undo the previous 16 actions.

Sometimes you may undo an action and then change your mind. Redo will step through the operations in reverse, in effect "undoing the undo"!

1   Close any workbooks that are open and then re-open Excel.

Excel keeps tabs on the last 100 actions taken. By closing and re-opening Excel we'll clear the existing list of actions available for undo.

2   Open *The World's Fastest Cars-8* from your sample files folder and select the World Cars worksheet.

3   Type **USA Cars** into cell A17 and bold face the text.

4   Copy row 3 into row 19.

5   Copy row 4 into row 20.

6   Copy row 7 into row 21.

The worksheet should now look like this:

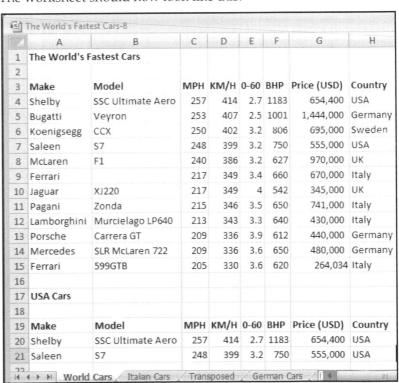

note

Using the keyboard to undo and redo

It is well worth remembering the undo keyboard shortcut :

<Ctrl>+<Z>

I use it all of the time. It is also the undo shortcut for the other Office applications.

You'll use the Redo action far less, but for completeness it is:

<Ctrl>+<Y>

If you forget them, you'll see the keyboard shortcuts in the tooltip when you hover over the undo and redo buttons.

Undo Paste (Ctrl+Z)

The World's Fastest Cars-8

7   Click the undo button on the quick access toolbar.

The Saleen details disappear from row 21.

8   Click the redo button on the quick access toolbar.

The Saleen details re-appear in row 21.

9   Click the drop-down arrow to the right of the undo button
     on the quick access toolbar.

A drop-down menu appears showing all of the actions that have
taken place (or the previous 100 actions if more than 100 actions
have taken place) since the workbook was opened.

10   Click the Bold action to *Undo 4 Actions*.

Only the text *USA Cars* remains on the worksheet and it is no
longer bold faced.

14	Mercedes	SLR McLaren 722	209	336
15	Ferrari	599GTB	205	330
16				
17	USA Cars			
18				

11   Click the drop-down arrow to the right of the redo button
     on the quick access toolbar.

A drop-down menu appears showing all of the actions that have
been undone and can be potentially re-done.

12   Click the last *Paste* action to redo four actions.

The worksheet reverts to its former state.

17	USA Cars							
18								
19	Make	Model	MPH	KM/H	0-60	BHP	Price (USD)	Country
20	Shelby	SSC Ultimate Aero	257	414	2.7	1183	654,400	USA
21	Saleen	S7	248	399	3.2	750	555,000	USA

13   Delete rows 17 to 21.

14   Save your work as *The World's Fastest Cars-9*.

Lesson 3-9: Insert cell comments

1 Open *The World's Fastest Cars-9* from your sample files folder (if it isn't already open) and select the *World Cars* worksheet.

2 Using Microsoft Word (not Excel), open *Car Descriptions* from your sample files folder.

   1. Open Microsoft Word.

   2. Click Office→Open and open *Car Descriptions* from your sample files folder.

3 Return to Excel without closing Word.

You will notice two buttons on the Windows status bar at the bottom of the screen:

Click the button with the Excel logo to return to Excel.

4 Set up the name that will appear in the comment box.

Whenever you enter a comment your name is added to the top. This allows other users to identify the source of each comment if you later distribute the workbook.

Click File→Options→General.

In the category *Personalize your copy of Microsoft Office* type your name into the *User Name* box and then click the OK button.

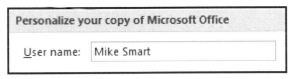

Personalize your copy of Microsoft Office
User name: Mike Smart

5 Copy the text for the Shelby SSC Ultimate Aero from the word document.

   1. Return to Word.

   2. Drag across the Shelby text with the mouse cursor.

   3. Right-click within the selected text and click *Copy* from the shortcut menu.

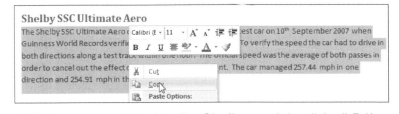

6 Add the comment text to the Shelby model cell (cell B4).

   1. Return to Excel.

   2. Right-click cell B4 and click *Insert Comment* on the shortcut menu.

---

note

Excel uses your log-in user name by default

If you don't set up your user name as described, Excel will use your Windows log-in user name instead.

This is the reason you'll often see cryptic user names (like JSmith93) in other people's worksheets.

---

note

Other ways to insert a comment

Click Review→Comments→ New Comment.

OR

Press <Shift>+<F2>

Car Descriptions

The World's Fastest Cars-9

A comment box with your name at the top is shown next to cell B4.

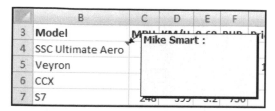

3. Paste into the comment box.

The text that you copied from the Word document appears in the box.

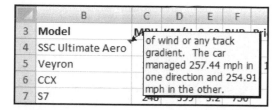

7   Enlarge the comment box, using the sizing handles, so that all text is visible.

The sizing handles are the small white dots that appear on the corners and edges of the comment box. When you hover over a sizing handle the cursor shape changes to a double headed arrow.

1. Hover carefully over the bottom-right sizing handle until you see the double-headed arrow.

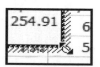

2. Click and drag to re-size the comment box.

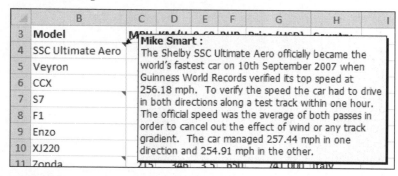

8   Click anywhere in the worksheet.

The comment disappears but a small red triangle has appeared in the top right corner of the cell.

9   Add two more comments for the Saleen S7 and Pagani Zonda.

10 Save your work as *The World's Fastest Cars-10.*

Lesson 3-10: View cell comments

1   Open *The World's Fastest Cars-10* from your sample files folder (if it isn't already open) and select the *World Cars* worksheet.

Cells with comments show a small red triangle in the top right-hand corner.

2   View the comment behind a single cell.

Hover the mouse cursor over any of the cells with a red triangle. The cell comment is displayed.

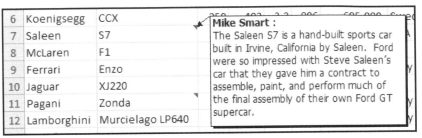

3   View all of the comments in a worksheet at the same time.

Click Review→Comments→Show All Comments.

Every comment on the worksheet is displayed.

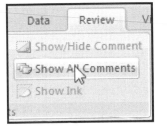

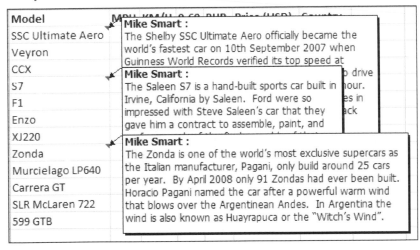

Unfortunately the comments overlap so you are unable to read them all at the same time. It is possible to view each comment by clicking it as this brings the window to the front but it isn't very elegant.

4   Move the comments so that they do not overlap.

Click a comment and then hover anywhere on the gray border *but not on a sizing handle* until you see a four headed arrow. When you see the four-headed arrow click and drag to move the comment.

The World's Fastest Cars-10

⊿	A	B	C	D	E	F	G	H	I	J
1	**The World's Fastest Cars**									
2										
3	**Make**	**Model**	**MPH**	**KM**						
4	Shelby	SSC Ultimate Aero	257							
5	Bugatti	Veyron	253							
6	Koenigsegg	CCX	250							
7	Saleen	S7	248							
8	McLaren	F1	240							
9	Ferrari	Enzo	217							
10	Jaguar	XJ220	217							
11	Pagani	Zonda	215							
12	Lamborghini	Murcielago LP640	213							
13	Porsche	Carrera GT	209							
14	Mercedes	SLR McLaren 722	209							
15	Ferrari	599 GTB	205							
16										
17										
18										
19										
20										
21										
22										

Mike Smart :
The Shelby SSC Ultimate Aero officially became the world's fastest car on 10th September 2007 when Guinness World Records verified its top speed at 256.18 mph. To verify the speed the car had to drive in both directions along a test track within one hour. The official speed was the average of both passes in order to cancel out the effect of wind or any track gradient. The car managed 257.44 mph in one direction and 254.91 mph in the other.

Mike Smart :
The Saleen S7 is a hand-built sports car built in Irvine, California by Saleen. Ford were so impressed with Steve Saleen's car that they gave him a contract to assemble, paint, and perform much of the final assembly of their own Ford GT supercar.

Mike Smart :
The Zonda is one of the world's most exclusive supercars as the Italian manufacturer, Pagani, only build around 25 cars per year. By April 2008 only 91 Zondas had ever been built. Horacio Pagani named the car after a powerful warm wind that blows over the Argentinean Andes. In Argentina the wind is also known as Huayrapuca or the "Witch's Wind".

> ## note
>
> ### Other ways to show/hide comments
>
> The right-click method is definitely the fastest but you can also show and hide comments using the Ribbon.
>
> To show or hide a comment:
>
> 1. Click cell B11 to make it the active cell.
>
> 2. Click:
>   Review→Comments→ Show/Hide Comment

5   Hide all of the comments.

Click: Review→Comments→Show All Comments.

The comments disappear.

6   Make the Zonda comment display all of the time.

Sometimes you will want to send somebody a worksheet and make sure that an important comment is on view when they open it.

Right click cell B11 and choose Show/Hide Comments from the shortcut menu.

The comment remains on display all of the time (even if you are not hovering over the comment cell).

7   Hide the Zonda comment.

Right click cell B11 and choose *Hide Comment* from the shortcut menu.

8   Save your work as *The World's Fastest Cars-11*.

Lesson 3-11: Print cell comments

One of the commonest requests asked by Excel users is: "how can I print a list of comments at the end of a worksheet".

Excel can do this but the feature is hidden away in the *Page Setup* dialog and missed by most users.

1 Open *The World's Fastest Cars-11* from your sample files folder (if it isn't already open) and select the *World Cars* worksheet.

2 Tell Excel to print comments at the end of the worksheet.

1. Click Page Layout→Page Setup→Dialog Launcher.

The *Page Setup* dialog is displayed.

2. Click the *Sheet* tab and then choose the option *At end of sheet* from the *Comments* drop-down.

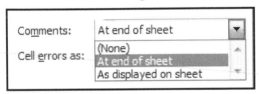

3 Click the *Print Preview* button to view the comments as they would print.

You can either click the *Print Preview* button on the *Page Setup* dialog or close the dialog and click File→Print. Whichever way you choose the *Backstage* view opens and displays a print preview of the worksheet in the right-hand pane.

Click the *Next Page* button to view Page 2 of the preview. The comments are displayed exactly as they would print.

Cell: B4
Comment: Mike Smart :
The Shelby SSC Ultimate Aero officially became the world's fastest car on 10th September 2007 when Guinness World Records verified its top speed at 256.18 mph. To verify the speed the car had to drive in both directions along a test track within one hour. The official speed was the average of both passes in order to cancel out the effect of wind or any track gradient. The car managed 257.44 mph in one direction and 254.91 mph in the other.

Cell: B7
Comment: Mike Smart :
The Saleen S7 is a hand-built sports car built in Irvine, California by Saleen. Ford were so impressed with Steve Saleen's car that they gave him a contract to assemble, paint, and perform much of the final assembly of their own Ford GT supercar.

Cell: B11
Comment: Mike Smart :
The Zonda is one of the world's most exclusive supercars as the Italian manufacturer, Pagani, only build around 25 cars per year. By April 2008 only 91 Zondas had ever been built. Horacio Pagani named the car after a powerful warm wind that blows over the Argentinean Andes. In Argentina the wind is also known as Huayrapuca or the "Witch's Wind".

The World's Fastest Cars-11

4   Click the *Home* tab on the Ribbon to return to the worksheet.

5   Make the Zonda comment display all of the time.

Right click cell B11 and choose *Show/Hide Comments* from the shortcut menu.

6   Move the Zonda comment so that it doesn't obscure the data in the worksheet.

This was covered in: *Lesson 3-10: View cell comments.*

7   Tell Excel to print comments exactly as they are displayed on the worksheet.

1.   Click Page Layout→Page Setup→Dialog Launcher.

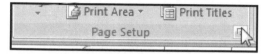

The *Page Setup* dialog is displayed.

2.   Click the *Sheet* tab and then choose the option *As displayed on sheet* from the *Comments* drop-down.

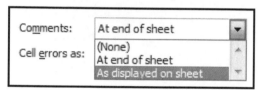

8   Click the *Print Preview* button to view the comment as it would print.

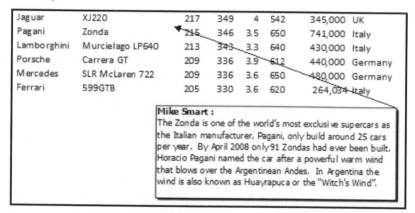

9   Click the *Home* tab on the ribbon to view the worksheet.

10   Hide the comment.

Right click cell B11 and choose *Hide Comment* from the shortcut menu.

11   Save your work as: *The World's Fastest Cars-12.*

Lesson 3-12: Understand absolute and relative cell references

You've seen how useful Excel's AutoFill is when copying formulas. Most of the time things work perfectly, as you normally want to increment row and column references when you AutoFill down and across.

Sometimes AutoFill can be a little too helpful when it adjusts cell references that you would like to be left alone. This lesson will illustrate the type of worksheet that requires *absolute cell references* as we convert USD (US Dollar) prices to GBP (Great Britain Pounds).

1   Open *The World's Fastest Cars-12* from your sample files folder (if it isn't already open) and select the *World Cars* worksheet.

2   Insert a column to the left of column H.

This skill was covered in: *Lesson 3-1: Insert and delete rows and columns.*

3   Type **Price (GBP)** into cell H3.

4   Type **USD/GBP** into cell G1.

5   Type **0.51195** into cell H1.

If you want more realism you can get the current exchange rate from www.oanda.com. If you are not in England or America it might be fun to change the exchange rate to match your own currency.

6   Place a formula in cell H4 that will calculate the price of a Shelby SSC Ultimate Aero in GBP (Great Britain Pounds).

Formulas were covered in: *Lesson 2-12: Create your own formulas.*

The correct formula is:

=G4*H1

We can now see that the Shelby costs £335,020 in Great Britain Pounds.

	G	H	I
1	USD/GBP	0.51195	
2			
3	Price (USD)	Price (GBP)	Country
4	654,400	335,020	USA

7   Consider what will happen if we AutoFill this formula.

(AutoFill was covered in: *Lesson 2-15: Use AutoFill to adjust formulas*).

As the formula is AutoFilled downward the number part of each formula will be incremented like this:

The World's Fastest Cars-12

	H
3	Price (GBP)
4	=G4*H1
5	=G5*H2
6	=G6*H3

Consider cell H5 (the price of the Bugatti Veyron). The formula in this cell is **=G5*H2**.

AutoFill has done a wonderful job with G5. It has changed the reference from the Shelby's price to the Bugatti and that's exactly what we wanted.

But AutoFill has seriously messed up with the H2 reference. The exchange rate is always in cell H1. It never moves.

To express this in "Excel-speak": G4 is a **relative reference** (ie we want AutoFill to adjust it) while H1 is an **absolute reference** (ie we want AutoFill to leave it alone).

8 Change the formula in cell H4 to make H1 into an absolute reference.

To make a reference absolute you simply add a dollar sign in front of both the letter and number.

So: H1 becomes $H$1.

Click cell H4 and then edit the formula (shown in the formula bar) so that it now reads.

=G4*$H$1

9 AutoFill the formula in cell H4 to the end of the list.

(AutoFill was covered in: *Lesson 2-15: Use AutoFill to adjust formulas*).

The price of each car is now displayed in both US Dollars and Great Britain Pounds.

	G	H	I
3	Price (USD)	Price (GBP)	Country
4	654,400	335,020	USA
5	1,444,000	739,256	Germany
6	695,000	355,805	Sweden

Click on each of the GBP prices and observe the formula shown in the formula bar at the top of the screen.

In every case Excel has adjusted the G4 part of the formula but left the H1 part of the formula alone.

H5				f_x	=G5*$H$1	
	C	D	E	F	G	H
3	MPH	KM/H	0-60	BHP	Price (USD)	Price (GBP)
4	257	414	2.7	1183	654,400	335,020
5	253	407	2.5	1001	1,444,000	739,256

10 Save your work as *The World's Fastest Cars-13*.

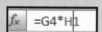

note

Don't worry if you're unable to understand this concept at first

In my "Essential Skills" classroom courses I've found that many students find mixed cell references a very difficult concept to understand.

I never waste a lot of time on this lesson if it is clear that some students are unable to easily follow the logic.

I'd advise that you take the same approach and don't waste a lot of time on this lesson if you find it difficult to follow.

You won't need to use mixed cell references anywhere else in the *Essential Skills* course and it's a skill that most office workers don't have.

If you do skip this lesson it's well worthwhile returning to it later, when you've completed the course and have been using Excel for a few months.

By then you will probably have encountered some of the real-world business problems that are more efficiently solved using mixed cell references.

International Price List

Lesson 3-13: Understand mixed cell references

Before we tackle mixed cell references I must warn you that this subject is a bit of a brain teaser (see sidebar). The skill is well worth mastering as you'll find it extremely useful in many types of real-world worksheets.

1 Open *International Price List* from your sample files folder.

This worksheet will calculate the price of each car for five more markets. The exchange rates are shown in row 4.

2 Add a formula to calculate the UK price of a Shelby SSC Ultimate Aero.

Formulas were covered in: *Lesson 2-12: Create your own formulas.*

The correct formula is:

=C6*D4

We can see that the Shelby costs £335,020.

	C	D	E	F	G	H
3		GBP	EUR	JPY	CAD	CHF
4		0.51195	0.64682	198.687	1.04422	1.05489
5	USA $	UK £	Euros €	Japan ¥	Canada $	Switzerland fr.
6	654,400	335,020				

3 Consider what will happen if we AutoFill this formula.

(AutoFill was covered in: *Lesson 2-15: Use AutoFill to adjust formulas*).

As the formula is AutoFilled downward the number part of each formula is incremented like this:

	C	D
6	654400	=C6*D4
7	1444000	=C7*D5
8	695000	=C8*D6

You may be thinking that this is just like the problem posed in: *Lesson 3-12: Understand absolute and relative cell references.*

Why not simply make D4 into an absolute reference? Like this:

	C	D	E
3		GBP	EUR
4		0.51195	0.64682
5	USA $	UK £	Euros €
6	654400	=C6*$D$4	

This will work just fine for the GBP prices but think carefully about what will then happen when you AutoFill to the right.

AutoFill knows that when you fill right you *usually* want the letter part of each formula incremented like this:

	C	D	E
3		GBP	EUR
4		0.51195	0.64682
5	USA $	UK £	Euros €
6	654400	=C6*$D$4	=D6*$D$4
7	1444000	=C7*$D$4	
8	695000	=C8*$D$4	

This is going to mess up the Euro price completely. AutoFill has made two errors.

1. It is still using the GBP exchange rate for the EUR prices because we made D4 an absolute reference.

2. It is referencing the UK price of the Shelby instead of the US dollar price because C6 is a relative reference.

Let's tackle each problem one at a time

1. We want the GBP exchange rate to adjust to the EUR exchange rate as the formula is filled to the right. In this case the D part of D4 should be relative but the 4 part should be absolute. This can be denoted by D$4 instead of $D$4.

2. We want the US Dollar price to always be used against the US Dollar Exchange rates in Row 4. Therefore we want the C part of C6 to be absolute. As AutoFill fills downward we need the price to be adjusted to the relevant car so the 6 part of C6 needs to be relative. This can be denoted by $C6 instead of $C$6.

4   Correct the formula so that it will AutoFill correctly.

Enter the formula =$C6*D$4 into cell D6.

This will AutoFill correctly like this:

	C	D	E
3		GBP	EUR
4		0.51195	0.64682
5	USA $	UK £	Euros €
6	654400	=$C6*D$4	=$C6*E$4
7	1444000	=$C7*D$4	=$C7*E$4
8	695000	=$C8*D$4	=$C8*E$4

5   AutoFill across to cell H6.

The correct Shelby prices are shown in five currencies.

6   AutoFill down to cell H17.

The correct prices are shown for all cars and all currencies.

7   Make the columns wide enough to display the prices.

8   Save your work as *International Price List-1*.

tip

A faster way to add dollar signs to create mixed references

3. Click on the formula bar so that the cursor is touching the cell reference you want to convert to mixed:

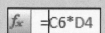

4. Press the <F4> key repeatedly on the keyboard.

Each time you press <F4> Excel cycles through all possible absolute and mixed references:

Lesson 3-14: Create a template

What is a template?

You'll often find yourself making copies of older workbooks that are nearly the same as the one you need. You'll then delete the bits you don't need and add the bits that you do.

If you find this happening it's time to make a template.

The template is just a normal workbook that contains the starting point for a task that you often need to do. You can put anything into a template that you can put into a regular workbook.

Templates are a great time saver.

Microsoft have even provided you with a set of templates that you may find useful, and there are more available for free via the Internet.

1　Open *First Quarter Sales and Bonus* from your sample files folder.

2　Delete the contents of cells *C6:D14.*

3　Replace the text in cell A1 with the words: *Bonus Calculator.*

<table>
<tr><td></td><td>A</td><td>B</td><td>C</td><td>D</td><td>E</td></tr>
<tr><td>1</td><td colspan="5">**Bonus Calculator**</td></tr>
<tr><td>2</td><td></td><td></td><td></td><td></td><td></td></tr>
<tr><td>3</td><td>Sales</td><td></td><td></td><td></td><td></td></tr>
<tr><td>4</td><td></td><td></td><td></td><td></td><td></td></tr>
<tr><td>5</td><td>First Name</td><td>Last Name</td><td>Sales</td><td>Target</td><td>Target Sales</td></tr>
<tr><td>6</td><td>Andrew</td><td>Fuller</td><td></td><td></td><td>-</td></tr>
<tr><td>7</td><td>Anne</td><td>Dodsworth</td><td></td><td></td><td>-</td></tr>
<tr><td>8</td><td>Janet</td><td>Leverling</td><td></td><td></td><td>-</td></tr>
<tr><td>9</td><td>Laura</td><td>Callahan</td><td></td><td></td><td>-</td></tr>
<tr><td>10</td><td>Margaret</td><td>Peacock</td><td></td><td></td><td>-</td></tr>
<tr><td>11</td><td>Michael</td><td>Suyama</td><td></td><td></td><td></td></tr>
<tr><td>12</td><td>Nancy</td><td>Davolio</td><td></td><td></td><td></td></tr>
<tr><td>13</td><td>Robert</td><td>King</td><td></td><td></td><td>-</td></tr>
<tr><td>14</td><td>Steven</td><td>Buchanan</td><td></td><td></td><td>-</td></tr>
<tr><td>15</td><td></td><td>Total:</td><td>-</td><td></td><td></td></tr>
<tr><td>16</td><td></td><td></td><td></td><td></td><td></td></tr>
<tr><td>17</td><td>Bonus</td><td></td><td></td><td></td><td></td></tr>
<tr><td>18</td><td></td><td></td><td></td><td></td><td></td></tr>
<tr><td>19</td><td>First Name</td><td>Last Name</td><td>Salary</td><td>Bonus</td><td>Total</td></tr>
<tr><td>20</td><td>Andrew</td><td>Fuller</td><td>2,500</td><td>-</td><td>2,500.00</td></tr>
<tr><td>21</td><td>Anne</td><td>Dodsworth</td><td>2,000</td><td>-</td><td>2,000.00</td></tr>
<tr><td>22</td><td>Janet</td><td>Leverling</td><td>2,600</td><td>-</td><td>2,600.00</td></tr>
<tr><td>23</td><td>Laura</td><td>Callahan</td><td>2,800</td><td>-</td><td>2,800.00</td></tr>
<tr><td>24</td><td>Margaret</td><td>Peacock</td><td>3,000</td><td>-</td><td>3,000.00</td></tr>
<tr><td>25</td><td>Michael</td><td>Suyama</td><td>1,800</td><td>-</td><td>1,800.00</td></tr>
<tr><td>26</td><td>Nancy</td><td>Davolio</td><td>4,500</td><td>-</td><td>4,500.00</td></tr>
<tr><td>27</td><td>Robert</td><td>King</td><td>2,000</td><td>-</td><td>2,000.00</td></tr>
<tr><td>28</td><td>Steven</td><td>Buchanan</td><td>3,000</td><td>-</td><td>3,000.00</td></tr>
<tr><td>29</td><td></td><td>Total:</td><td>24,200</td><td>-</td><td>24,200.00</td></tr>
</table>

note

This worksheet looks flashy!

If you are wondering how to make your own worksheets look as flashy as this one you'll only need a little more patience.

You'll learn every skill you need to make your worksheets look as good, and even a lot better, than this one in the next session: *Session Four: Making Your Worksheets Look Professional.*

First Quarter Sales and Bonus

This is exactly the type of workbook you'd probably want to convert into a template. The bonus has to be calculated every quarter and it will save a lot of work.

4   Save your work as: *Bonus Calculator*.

5   Save the workbook as a template.

Every quarter you could simply open last quarter's spreadsheet, save it with a new name and then delete the cell values. But you'd have to do that every quarter and then, one day, you might forget the *save it with a new name* step and end up over writing the old file.

A much better solution is to save the empty workbook as a template.

1.   Click File→Save As.

2.   Click the drop down list arrow labeled *Save as Type* at the bottom of the *Save As* dialog.

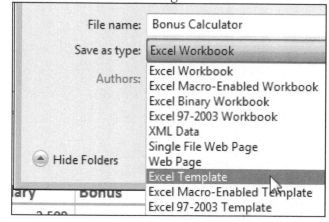

3.   For this workbook the best choice is *Excel Template*.

If this template needs to be used by users with older versions of Excel you'd choose *Excel 97-2003* template.

If the workbook contained macros (working with macros is an Expert level skill covered fully in the *Expert Skills* book in this series) you'd need to choose *Excel Macro-Enabled Template*.

4.   Click the *Save* button to save the template to the default template folder. The existing name: *Bonus Calculator* is fine.

The default template folder is

C:\Users\ user name \AppData\Roaming\Microsoft\Templates

If you want to change this location see the sidebar for instructions.

6   Close the template.

Lesson 3-15: Use a template

1   Click File→New.

2   Click the *My templates...* list item in the center window of the Backstage view.

A dialog appears showing all of the templates in your personal templates folder:

3   Either double-click *Bonus Calculator* (the template saved in the last lesson) or click *Bonus Calculator* once and then click the *OK* button.

A new workbook is created from the template.

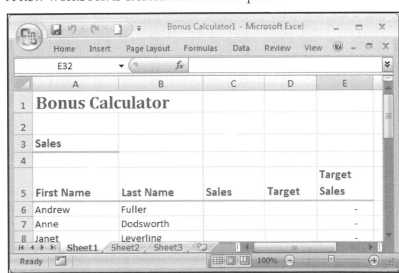

Notice that the workbook has been named *Bonus Calculator1*. You are not looking at the template but a new workbook created from the template.

4   Use a sample template.

Sample templates are a set of Microsoft sample templates that were created when you installed Excel.

Create a new workbook in exactly the same way as you did using the *Bonus Calculator* template but choose *Sample Templates* and then select one of Microsoft's templates.

Some of Microsoft's templates may seem a little overwhelming at the moment but they'll seem far less intimidating by the time you reach the end of this book!

5   Create a new workbook using an existing workbook as a template.

This is really the equivalent of opening the existing workbook and then saving it with a different name.

Proceed as before but, this time, choose *New from existing…* instead of *My Templates*.

You are then able to navigate to any Excel workbook and copy it into a new workbook without altering the original.

6   Create a workbook from Microsoft's on-line library of templates.

The Internet is a wonderful thing. Microsoft have a huge library of templates that they add to all of the time and make available to you for free.

Proceed as before, but this time choose any of the categories from the *Office.com Templates* section.

Some of their templates are very interesting but do read the cautionary note in the sidebar before using any of them.

note

If you don't fully understand how a template works don't use it

Many of Microsoft's templates contain program code written in a language called Visual Basic for Applications (VBA).

VBA programming is way beyond the skills of nearly all Excel users (I would estimate that far less than 1% of Excel users can hand-craft VBA code).

If you can use this type of template "as is", or if you have a VBA programmer on your staff who is also an Excel expert, you may find templates containing VBA code useful. Otherwise there's a danger that you may end up with a worksheet you don't understand and are unable to maintain.

For this reason I'd always advise you to create your own worksheets (and templates) from scratch so that you fully understand how they are built and are able to maintain them.

A Smart Method *Excel VBA* book will be available soon. This will be of interest to Excel Expert Level users who have very advanced requirements.

Lesson 3-16: Freeze columns and rows

1   Open *Sales First Quarter 2008* from your sample files folder.

Notice that it is easy to see which data is in each column when you are at the top of the worksheet and can see the header row:

	A	B	C	D
1	Date	First Name	Last Name	Company Name
2	01-Jan-08	Nancy	Davolio	Eastern Connection
3	01-Jan-08	Nancy	Davolio	Eastern Connection

But things get confusing when you scroll further down the list:

	A	B	C	D
128	17-Feb-08	Margaret	Peacock	Rancho grande
129	17-Feb-08	Margaret	Peacock	Rancho grande
130	18-Feb-08	Janet	Leverling	Blondel père et fils

It is no longer clear what information is contained in each column because the header row has disappeared.

2   Press **<Ctrl>+<Home>** to quickly move to Cell A1.

3   Click View→Window→Freeze Panes.

A rich menu is displayed:

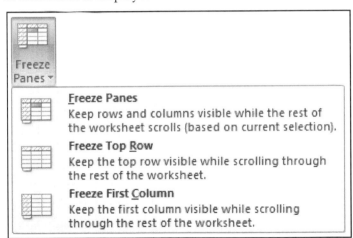

With Excel's new rich menus the meaning of each option is quite clear.

4   Click the *Freeze Top Row* list item.

A small black line appears beneath the first row.

5   Scroll down the list.

Notice that as you scroll down, the top row remains in place.

Sales First Quarter 2008

A	A	B	C	D
1	Date	First Name	Last Name	Company Name
47	16-Jan-08	Margaret	Peacock	Simons bistro
48	16-Jan-08	Margaret	Peacock	Simons bistro
49	16-Jan-08	Margaret	Peacock	Simons bistro
50	17-Jan-08	Margaret	Peacock	QUICK-Stop

6   Unfreeze the top row.

Click View→Window→Freeze Panes once more. The first choice has now changed to *Unfreeze Panes*. Click this menu item to put things back to normal.

7   Freeze the first column.

Do exactly as you did before but, this time, select *Freeze First Column* from the rich menu.

Notice that the date column is now locked into place. As you scroll to the right the date remains in the first column.

A	A	F	G	H
1	Date	Country	Product Name	Quantity
2	01-Jan-08	UK	Thüringer Rostbratwurst	21
3	01-Jan-08	UK	Steeleye Stout	35

8   Unfreeze the panes.

9   Freeze the first two rows and the left most three columns.

Whilst a simple freezing of the top row or first column may sometimes be what you need, you'll often want to freeze columns *and* rows.

You'll sometimes also want to freeze more than one column and/or row.

1. Click in cell D3 to make it the active cell. This is your way of telling Excel that you want to freeze all cells above, and to the left of, cell D3.

2. Click: View→Window→Freeze Panes again but, this time, select the first option from the rich menu: *Freeze Panes*.

The first two rows and first three columns are frozen.

A	A	B	C	D
1	Date	First Name	Last Name	Company Name
2	01-Jan-08	Nancy	Davolio	Eastern Connection
3	01-Jan-08	Nancy	Davolio	Eastern Connection
4	01-Jan-08	Nancy	Davolio	Eastern Connection

10   Unfreeze the panes.

Lesson 3-17: Split the window into multiple panes

1   Open *Sales First Quarter 2008* from your sample files folder (if it isn't already open).

2   Press **<Ctrl>+<End>** to quickly move to the end of the worksheet (cell J242).

This is quite a long list. Imagine that you need to compare sales for 3rd February to sales for 3rd March.

This could involve a lot of scrolling unless you split the window into two panes.

3   Drag a horizontal split bar down to the center of the screen.

The split bar is located at the top of the vertical scroll bar. Hover the mouse cursor over it until you see the following cursor shape.

(If you can't see the split bar you probably forgot to unfreeze the panes at the end of the last session).

When you see the  shape, click and drag down to the center of the screen.

The screen is split into two independently scrolling horizontal panes.

4   Scroll the lower pane so that the first sale on 3rd March 2008 is shown on the first line.

Sales First Quarter 2008

5   Scroll the upper pane so that the first sale on 3rd February 2008 is shown on the first line.

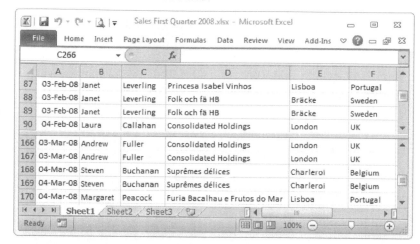

note

Other ways to add and remove split bars

Using the Ribbon

1. Click in a cell so that the active cell indicates where you want to split the screen.

   If you click a cell in row 1 the screen will be split into two vertical panes.

   If you click a cell in column A, the screen will be split into two horizontal panes.

   If you click a cell that is not contained in Row 1 or Column A, the screen will split into four panes as both a horizontal and vertical split bar will be added.

2. Click View→Window→ Split.

   The window will then be split into two or four windows depending upon the location of the active cell.

3. To remove the split bars :

   Click:

   View→Window→Split

   … one more time.

Remove split bars using the mouse

You can remove split bars by double-clicking them with the mouse.

6   Remove the split window view by returning the split bar to its original location.

Drag the bar up to the top of the screen. It then disappears, returning the view to normal.

7   Drag a vertical split bar to the intersection of columns C and D.

The vertical split bar is located on the right hand side of the horizontal scroll bar. Hover the cursor over it until you see the following cursor shape.

When you see the ⬌ shape, click and drag left until the gray indicator bar is at the intersection of columns C and D.

You can then release the mouse button to split the window into two independently scrolling vertical panes.

8   Remove the split window view by returning the split bar to its original location.

Drag the bar to the right-hand side of the screen. It then disappears returning the view to normal.

Lesson 3-18: Check spelling

anecdote

Fun with dictionaries

I used to tell my students that the Australian English dictionary included such words as G'day which I thought was a joke.

One day, one of my students checked it out in a coffee break and it's actually true!

Excel shares the same powerful spell checker included with Word and other Office applications.

Most European companies have a corporate standard for their spelling, often American English or British English. Excel also includes standard support for eighteen different dialects of English as well as other languages.

While most words are included in Excel's dictionary, you will often be warned that a correct spelling is misspelled. When this is the case you can add the word to the dictionary so that Excel doesn't keep nagging you about it in the future.

1   Open *Empire Car Sales Stock List* from your sample files folder.

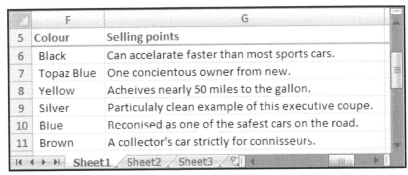

	F	G
5	Colour	Selling points
6	Black	Can accelarate faster than most sports cars.
7	Topaz Blue	One concientous owner from new.
8	Yellow	Acheives nearly 50 miles to the gallon.
9	Silver	Particulaly clean example of this executive coupe.
10	Blue	Reconised as one of the safest cars on the road.
11	Brown	A collector's car strictly for connisseurs.

We'll have to hope that Empire's cars are better than their spelling!

You may find it fun to try to identify their spelling errors before we set the Spell Checker loose on the job. The *Selling points* column contains many frequently incorrectly spelt words.

2   Check the spelling for the words in the range F5:G7.

If you select a range of cells before invoking the spell checker, only the selected range will be checked.

1. Select the range F5:G7

2. Click Review→Proofing→Spelling to start the spell checker.

If all of the words are spelt correctly the spell checker does not display. In this case there are errors so the Spell Check dialog is displayed.

note

Another way to start the spell checker

Press the <**F7**> key.

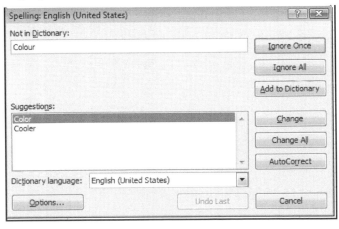

note

Setting the default language

Click File➔Options➔Proofing.

You are then able to set the Excel default dictionary language.

note

Dictionaries for other languages

The English version of Excel includes support for English, French and Spanish.

Microsoft also offer language packs for 35 other languages ranging from Chinese to Ukrainian.

In the example above note that the *Dictionary language* was set to English (United States). The British spelling of the word *colour* does not appear in the American English dictionary because, in America, it is spelt: *color*.

If your dictionary is set to English (United Kingdom) you will not see this error because *colour* is the correct UK English spelling.

See the sidebar if you want to change your dictionary to a different language.

3   Click *Change* to accept Excel's suggested correction.

4   Click *Change* twice more to accept Excel's suggestions for *accelerate* and *conscientious*.

5   Click the *Close* button to close the Spell Checker.

6   Spell check the single word *Particulaly* in cell G9.

Sometimes you'll spell a single word and be unsure that it is correctly spelt. You will want to be able to quickly check the single word.

1. Click cell G9 and then select the word Particulaly in the formula bar at the top of the window.

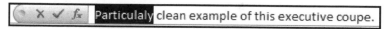

2. Click Review➔Proofing➔Spelling to start the Spell Checker.

3. Chick the *Change* button to accept the correct spelling.

7   Spell check the entire worksheet.

1. Click in any cell on the worksheet. When you don't select a range, or a single word, the spell checker checks the entire worksheet.

   If you didn't click cell A1, cells to the right and beneath the selected cell are checked first and then Excel asks: *Do you want to continue checking at the beginning of the sheet?*

2. Click Review➔Proofing➔Spelling to start the Spell Checker.

8   Click *Change* to accept each change until you are prompted for Alfasud.

Alfasud is a real word for a car (a model produced by Alfa Romeo between 1976 and 1989) but it isn't in the Excel dictionary. Perhaps Empire sells a lot of Alfasuds and don't want to be pulled up by the spell checker every time the word is used.

To prevent this happening, click the *Add to Dictionary* button so that Excel will recognize the word in the future.

When the spell check is completed a dialog will display.

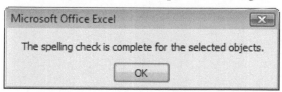

9   Save your work as *Empire Car Sales Stock List-1*.

Session 3: Exercise

1   Open *The Best Selling Albums of All Time* from your sample files folder.

2   Insert one row above row 7, type *AC/DC* for the Artist and *Back in Black* for the Album.

3   Use AutoComplete to put the text *Rock* into cell C7 and type *42* for copies sold (millions).

4   Delete rows 10 and 11 to remove the *The Bee Gees* and *Pink Floyd* from the list.

5   Insert a formula in cell E6 to calculate how much revenue the album sales would have generated if sold at the Average Album Price shown in cell E3.

      Don't forget that the reference to cell E3 will have to be an absolute reference.

6   AutoFill the formula to the end of the list to see the estimated revenue for the top four selling albums.

7   Use AutoSum to add a value for total copies sold and total revenue to cells D10 and E10.

8   Remove decimal places displayed in cells E6:E10 so that the revenue is rounded to the nearest million.

9   Add a comment to cell B6 saying "Thriller was Michael Jackson's sixth studio album and was produced with a budget of $750,000".

10   Save your work as *The Best Selling Albums of All Time-1*.

	A	B	C	D	E
1	**Best Selling Albums of All Time**				
2					US$
3				Average Album Price	14.99
4					
5	Artist	Album	Genre	Copies Sold (millions)	Revenue (Million USD)
6	Michael Jackson	Thriller	Pop/R&B	108	1619
7	AC/DC	Back in Black	Rock	42	630
8	Whitney Houston	The Bodyguard	Pop/R&B	42	630
9	Eagles	Their Greates Hits (1971-1975)	Rock	41	615
10		Total:		233	3493
11					
12					
13					
14					
15					

Mike Smart :
Thriller was Michael Jackson's sixth studio album and was produced with a budget of $750,000.

The Best Selling
Albums of All Time

If you need help slide the page to the left

Session 3 Exercise answers

These are the four questions that most students find the most difficult to remember:

Q 7	Q 5	Q 4	Q 2
1. Click in cell D10. 2. Click Home→Editing→AutoSum 3. Either press the <Enter> key or click: Home→Editing→AutoSum one more time. This was covered in: *Lesson 2-3: Use AutoSum to quickly calculate totals.*	1. Type the following formula into cell E6: =D6*$E$3 2. Press the <Enter> key. This was covered in: *Lesson 3-12: Understand absolute and relative cell references.*	1. Right-click on the row header for row 7. 2. Click *Delete* from the shortcut menu. This was covered in: *Lesson 3-1: Insert and delete rows and columns.*	1. Right-click on the row header for row 7. 2. Click *Insert* from the shortcut menu. This was covered in: *Lesson 3-1: Insert and delete rows and columns.*

If you have difficulty with the other questions, here are the lessons that cover the relevant skill:

1   Refer to: Lesson 1-4: Download the sample files and open/navigate a workbook.

3   Refer to: Lesson 3-2: Use AutoComplete and fill data from adjacent cells.

6   Refer to: Lesson 2-15: Use AutoFill to adjust formulas.

8   Refer to: Lesson 3-5: Use Paste Values and increase/decrease decimal places displayed.

9   Refer to: Lesson 3-9: Insert cell comments.

10   Refer to: Lesson 1-5: Save a workbook.

4

Session Four: Making Your Worksheets Look Professional

> It is only shallow people who do not judge by appearances.
>
> *Oscar Wilde (1854 - 1900)*

Never under-estimate the importance of presentation. In many areas of life it is valued more than content.

This session will enable you to make your worksheets get noticed.

By the end of this session everybody will be convinced that you are an Excel genius because your worksheets will be visually excellent.

Session Objectives

By the end of this session you will be able to:

- Format dates
- Understand date serial numbers
- Format numbers using built-in number formats
- Create custom number formats
- Horizontally and Vertically align the contents of cells
- Merge cells, wrap text and expand/collapse the formula bar
- Understand themes
- Use cell styles and change themes
- Add color and gradient effects to cells
- Add borders and lines
- Create your own custom theme
- Create your own custom cell styles
- Use a master style book and merge styles
- Use simple conditional formatting
- Manage multiple conditional formats using the Rules Manager
- Bring data alive with visualizations
- Create a formula driven conditional format
- Insert a Sparkline into a range of cells
- Apply a common vertical axis and formatting to a Sparkline group
- Apply a date axis to a Sparkline group and format a single Sparkline
- Use the format painter
- Rotate text

Lesson 4-1: Format dates

You may notice that I've been very careful in using internationally safe date formats throughout this book.

A classic cause of errors when dealing with international worksheets is the use of a date such as the following:

10/03/2008

This means *10th March 2008* in some countries (such as the UK) and *3rd October 2008* in others (such as the USA).

If your work may be viewed by an international audience it is far better to use a date format that cannot possibly cause confusion.

In this lesson we'll re-format a date into the compact and universally readable format of: *10-Mar-08*.

1 Open *Sales Week Ended 14th March 2008* from your sample files folder.

Notice the hashes in the date column. This tells you that the column isn't wide enough to display the date.

	A	B	C	D
1	Invoice No	Date	Customer	Country
2	10918	##########	Bottom-Dol	Canada
3	10917	##########	Romero y tc	Spain
4	10926	##########	Ana Trujillo	Mexico

If you're used to calling the hash (#) a **pound sign** or **number sign** see the sidebar in: *Lesson 2-9: Re-size rows and columns* for an explanation.

2 Auto-resize cells A1:G17 so that their contents are fully visible.

This was covered in: *Lesson 2-9: Re-size rows and columns.*

At present the dates are formatted with the month spelled out in full:

	A	B	C
1	Invoice No	Date	Customer
2	10918	10 March 2008	Bottom-Dollar Markets
3	10917	10 March 2008	Romero y tomillo
4	10926	10 March 2008	Ana Trujillo Emparedados y helados

We're going to re-format them to the shorter form: *10 Mar 08*.

3 Select cells B2:B17.

4 Right-click anywhere in the selected range and choose *Format Cells…* from the shortcut menu.

You can also do this from the Ribbon (see sidebar).

The *Format Cells* dialog appears.

note

Other ways of launching the Format Cells dialog

Click:

Home→Number→ Dialog Launcher

The dialog launcher is the small button on the bottom right of the *Number* group.

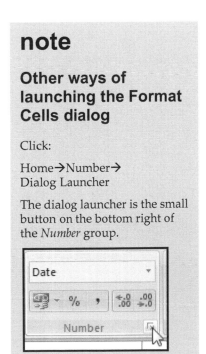

Sales Week Ended
14th March 2008

5   Click the *Number* tab (if it isn't already selected) and then choose *Date* from the *Category* list box.

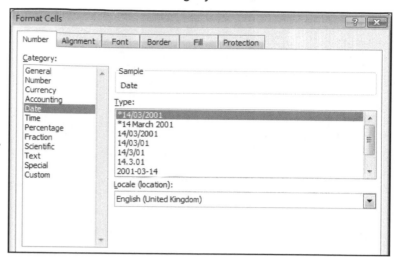

The dates you see may be different from those shown above (see sidebar).

I wanted the format 14-Mar-2008 but that isn't in the list. When you need a slightly special format it is worth checking the *Custom* category to see whether there is a pre-defined format available.

6   Click *Custom* in the category list box.

7   Apply a custom format so that the dates display in the format: 10-Mar-08.

Scroll through each of the entries in the *Type* list box, keeping your eye on the preview in the *Sample* frame.

When you reach the format *dd-mmm-yy* you will see *10-Mar-08* in the sample box. That's just what you need so click the OK button to accept.

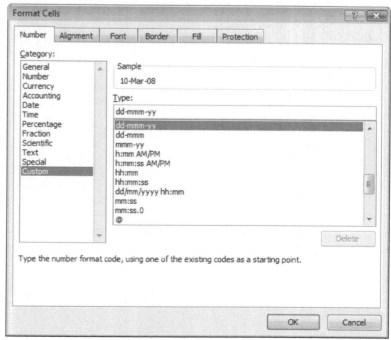

8   Save your work as *Sales Week Ended 14th March 2008-1.*

trivia

The Julian and Gregorian calendars

When you work with very old dates you can run into a problem with the Julian and Gregorian calendars.

In 1582 it was noticed that the seasons had drifted by 10 days because the Julian system (named after Julius Caesar who adopted it in 45 BC) had incorrectly miscalculated a year as being 365 ¼ days. It is actually slightly shorter than this.

Pope Gregory XIII decreed that, in order to put things right, the world had to lose 10 days to make up for all of those extra leap years.

The reformed Gregorian calendar also adopted a new leap year rule, skipping the leap year every millennium to keep things on track in future years.

It took nearly 200 years for everybody to get on board with the Gregorian calendar. The Catholic countries of Spain, Italy and Portugal went for it at once but England and parts of America didn't convert until September 14th 1752.

This means that in Spain the dates October 5th 1582 to October 14th 1582 never actually existed. In England it was the dates Sept 3rd 1752 to September 14th 1752.

The strangest case of all was Sweden who decided to "phase it in gradually" between 1700 and 1740 meaning that their calendar was out of step with the rest of the world for 40 years.

If you work with historical data from this era you have to be very careful indeed.

Lesson 4-2: Understand date serial numbers

Excel stores dates in a very clever way. Understanding Excel's date storage system empowers you to use date arithmetic. You can use date arithmetic to compute the difference between two dates (in days) or to shift date ranges by a given time interval.

How Excel stores dates

Dates are stored as simple numbers called *date serial numbers*. The serial number contains the number of days that have elapsed since 1st January 1900 (where 1st January 1900 is 1).

The world began in 1900

An interesting shortcoming of Excel is its inability to easily work with dates before 1900. Excel simply doesn't acknowledge that there were any dates before this time. If you work with older dates you will have to work-around this limitation.

In Excel every time is a date, and every date is a time

This one is an eye opener! We've already realized that 5th January 1900 is stored as the number 5. What would the number 5.5 mean? It would mean midday on 5th January 1900.

It is possible to format a date to show only the date, only the time, or both a time and a date.

When you enter a pure time into a cell, the time is stored as a number less than one. Excel regards this as having the non-existent date of 00 January 1900!

When you enter a pure date into a cell, the time is stored as midnight at the beginning of that day.

1   Create a new blank workbook and put the numbers 1 to 5 in cells A1:A5.

2   Type the formula **=A1** into cell B1 followed by the **<Enter>** key, and then AutoFill the formula to the end of the list.

AutoFill was covered in: *Lesson 2-14: Use AutoFill for text and numeric series.*

	A	B
1	1	1
2	2	2
3	3	3
4	4	4
5	5	5

3 Apply a date format to column A that will show a four digit year.

This was covered in: *Lesson 4-1: Format dates.*

	A	B
1	01 January 1900	1
2	02 January 1900	2

This reveals that the numbers 1 to 5 represent the dates 1-Jan-1900 to 05-Jan-1900.

4 Change the date format in column A so that it shows both dates and times.

Setting a custom format was covered in: *Lesson 4-1: Format dates.*

Choose the custom format: **dd/mm/yyyy hh:mm.** (If it isn't shown in the list you will need to type it into the *Type* box).

Notice that when you enter a date without a time, the time is set to midnight at the beginning of that day.

	A	B
1	01/01/1900 00:00	1
2	02/01/1900 00:00	2

5 Change the time in cell A2 to 12:00.

Notice that the number in cell B2 has altered to 2.5 showing that times are stored by Excel as the decimal part of a number.

1	01/01/1900 00:00	1
2	02/01/1900 12:00	2.5

6 Compute the number of days that occurred between 01/01/1900 and 01/01/2000.

Now that you have a good grasp of Excel's serial numbers this task is easy.

1. Enter the two dates in cells A7 and A8, one beneath the other.

2. Click in cell A9 to make it the active cell.

3. Click Home→Number→Comma Style. [,]

   We'll be learning more about the comma style in: *Lesson 4-3: Format numbers using built-in number formats.*

4. Subtract one date from the other by entering the formula: **=A8-A7** into cell A9.

	A
7	01/01/1900 00:00
8	01/01/2000 00:00
9	36,525.00

You now know that 36,525 days occurred during the last millennium (actually 36,524 due to the Lotus 1-2-3 bug – see sidebar).

7 Close the workbook without saving.

Lesson 4-3: Format numbers using built-in number formats

Formatting fundamentals

When you format a number you never change its value. For example if you format the number:

> 483.45495

... so that it only displays two decimal places. The number displays like this:

> 483.45

It is important to realize that the actual value in the cell remains at the old value of 483.45495. All we have done is to change the way in which the value is presented to the user.

1   Open *Sales Week Ended 14ᵗʰ March 2008-1* from your sample files folder.

2   Apply the comma style to column E.

There is an extremely useful quick format button called the *comma style*. This is perfect for formatting monetary values with a single click. The comma style places a comma after thousands and displays exactly two decimal places.

1.   Select all of Column E.

2.   Click Home→Number→Comma Style.

All of the values in Column E now display correctly.

D	E	F	G
Country	Amount	Tax	Total
Canada	1,447.50	0.175	1700.8125
Spain	365.89	0.175	429.92075

Note that there is also a very similar *Accounting Number Format* style (I think that Microsoft should have more intuitively named it the Currency Style).

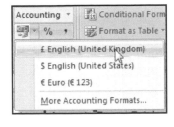

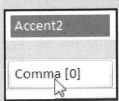
Sales Week Ended
14ᵗʰ March 2008-1

note

Solutions to the "penny rounding" problem

Formatting a floating point number to two decimal places often results in the *penny rounding problem* when you sum a column of numbers.

There are two solutions to the problem. One is a very good solution, the other can cause problems.

Best practice

The best solution to the problem is to address it when the column is first calculated.

In this lesson's example worksheet the formula used to calculate G2 is:

=E2*(F2+1)

Excel has a Round() function that can be used to round the result to two decimal places at the point of calculation.

The new formula would become:

=ROUND(E2*(F2+1),2)

Changing precision

Click:

File→Options→Advanced

In the *When Calculating This Workbook* group click the *Set precision as displayed* check box.

This alters the default behaviour of Excel so that each value in the worksheet is regarded as being precisely the same as its display value when performing calculations.

Using this option can cause data to become inaccurate as it is a global setting affecting the entire worksheet (and any other worksheets you may open before turning it off).

Use this feature with extreme caution, or better still, don't use it at all!

This is very similar to the comma style but adds a leading currency symbol and an appropriate number of decimal places. The *More Accounting Formats…* option supports a vast number of international currency styles.

Try the currency style out to see how it works. I've found that the comma style is more appropriate for most of my work as I'm usually working in one country and one currency making the currency type obvious.

3   Apply the comma style to column G.

Column G has many decimal places, in some cases, as the sales tax calculation results in as many as six decimal places.

Apply the comma style to column G and notice how all of the values are displayed rounded to the nearest two decimal places.

| 2779.677725 | Becomes | 2,779.68 |

| 372.293075 | Becomes | 372.29 |

It is a key concept (as discussed in the introduction to this lesson) to realize that the values in the cells have not changed. For example, if you add two cells containing the value 1.4, the result will be 1.4+1.4=2.8. If you then format the cells as whole numbers you'll see that 1+1=3 as each number is rounded up or down.

See the sidebar for potential solutions to this problem.

4   Apply the percentage style to column F.

The example sales tax rate is 17.5%. When working with percentages it is useful to enter them so that you can calculate a percentage simply by multiplying by the cell.

Instead of 17.5 (more readable) the values are entered as 0.175 (easier to use in formulas). In order to make percentages both readable and easy to use Microsoft has created the percentage style. If you type 17.5% into a cell the actual value within the cell will be 0.175.

1.   Select column F.

2.   Click Home→Number→Percentage Style.

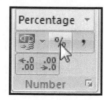

3.   Click Home→Number→Increase Decimal  once, to make the values in column F display more accurately.

D	E	F	G
Country	Amount	Tax	Total
Canada	1,447.50	17.5%	1,700.81
Spain	365.89	17.5%	429.92

5   Save your work as *Sales Week Ended 14th March 2008-2*.

Lesson 4-4: Create custom number formats

The built-in number formats are very quick and convenient but are also quite limited.

For example, there was a credit note on 11-Mar-08 for 637.49 plus tax. You could easily miss the little minus sign to the left of the amount.

Germany	500.00	17.5%	587.50
Italy	637.49	17.5%	749.05
Italy	- 637.49	17.5%	- 749.05

Old-school accountants like to show brackets around negative values. You just can't miss those brackets! Here's what we want to see:

Germany	500.00	17.5%	587.50
Italy	637.49	17.5%	749.05
Italy	(637.49)	17.5%	(749.05)

There's one little problem with this requirement. Excel 2010 doesn't support brackets in any of the built-in or pre-defined custom formats.

Fortunately it is possible to create your own custom format when none of the built-in styles fit your requirement.

Overview of custom formats

There's plenty of documentation in the help system and on the Internet about the rather cryptic formatting codes provided with Excel 2010. Just about everything is possible once you've got to grips with the basic concepts.

To communicate the custom format to Excel, you must construct a custom format string.

Zeros mean "Display significant zeros". You tell Excel how many you want within the format string. For example, 0.00 means *display one leading zero and two decimal places*. The following examples should make things clear:

Custom Format String	Value	Display
0	1234.56	1235
0.0	1234.56 1234.5	1234.6 1234.5
0.00	1234.56 1234.5	1234.56 1234.50
00.000	4.56	04.560
0.000	1234.56	1234.560

Sales Week Ended 14th March 2008-2

© 2011 The Smart Method® Ltd

The hash symbol (#) is mainly used to add comma separators to thousands and millions.

Custom Format String	Value	Display
#	123.4500	123
#.##	123.45 123.50	123.45 123.5
#,#	1234.56	1,235
#,#.##	1234.56 1234.50 12341234.56	1,234.56 1,234.5 12,341,234.56

Because the hash symbol can be used in conjunction with zeroes it is also possible to indicate that you want both thousand separators *and* a specific number of leading or trailing zeroes.

Custom Format String	Value	Display
#,#0.00	12341234.5	12,341,234.50

You can also specify two different format strings separated by a semi colon. The first provides formatting for positive values and the second for negative values. This information enables us to construct the custom format string required.

Custom format string	Value	Display
#,#0.00;(#,#0.00)	12341234.5 -12341234.5	12,341,234.50 (12,341,234.50)

1 Open *Sales Week Ended 14th March 2008-2* from your sample files folder (if it isn't already open).

2 Select columns E and G.

This was covered in: *Lesson 2-6: Select adjacent and non-adjacent rows and columns.*

3 Right-click anywhere in column E or G and then select *Format Cells…* from the shortcut menu.

4 Select *Custom* from the *Category* list on the left of the dialog.

5 Type the custom format: **#,#0.00;(#,#0.00)** into the box labeled *Type* and click the OK button.

Type:
#,#0.00;(#,#0.00)

The negative values on the worksheet are now surrounded by brackets.

Italy	637.49	17.5%	749.05
Italy	(637.49)	17.5%	(749.05)

6 Save your work as *Sales Week Ended 14th March 2008-3.*

© 2011 The Smart Method® Ltd

157

---

note

More about custom number formats

It is only possible to give you a broad overview of number formats in a single lesson. This should be all that you need to discover more using Excel's help system or the Internet.

Here are a couple of other insights that may help if you want to explore them further:

- You can embed colors into number formats. For example, to make every negative value red you could use:

  0.00;[Red]0.00

- There are four possible parts to a number format. They are:

  Positive format; Negative format; Zero format; Text format

  You could, for example, use the custom format string:

  0.00;-0.00;"Zero";[Blue]

  On these cells:

Mike	0	120.119	-345.5744

  Resulting in:

Mike	Zero	120.12	-345.57

  (Text above is colored blue).

note

Hiding values with the three semicolon trick

You will often want to hide the values in specific cells, even though you want other values in the same column to display.

A common way of doing this is to format the cell as a white foreground color upon a white background.

A better solution is to create a custom format consisting of three semicolons:

;;;

Lesson 4-5: Horizontally align the contents of cells

This table summarizes Excel's different horizontal alignment options.

Icon	Description	What it does	Example
General ▾	General (the default)	Aligns numbers and dates to the right and text to the left.	Canada 1,447.50 / Spain 365.89
▤	Align Left	Aligns cell contents left. If the cell contains text and the adjacent cell is empty, text spills to the right. If the cell contains text and the adjacent text isn't empty, text is truncated.	Bottom-Dollar Markets / Bottom-Dollar Markets / Bottom-Dollar M Canada
▥	Align Center	Aligns cell contents to the center. If the cell contains text and the adjacent cells are empty, text spills to the left and right. If the cell contains text and the adjacent cells are not empty, text is truncated.	Bottom-Dollar Markets / Bottom-Dollar Markets / 10-Mar-08 om-Dollar Mar Canada
▤	Align Right	Aligns cell contents to the right. If the cell contains text and the adjacent cell is empty, text spills to the left. If the cell contains text and the adjacent cell isn't empty, text is truncated.	Bottom-Dollar Markets / Bottom-Dollar Markets / 10-Mar-08 om-Dollar Markets C
▤	Justify	Text lines up to the left and right of the cell (like a newspaper)	to be or not to be, that is the question.
▤	Distributed	Words are distributed evenly across the cell.	City of London
No icon	Fill	Text is repeated until the cell is filled	CatCatCatCatCatCat

**Sales Week Ended
14th March 2008-3**

note

How to access the justified, distribute, and fill options

The justify and distributed option are not on the Ribbon as most users wouldn't find a need for them.

If you find them useful you can add buttons to the Quick Access Toolbar. Refer to: *Lesson 1-13: Customize the Quick Access Toolbar and preview the printout.*

The Fill option doesn't even have a toolbar button. This needs to be accessed from the Format Cells dialog.

To access the Format Cells dialog right-click any cell and choose *Format Cells...* from the shortcut menu.

You'll then find a *Horizontal Alignment* drop-down list on the *Alignment* tab.

1 Open *Sales Week Ended 14th March 2008-3* from your sample files folder (if it isn't already open).

2 Notice that the text in row one doesn't align with the column contents.

Numerical and date values are, by default, right aligned.

Columns E, F and G contain numerical data but the text headings of their columns are left aligned.

You can see the problem more clearly if the columns are widened:

D	E	F	G
Country	Amount	Tax	Total
Canada	1,447.50	0.175	1,700.81
Spain	365.89	0.175	429.92

3 Right-align the column headers for columns E, F and G.

Select cells E1:G1 and then click:

Home→Alignment→Align Text Right

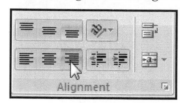

The column headers now look much better.

E	F	G
Amount	Tax	Total
1,447.50	1.75%	1,472.83

4 Right-align cell B1.

Column B also has a problem as the dates and column header do not align.

Select cell B1 and then click Home→Alignment→Align Text Right.

	B	C
1	Date	Customer
2	10-Mar-08	Bottom-Dollar Markets
3	10-Mar-08	Romero y tomillo

You will normally align column headers to the right for numeric/date columns, and to the left for text columns.

5 Bold-face row 1.

Select row 1 and then click Home→Font→Bold.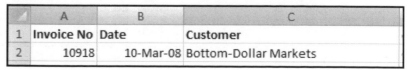

	A	B	C
1	Invoice No	Date	Customer
2	10918	10-Mar-08	Bottom-Dollar Markets

6 Save your work as *Sales Week Ended 14th March 2008-4.*

Lesson 4-6: Merge cells, wrap text and expand/collapse the formula bar

1   Open *Sales Week Ended 14th March 2008-4* from your sample files folder (if it isn't already open).

2   Insert three blank rows above row 1.

This was covered in: *Lesson 3-1: Insert and delete rows and columns.*

3   In cell A1 type: **Sales Week Ended 14th March 2008**.

4   Center the title across columns A to G.

The title cell (A1) doesn't look bad but wouldn't it be nice to center it above the transactions listed beneath? You could simply copy and paste it into cell D1 but it still wouldn't be perfectly central.

The solution is to merge cells A1:G1 so that they turn into one big cell. It will then be possible to center the text inside the merged cell. Excel provides a handy *Merge and Center* button to do this in one click.

1.   Select cells A1:G1.

2.   Click Home→Alignment→Merge & Center.

The title appears at the center of the merged cell.

	A	B	C	D	E	F	G
1			Sales Week Ended 14th March 2008				
2							

5   View the text in cell A22.

There is a long description in cell A22. You probably can't see all of it on your screen.

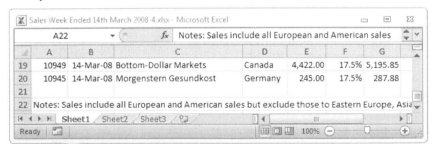

Re-sizing the formula bar allows all of the text to be read.

Click cell A22 and then click the *Expand Formula Bar* button.

The text becomes visible in the enlarged formula bar:

6   Re-size the formula bar.

Sales Week Ended 14th March 2008-4

Sometimes there isn't enough space in the expanded formula bar to view all of the text.

If this is the case hover the mouse over the bottom border of the formula bar until you see the double-headed arrow cursor shape.

When the double-headed arrow is visible, click and drag downward or upward to re-size the formula bar as required.

7 **Collapse the formula bar.**

When you have read the text there is no need to keep the formula bar expanded. Click the same button used to expand the formula bar ⌃ and the bar will collapse.

8 **Merge cells A22:G22.**

1. Expanding the formula bar isn't a great solution. We will create a box at the bottom of the report to contain all of the text.

2. Select cells A22:G22.

3. Click Home→Alignment→Merge & Center Drop Down.

    A drop-down menu is displayed.

    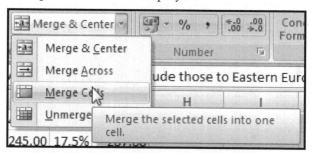

4. Click *Merge Cells* to make all of the selected cells into one large cell.

9 **Make row 22 deep enough to accommodate all of the text.**

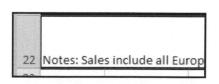

This was covered in: *Lesson 2-9: Re-size rows and columns.*

The cell is now deep enough to accommodate the text but you can still only see one line. This is because the text isn't *wrapping*.

10 **Wrap the text within the merged cells.**

Click Home→Alignment→Wrap Text.

The text now displays well except that it appears at the bottom of the cell. We'll discover how to fix this later, in: *Lesson 4-7: Vertically align the contents of cells.*

> Notes: Sales include all European and American sales but exclude those to Eastern Europe, Asia and South Africa. Salesmen reported that clients are not ordering as much stock as
> 22 usual because we are nearing the end of the first quarter.

11 **Save your work as *Sales Week Ended 14ᵗʰ March 2008-5.***

Lesson 4-7: Vertically align the contents of cells

This table summarizes Excel's different vertical alignment options.

Icon	Description	What it does	Example
General ▾	General (the default)	Aligns cell contents to the bottom of the cell.	Bottom-Dollar Markets
≡	Top Align	Aligns cell contents to the top of the cell	Bottom-Dollar Markets
≡	Middle Align	Aligns cell contents to the middle of the cell.	Bottom-Dollar Markets
≡	Bottom Align	Aligns cell contents to the bottom of the cell	Bottom-Dollar Markets
No icon	Justify	Lines of text are spread out so that the space between each is equal, the first line is at the top and the last line is at the bottom.	to be or not to be, that is the question.
No Icon	Distributed	The same as Justify!	to be or not to be, that is the question.

1　Open *Sales Week Ended 14th March 2008-5 from* your sample files folder (if it isn't already open).

2　Top align the contents of cell A22.

The contents of cell A22 are currently bottom aligned (the default).

22　Notes: Sales include all European and American sales but exclude those to Eastern Europe, Asia and South Africa. Salesmen reported that clients are not ordering as much stock as usual because we are nearing the end of the first quarter.

When you place a block of text into a cell in this way you will typically want it to be top-aligned.

1. Select cell A22.

Sales Week Ended 14th March 2008-5

2. Click Home→Alignment→Top Align  to align the text to the top of the cell.

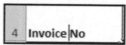

Notes: Sales include all European and American sales but exclude those to Eastern Europe, Asia and South Africa. Salesmen reported that clients are not ordering as much stock as usual because we are nearing the end of the first quarter.

3   Increase the height of row 4 so that it is about twice its present height.

This was covered in: *Lesson 2-9: Re-size rows and columns.*

3			
4	Invoice No	Date	Customer
5	10918	10-Mar-08	Bottom-Dollar Markets

You can see why the default vertical alignment is *bottom align*. This alignment works really well for title rows.

4   Wrap the text in cell A4.

This was covered in: *Lesson 4-6: Merge cells, wrap text and expand/collapse the formula bar.*

5   Split the words *Invoice* and *No* so that they appear on separate lines.

1. Double-click cell A4 to enter Edit mode and then position the cursor to the left of the word *No*.

2. Press **<Alt>+<Enter>**.

3. Press the **<Enter>** key again to exit Edit mode.

The two words appear on separate lines.

6   Horizontally right-align the text in cell A4.

This was covered in: *Lesson 4-5: Horizontally align the contents of cells.*

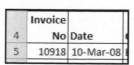

7   Automatically re-size columns A to G so that each column is just wide enough for the cell contents.

This was covered in: *Lesson 2-9: Re-size rows and columns.*

	Invoice		
4	No	Date	
5	10918	10-Mar-08	

8   Save your work as *Sales Week Ended 14th March 2008-6.*

note

What are serifs?

They are the little lines at the edges of text that allow the eye to more easily scan words.

Serifs

Sans
Serif

note

Can I change the default theme?

Yes you can, along with any other Excel default settings.

Open a new empty Excel workbook and apply your chosen default theme.

Save the workbook as a template to the xlStart folder with the name: *book*.

There are two xlStart folders. One of them determines the settings when you are logged in to your computer and the other determines settings for all users of your computer.

If you are using Vista or Windows 7 you'll find the xlStart folder at:

C:\Users\Username\ AppData\Roaming\ Microsoft\Excel

and C:\Program Files\Microsoft Office\Office 12 folders

Windows XP users will find them at:

C:\Documents and Settings\Username\ Application Data\ Microsoft\Excel

and C:\Program Files\Microsoft Office\Office 12

Lesson 4-8: Understand themes

A theme is simply a set of fonts, colors and effects that go very nicely together. This feature was added for the first time in Office 2007.

Font sets

A font set consists of two complementary fonts that work well as a pair.

A golden rule of typesetting is to never have more than two fonts in a document. Old school typesetters would always use a serif font for the body text (also called the *Normal* text) and a sans-serif font for the titles (just as this book does). See sidebar for the difference between serif and sans-serif fonts.

There's a modern school of thought that suggests that breaking this rule is cool and Microsoft have done just that with their default set for Excel 2010 (called the *Office* set) by choosing a serif font (Cambria) for their titles and a sans-serif (Calibri) for normal text. To avoid upsetting purists they also include the *Office2* set that has them the conventional way around!

You can see all 23 pre-defined font sets by clicking:

Page Layout→Themes→Fonts

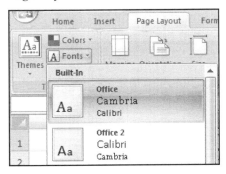

You can also create your own font sets if you don't like any of the pre-defined ones. You'll learn how to do this in: *Lesson 4-12: Create your own custom theme.*

Color sets

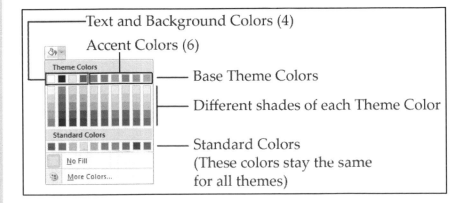

trivia

Times New Roman is probably the most widely used and successful serif typeface in the world.

This font was commissioned by the British Times newspaper in 1931 and was used to print the Times until 1982 when it was replaced due to incompatibility with faster printing presses. It is still widely used in book publishing.

Times New Roman was the default font in Word for all versions right up to 2007 and is still available in Excel's *Office Classic* font set.

Helvetica is probably the most widely used and successful sans-serif font. It was designed in Switzerland in 1957. Windows doesn't include Helvetica but uses *Arial,* a very similar font that most non-experts cannot distinguish from Helvetica.

I used to advise my students that if they stuck to the "killer combination" of Arial/Times New Roman they would never go far wrong, because readers are very used to them and thus find them extremely easy to read

Microsoft has now changed all of the rules by introducing the Cambria/Calibri font pair.

Just as the Times newspaper designed their font to optimize reading at small type sizes in newspapers, Cambria/Calibri were designed specifically to be easy to read on computer screens using Microsoft's *Clear Type* rendering technology.

Office 2007 was the first Office version to have *Clear Type* rendering switched on by default. It works particularly well on LCD flat-panel displays.

Clear Type has saved me reams of paper because now, for the first time, I am able to proof read my books on-screen without causing eye strain. This has saved the life of several trees.

Color sets are a little more involved than font sets

The ten colors along the top row are the *Theme colors*. The left most four are used for *Text and Background colors* and the other six are *Accent colors*. This set of colors has been selected by design professionals to work well together. There are actually twelve theme colors but you can only see ten of them. The two hidden theme colors are used for hyperlinks.

The *Standard colors* are best avoided. They are colors that will remain the same no matter what theme is in use. If you use standard colors (or the *More Colors…* option) the worksheet may look odd if the theme needs to be changed in the future. You can see all 21 pre-defined color sets by clicking:

Page Layout→Themes→Colors

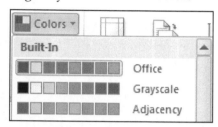

Effects

You'll only notice a change in theme effects if you have graphic elements on your worksheet such as drawing shapes or chart objects. We'll see this working later in: *Lesson 5-5: Format 3-D elements and add drop shadows.*

Theme effects are applied to the outline and fill of shapes. You can see all 21 pre-defined effects by clicking:

Page Layout→Themes→Effects

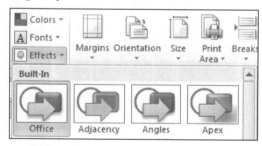

Themes

Themes are simply a group of one *color* set, one *font* set and one *effects* set.

Because Microsoft have consistently named their Colors, Fonts, Effects and Themes the *Office* theme consists of the *Office* color set, the *Office* font set and the *Office* effects set.

Themes aren't just for Excel

The Themes feature is also included in Excel, Word, PowerPoint and Outlook. Choosing the same theme for your documents, spreadsheets, presentations and Emails can give all of your communications a consistent and professional appearance.

Lesson 4-9: Use cell styles and change themes

In order for themes to work their magic you must get into the habit of using cell styles to format cells based only upon the options available in the current theme.

For many years expert Word users have used styles to quickly produce professional documents. Their mortal sin would be to apply a font size or color directly to a document.

Now that Excel also supports styles, professional users should adopt the same discipline.

1   Open *Sales Week Ended 14th March 2008-6* from your sample files folder (if it isn't already open).

2   Apply the *Title* style to cell A1.

Even though cell A1 now encompasses cells A1:G1 it retains the cell reference A1.

A novice user might apply a font and color to cell A1 but we're going to do things the professional way and use the *Title* style.

1.   Select cell A1.

2.   Click Home→Styles→Cell Styles.

The styles gallery appears.

3.   Click *Title* to apply the Title style to cell A1.

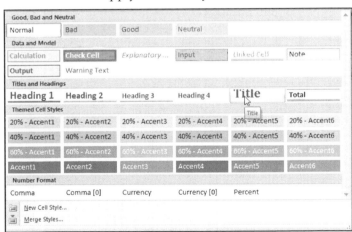

Cell A1 is formatted with the Title style.

3   Apply the *Heading 3* style to cells A4:G4.

1.   Select cells A4:G4.

2.   Click Home→Styles→Cell Styles→Heading 3.

4   Apply the *Note* style to cell A22.

Select cell A22 and then click Home→Styles→Cell Styles→Note.

5   Apply the *20% - Accent 5* style to cells A5:D20.

Select cells A5:D20 and then click:

note

Removing a style from a cell

All cells have the *Normal* style by default. Select a cell or range of cells and click:

Home→Styles→
Cell Styles→Normal

You will then remove the cell style, and all other cell formatting such as bold face or underline, from the cell or range.

Sales Week Ended 14th March 2008-6

Home→Styles→Themed Cell Styles→20% - Accent 5

6   Apply the *20% - Accent 6* style to cells E5:G20.

Select cells E5:G20 and then click:

Home→Styles→Cell Styles→20% - Accent 6

The worksheet now looks very different

7   Insert a row above row 21.

This was covered in: *Lesson 3-1: Insert and delete rows and columns.*

8   Use AutoSum to place a total in cell G21.

This was covered in: *Lesson 2-3: Use AutoSum to quickly calculate totals.*

9   Apply the *Total* style to cell G21.

Select cell G21 and then click Home→Styles→Cell Styles→Total.

The total cell is neatly formatted.

Canada	4,422.00	17.5%	5,195.85
Germany	245.00	17.5%	287.88
			18,137.37

10   Preview your finished work under different themes.

Because you did things the professional way, using styles instead of directly formatting cells, it is now possible to cycle through the themes. You may find one of the other themes more attractive.

1. Click Page Layout→Themes→Themes.

    The *Themes* gallery appears.

2. Hover over each theme in turn. You'll be amazed at how your work completely changes as each theme's style set is applied.

11   Save your work as *Sales Week Ended 14th March 2008-7.*

Lesson 4-10: Add color and gradient effects to cells

Excel 2007 added the ability to add gradient effects (instead of solid colors) to cells.

Most of the time solid colors are all you need, but you may want to make data look more interesting for a PowerPoint presentation, or for publication in a newsletter or a web page.

When you add colors it is usually best to stay within those of the current theme. This enables you to quickly change the appearance of the worksheet to match that of a PowerPoint presentation or Word document that uses a different theme (see sidebar for an example of this in action).

In this lesson we'll add a gradient to the sharp transition between the orange (pink) totals section and the aqua transaction details section of the worksheet.

1 Open *Sales Week Ended 14th March 2008-7* from your sample files folder (if it isn't already open).

2 Check the colors that are currently being used for the transaction and totals section in your worksheet.

1. Click anywhere in the blue area of your worksheet (cells A5:C21).

2. Click the drop-down arrow next to Home→Font→Fill Color.

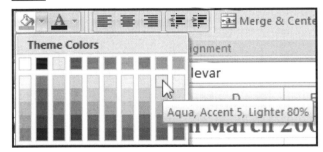

Notice that one color has a small square around it. When you hover over this button you will see that the fill color for the left-hand side of the worksheet is *Aqua, Accent 5, Lighter 80%*.

3. Do the same for the orange (pink) colored cells (in cells D5:G21). You'll find that they are *Orange, Accent 6, Lighter 80%*. The cells appear to be pink, of course, but they are really a 20% tint of orange that appears to be pink to the eye.

3 Set a gradient fill in column D.

1. Select cells D5:D21.

2. Right-click inside the selected range and click Format Cells... from the shortcut menu.

3. Click the *Fill* Tab.

note

Why it is a good idea to restrict custom style colors to theme colors

If you restrict your color choice to the 60 Theme Colors you will make your worksheets design-compatible with documents that use other themes.

If you use non-theme colors your worksheets will not seamlessly integrate (from a design point of view) with PowerPoint presentations, Word documents, and other Office documents, that use a different theme.

Example

John creates a worksheet using the default *Office* theme.

Mary wants to use this in her PowerPoint presentation that uses the *Opulent* theme. John emails the worksheet to her and then she simply pastes the required cells into her presentation and changes the theme to *Opulent*.

Joe sees the presentation and wants to use the same worksheet in his Word report that uses the *Verve* theme. Mary emails the presentation to him and then he simply pastes the required slides into his Word document and changes the theme to *Verve*.

The same worksheet has been used without modification and it blends perfectly into both Joe and Mary's work because John followed best practice and restricted his color choices to theme colors.

Sales Week Ended 14th March 2008-7

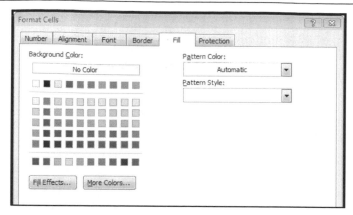

4. Click the *Fill Effects...* button.

5. In the *Colors* frame, choose *Aqua, Accent 5, Lighter 80%* for *Color 1*.

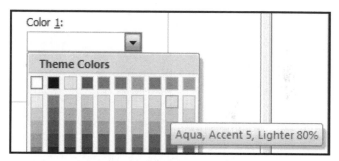

6. In the *Colors* frame, choose *Orange, Accent 6, Lighter 80%* for *Color 2*.

7. Select the *Vertical* shading style.

8. Select the top left variant.

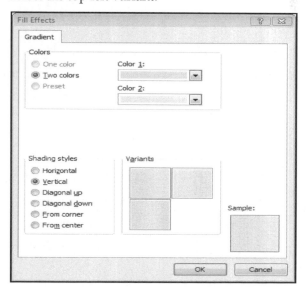

9. Click OK and then OK again.

A smooth gradient fill has been added to column D.

4   Save your work as *Sales Week Ended 14th March 2008-8*.

Lesson 4-11: Add borders and lines

1 Open *Sales Analysis* from your sample files folder.

We're going to use the powerful *borders and lines* feature to make this worksheet more readable.

Before	After

	A	B	C	D	E
1					
2			Total		
3		Analysis Type	Cash	Percent	
4		By Category			
5		Beverages	25,326	20%	
6		Meat/Poultry	65,780	52%	
7		Vegetables	35,679	28%	
8		Total	126,785		
9		By Month			
10		Oct	45,300	36%	
11		Nov	36,800	29%	
12		Dec	44,685	35%	
13		Total	126,785		
14		By Country			
15		UK	56,175	44%	
16		USA	42,368	33%	
17		Canada	28,242	22%	
18		Total	126,785		
19					

	A	B	C	D	E
1					
2			Total		
3		Analysis Type	Cash	Percent	
4		By Category			
5		Beverages	25,326	20%	
6		Meat/Poultry	65,780	52%	
7		Vegetables	35,679	28%	
8		Total	126,785		
9		By Month			
10		Oct	45,300	36%	
11		Nov	36,800	29%	
12		Dec	44,685	35%	
13		Total	126,785		
14		By Country			
15		UK	56,175	44%	
16		USA	42,368	33%	
17		Canada	28,242	22%	
18		Total	126,785		
19					

2 Add cell styles to rows 2,3,4,9 and 14.

1. Select cells B2:D3.

2. Click Home→Styles→Cell Styles→60% Accent 3.

3. Select Cells B4:D4, B9:D9 and B14:D14.

This was covered in: *Lesson 2-7: Select non-contiguous cell ranges and view summary information.*

4. Click Home→Styles→Cell Styles→40% Accent 3.

5. Select cells B2:D3.

6. Click Home→Styles→Cell Styles→Heading 4.

3 Switch off the worksheet gridlines.

When you are working with borders it is always a good idea to switch off the gridlines so that you can have a better idea of how the worksheet will print.

This feature appears in two different places on the Ribbon. Uncheck either of the following check boxes:

View→Show→Gridlines

OR

Page Layout→Sheet Options→Gridlines→View

4 Add a solid border around the entire range.

Sales Analysis

1. Select cells B2:D18.

2. Click Home→Font→Borders drop-down arrow→ Outside Borders.

tip

Use the draw border line tool to quickly add complex borders

The fastest way to quickly add borders is to simply draw them into place using the *Draw Border* tool.

Click:

Home→Font→ Borders drop-down arrow→ Draw Border

You can then simply draw borders straight onto the grid. There's also an *Erase Border* tool available on the same menu.

note

Changing the border line or color from the drop-down menu

The *Format Cells* dialog method of adding borders is more powerful than the menu method.

The ability to change line style and color from the menu (a new feature introduced in Excel 2007) means you'll rarely have to resort to using *the Format Cells* dialog for borders.

To change line style or color from the Borders drop-down menu select *Line Color or Line Style*.

The selected color and/or style will remain active until you close Excel. Next time you open Excel it will have returned to the default.

5   Add solid borders inside cells C2:D3.

    1. Select cells C2:D3.

    2. Click Home→Font→Borders drop-down arrow→All Borders.

6   Add top and bottom borders to *By Category, By Month* and *By Country*.

    1. Select Cells B4:D4, B9:D9 and B14:D14.

    2. Click Home→Font→Borders drop-down arrow→ Top and Bottom Border.

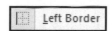

7   Add dotted underlines to the borders of cells B5:D8, B10:D13 and B15:D18.

    1. Select cells B5:D8, B10:D13 and B15:D18.

    2. Right-click any of the selected cells and click *Format Cells…* from the shortcut menu.

     The *Format Cells* dialog appears.

    3. Click the *Border* tab of the *Format Cells* dialog.

    4. Click the *Dotted Line* style.

    5. Click the *Inside* button.

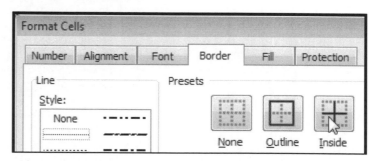

    6. Click the OK button.
     The dotted lines are displayed within the cells.

8   Add left and right borders to cells C5:C8, C10:C13 and C15:C18.

    1. Select cells C5:C8, C10:C13 and C15:C18.

    2. Click Home→Font→Borders→Left Border.

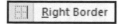

    3. Click Home→Font→Borders→Right Border.

Right Border

9   Save your work as *Sales Analysis-1*.

Lesson 4-12: Create your own custom theme

If none of the 40 built-in themes suffice you can click:

Page Layout→Themes→From Office.com (scroll down the list)

The last time that I looked there were another thirteen themes available for download.

Some clients have a defined corporate style and are extremely particular that colors, fonts and other layout items reinforce their corporate identity.

When individuality is important, you need your own custom theme.

1   Open *Sales Week Ended 14th March 2008-8* from your sample files folder (if it isn't already open).

2   Select a different set of theme colors.

Click Page Layout→Themes→Colors.

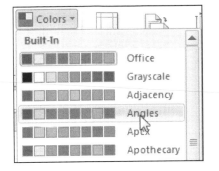

All of the pre-defined sets of colors are displayed (see sidebar). Try hovering your mouse over them one at a time, to see how your worksheet would look if you changed the theme colors.

Choose a different set that you think look attractive.

3   Create a custom set of theme colors.

Click Page Layout→Themes→Colors→Create New Theme Colors.

The *Create New Theme Colors* dialog appears.

Click any of the colors on the left of the dialog and select a different color. Notice that, as you do, the Sample frame shows a preview of how your theme looks. Let your imagination run wild and create your own custom color theme.

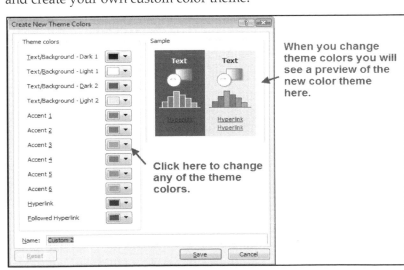

Type **TSM Corporate** into the *Name* box and then click the *Save* button to create your own personalized set of custom colors.

4   Select a different set of fonts.

As discussed in: *Lesson 4-8: Understand themes,* a theme consists of a color set, a font set and an effects set.

Sales Week Ended
14th March 2008-8

A font set consists of two fonts: a heading font and a body font.

Click Page Layout→Themes→Fonts.

All of the pre-defined sets of fonts are displayed (see sidebar). Try hovering your mouse over them one at a time, to see how your worksheet would look if you changed the theme fonts.

Choose a different set that you think look attractive.

5 Create a custom set of theme fonts.

Click Page Layout→Themes→Fonts→Create New Theme Fonts.

The *Create New Theme Fonts* dialog appears.

Select two complimentary fonts. Ideally one should be a serif font and one should be a sans-serif font (this issue is discussed in the sidebar within: *Lesson 4-8: Understand themes*).

Type **TSM Corporate** into the *Name* box and then click the *Save* button to create your own personalized set of custom fonts.

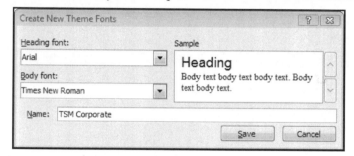

6 Select a different set of effects.

Unlike colors and fonts you can't create a custom set of effects. You have to choose from the pre-defined ones.

Effects change the appearance of drawing objects and we haven't yet covered these (they will make an appearance in: *Lesson 5-5: Format 3-D elements and add drop* shadows).

You can change the theme effects by clicking:

Page Layout→Themes→Effects

Choose a different set at random to see how this works.

7 Save the corporate theme.

1. Click Page Layout→Themes→Themes→Save Current Theme.

2. Enter the name *TSM Corporate* in the *File Name* text box.

3. Click the *Save* button.

8 Revert to the standard Office theme.

1. Click Page Layout→Themes→Themes.

Notice that your custom theme is listed at the top in the Custom group.

2. Click the *Office* theme to put things back the way they were.

173

tip

Naming your themes

The built-in themes follow a sensible naming convention.

The *Office* theme has the *Office* font set, the *Office* color set and the *Office* effects set.

In this lesson we followed the same convention with the *TSM Corporate* theme containing the *TSM Corporate* color set and the *TSM Corporate* font set.

It is a good convention to maintain consistent naming across your own custom themes.

Lesson 4-13: Create your own custom cell styles

Excel 2010 has a large number of pre-defined cell styles grouped into:

- Good, Bad and Neutral – to mark particularly good or bad results.

- Data and Model – usually used in a worksheet containing formulas to mark cells that require user input or contain formula results.

- Titles and Headings – for section titles and column headers.

- Themed Cell Styles - to color cells based upon the theme colors.

- Number Format – to quickly apply number formats, like the Comma[0] number format that is just like the comma style but with no decimal places.

Custom styles are only available in the workbook within which they were originally created. In order to use them in another workbook you need to use Excel's *merge styles* feature that will be covered in: *Lesson 4-14: Use a master style book to merge styles.*

1 Open *Sales Week Ended 14th March 2008-8* from your sample files folder (if it isn't already open).

2 Modify an existing cell style.

Click cell A23 to make it the active cell. This is the cell containing the Note text.

Note: Sales include all European and American and South Africa. Salesmen reported that clien because we are nearing the end of the first qua

23

1. Click Home→Styles→Cell Styles.

2. Right-click the *Note* style and click *Modify* from the shortcut menu.

3. The *Style* dialog appears (see sidebar).

4. Click the *Format…* button. The *Format Cells* dialog appears.

5. Click the *Fill* tab and select a light green background color:

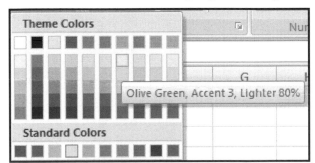

6. Click the OK button and then the OK button once more.

7. If cell A23 isn't green, click Home→Styles→Cell Styles and click once on the *Note* style.

tip

Change the default font (of this workbook) by modifying the normal style

When you modify a cell style the change affects every cell that depends upon that style.

For example, suppose you wanted to change the default font of a worksheet to Times New Roman, 12 point.

You'd simply modify the Normal style's font and then every un-formatted cell in the entire workbook would change to the new default font.

Sales Week Ended 14th March 2008-8

Note that the background color of cell A23 (which has the *Note* style applied to it) has now turned light green.

You haven't permanently changed the *Office* theme's *Note* style. You've simply changed it for this workbook only. When you open another workbook that uses the *Office* theme the *Note* style will be light yellow once again.

3 Duplicate the *Note* built-in cell style.

1. Click Home→Styles→Cell Styles to display the Cell Styles gallery.

2. Right-click the *Note* cell style and then click *Duplicate* from the shortcut menu.

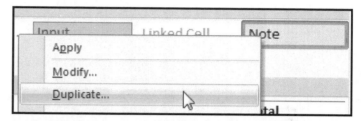

3. The Style dialog appears suggesting the name *Note 2* for your new cell style. Change this to *Blue Note* (we're going to change the color in a moment) and click the OK button.

4. Click Home→Styles→Cell Styles to display the Cell Styles gallery once more. Notice that the *Blue Note* style is at the top of the gallery in the *Custom* section.

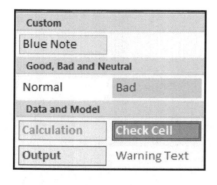

5. Change the background color of the new *Blue Note* style to light blue using the technique learned in: *Step 2-Modify an existing cell style.*

4 Create a custom cell style *By Example*.

This is the easiest way to create custom cell styles.

1. Select Cell A23.

2. Click Home→Font→Fill Color Drop-down and choose the *Purple, Accent 4, Lighter 80%* theme color.

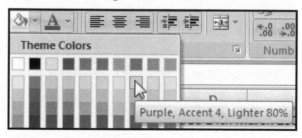

3. Click Home→Styles→Cell Styles→New Cell Style.

The *Style* dialog appears but notice the words: *By Example*. This means that the style already contains all of the formatting information for cell A23.

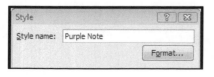

4. Change the style name to **Purple Note** and click the OK button.

5 Save your work as *Sales Week Ended 14th March 2008-9*.

Lesson 4-14: Use a master style book to merge styles

When you create custom styles they are only available within the workbook in which they were created. Sometimes it is useful to have the same set of custom styles available across multiple workbooks.

In this lesson we'll cater for the following scenario at Empire Car Sales:

Syd Slater, the owner of Empire Car Sales, knows that you have to keep your stock turning over.

His salesmen are allowed to discount 10% of the sticker price on all cars. If the car has been on the forecourt for more than two weeks they are allowed to discount 15%, after three weeks 20%, and after four weeks the car goes back to auction.

Syd's salesmen need to know the maximum discount they can offer, but Syd doesn't want the customers to find this out, so they use a cunning system of color coding on the stock list:

10% Max Discount: Blue

15% Max Discount: Green

20% Max Discount: Red

The stock list is produced each week in Excel with three custom cell styles, one for each discount.

To avoid having to constantly re-create custom cell styles they are stored in a master style book called *Empire Styles* which Syd merges with his worksheets so that the three styles are always available.

1   Open a new blank workbook.

2   Create a custom style called *10% Max Discount* with a background color of Light Blue.

   This was covered in: *Lesson 4-13: Create your own custom cell styles.*

3   Create a custom style called *15% Max* Discount with a background color of Light Green.

4   Create a custom style called *20% Max* Discount with a background color of Light Red.

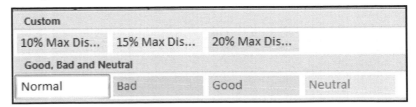

Because you have used theme colors for the custom styles their color will change if the theme is changed.

For example, if you change the theme to *Solstice,* the 10% Max Discount becomes orange, 15% becomes red and 20% becomes Yellow.

Empire Car Sales
Stock List-1

For this reason you could argue that it would be better to set the colors using the *More Colors* option so that the colors remained the same even if the theme was changed.

For the purposes of this lesson we will assume that Syd will not change from the Office theme and follow the normal rule of restricting color choice to theme colors. (See the sidebar in: *Lesson 4-10: Add color and gradient effects to cells* for an explanation of why this is best practice).

5 Save the workbook as *Empire Styles* but don't close it.

6 Open *Empire Car Sales Stock List-1* from your sample files folder.

7 Merge the styles from the *Empire Styles* master style book.

    1. Click Home→Styles→Cell Styles→Merge Styles.

    2. The *Merge Styles* dialog appears.

    3. Select *Empires Styles.xlsx* and then click the OK button.

The three custom styles are now available within the current workbook.

8 Apply the 20% style to the Volkswagen and Mercedes.

9 Apply the 15% style to the BMW and Alfa Romeo.

10 Apply the 10% style to the Volvo and Ford.

Syd's salesmen are now ready to start selling!

11 Save your work as *Empire Car Sales Stock List-2*.

Lesson 4-15: Use simple conditional formatting

Simple conditional formatting applies a format to a cell based upon the value of the cell. In this lesson we'll change the cell background color to red if the cell has a value of less than 5,000 and to green if the value is over 30,000.

The same technique learned in this lesson can be used to apply conditional formats based upon text that begins with, ends with, or contains, specific characters.

You can also apply conditional formats to cells containing dates. For example, you can highlight dates such as today, tomorrow, in the last seven days, last week and this week. Conditional formatting will then cause the worksheet to change every time that you open it based upon the current date.

1   Open *Sales Report* from your sample files folder.

2   AutoFit cells A4:A26.

    1.   Select cells A4:A26.

    2.   Click Home→Cells→Format→AutoFit Column Width.

3   AutoFit cells D4:D13.

4   Apply the comma style to column B and Column E.

This was covered in: *Lesson 4-3: Format numbers using built-in number formats.*

5   Merge cells A3:B3, D3:E3 and D18:E18.

This was covered in: *Lesson 4-6: Merge cells, wrap text and expand/collapse the formula bar.*

6   Apply the *Title* style to cell A1.

This was covered in: *Lesson 4-9: Use cell styles.*

7   Apply the *Heading 2* style to cells A3, D3 and D18.

8   Apply the *Heading 3* style to cells A4:B4, D4:E4 and D19:E19.

9   Apply the *Total* style to cells A26:B26, D13:E13 and D26:E26.

10   Change the theme to the *Flow* theme.

This was covered in: *Lesson 4-9: Use cell styles and change themes.*

The worksheet is now well formatted and has a professional appearance:

	A	B	C	D	E
1	Sales Report - 6 Months ended March 2008				
2					
3	Sales By Country			Sales by Category	
4	Country	Total Sales		Category	Total Sales
5	Argentina	762.60		Beverages	70,168.10
6	Austria	33,462.58		Condiments	24,938.06

Sales Report

note

You can have as many conditional formats as you need

Excel versions prior to Excel 2007 were limited to three conditional formats per cell.

In Excel 2010 you can have an infinite number of conditional formats.

3	Sales By Country	
4	Country	Total Sales
5	Argentina	762.60
6	Austria	33,462.58
7	Belgium	6,109.48
8	Brazil	20,524.42
9	Canada	21,306.29
10	Denmark	16,658.80
11	Finland	5,525.00
12	France	26,155.54
13	Germany	28,361.38
14	Ireland	6,157.76
15	Italy	2,585.69
16	Mexico	3,524.30
17	Norway	1,058.40
18	Poland	459.00
19	Portugal	5,584.13

3	Sales By Country	
4	Country	Total Sales
5	Argentina	762.60
6	Austria	33,462.58
7	Belgium	6,109.48
8	Brazil	20,524.42
9	Canada	21,306.29
10	Denmark	16,658.80
11	Finland	5,525.00
12	France	26,155.54
13	Germany	28,361.38
14	Ireland	6,157.76
15	Italy	2,585.69

11 Select cells B5:B25.

12 Conditionally format the selected range so that any country with sales below 5,000 has a light red fill with dark red text.

1. Click Home→Styles→Conditional Formatting→ Highlight Cell Rules→Less Than...

   The *Less Than* dialog appears.

2. Type 5,000 in the left-hand text box and choose *Light Red Fill with Dark Red Text* for the font and fill color.

   Notice that if you change the value in the text box the worksheet adjusts in the background to preview what will happen with this conditional format.

   Note also that there's a *Custom Format...* option (in the drop-down list) which enables you to choose effects such as underlines and theme colors. The advantage of restricting color choice to theme colors is discussed in: *Lesson 4-10: Add color and gradient effects to cells (sidebar).*

3. Click the OK button.

   Cells that have a value of less than 5,000 are now highlighted in red (see sidebar).

13 Add another conditional format to the same range so that any country with sales above 30,000 has a green fill with dark green text.

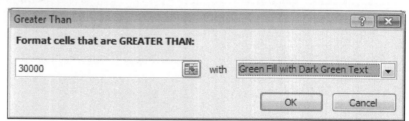

   Both conditional formats now display with the two sales values over 30,000 displayed in green (see sidebar).

14 Remove both conditional formats.

1. Select cells B5:B25.

2. Click Home→Styles→Conditional Formatting→ Clear Rules→Clear Rules from Selected Cells.

   The conditional formats are removed.

15 Save your work as *Sales Report-1.*

Lesson 4-16: Manage multiple conditional formats using the Rules Manager

The conditional formats applied in the last lesson depended upon the value of a single cell.

Often you will want a cell to be formatted based upon its relationship to other cells in a range.

In this lesson we'll color the top 25% of sales green, the middle 50% yellow and the bottom 25% red.

This lesson also introduces the *Rules Manager* that allows you to edit conditional format rules and to specify the order in which conditional formats are applied.

1   Open *Sales Report-1 from* your sample files folder (if it isn't already open).

2   Select cells B5:B25.

3   Conditionally format the selected range so that any country whose sales are in the top 25% has a green fill with dark green text.

> 1.   Click Home→Styles→Conditional Formatting→ Top/Bottom Rules→Top 10%.
>
> The *Top 10%* dialog appears.
>
> 2.   Change the value to 25% and choose *Green fill with Dark Green Text* for the fill.

> 3.   Click the OK button.

4   Conditionally format the selected range so that any country whose sales are in the bottom 25% has a light red fill with dark red text.

The top and bottom 25% of sales are now highlighted as specified in the conditional formats (see sidebar).

3	Sales By Country	
4	Country	Total Sales
5	Argentina	762.60
6	Austria	33,462.58
7	Belgium	6,109.48
8	Brazil	20,524.42
9	Canada	21,306.29
10	Denmark	16,658.80
11	Finland	5,525.00
12	France	26,155.54
13	Germany	28,361.38
14	Ireland	6,157.76
15	Italy	2,585.69

Sales Report-1

5 Add another conditional format so that any country with sales greater than zero has a yellow fill with dark yellow text.

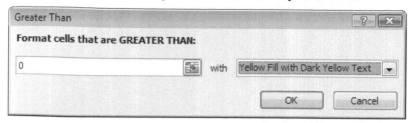

Remember that the specification was to color the middle 50% of sales yellow?

Unfortunately all sales are now yellow because the yellow cells are over-writing the red and green cells.

6 Use the *Rules Manager* to control the order in which conditional formats are applied.

1. Select cells B5:B25.

2. Click Home→Styles→Conditional Formatting→Manage Rules.

   The *Conditional Formatting Rules Manager* dialog is displayed.

3. Click the first rule (the Cell Value > 0 rule).

4. Use the Move Down button to move the rule to the bottom of the list (if you don't see the Move Down button it is because you haven't selected the rule).

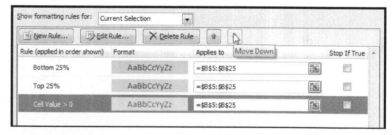

5. Click the OK button.

   The red, green and yellow formatting rules are now applied as required. This works because of the conflict resolution rules (see sidebar).

7 Use the *Rules Manager* to edit the rules so that the top and bottom 30% values are now highlighted.

1. Select cells B5:B25.

2. Click Home→Styles→Conditional Formatting→Manage Rules.

3. Select the *Bottom 25%* rule.

4. Click the *Edit Rule...* button and change the criteria to: *30%*.

5. Edit the *Top 25%* rule in the same way so that it will show the top 30% values.

8 Remove all three conditional formats.

This was covered in: *Lesson 4-15: Use simple conditional formatting.*

181

---

note

Conflict resolution rules

In this lesson we applied three different conditional formats to the selected range.

Sometimes there will be a conflict between different conditional formatting rules.

Consider this specification:

- Format every value over 50 as blue underlined and bold.

- Format every value over 75 as red and italic.

The rules manager has a dilemma with a value of 80. Should it be blue or red, bold, italic, underlined or all three?

To resolve the conflict, rules are applied in the order listed in the rules manager. Attributes are applied only if an earlier conditional format has not set a conflicting condition.

1. The value is over 50 so apply blue, underlined, bold-face.

2. The value is over 75. Can't format red because the earlier condition has made the cell blue.

3. The value is over 75. Apply italics.

Lesson 4-17: Bring data alive with visualizations

Visualizations are a fantastic new feature that was introduced in Excel 2007. Excel 2010 has enhanced the feature with even more visualization options.

Visualizations are a half-way house between raw data and charts. With a few clicks of the mouse they allow you to express numbers in a visual manner.

1   Open *Sales Report-1* from your sample files folder (if it isn't already open).

2   Add a data bar visualization to the *Sales by Country* figures.

1. Select cells B5:B25.

2. Click Home→Styles→Conditional Formatting→ Data Bars→Gradient Fill→Red Data Bar.

The visualization is applied (see sidebar).

3   Add a color scale visualization to the *Sales by Category* figures.

1. Select cells E5:E12.

2. Click Home→Styles→Conditional Formatting→ Color Scales→Green/Yellow Color Scale.

The visualization is applied (see sidebar).

4   Add an icon set visualization to the *Sales by Month* figures.

1. Select cells E20:E25.

2. Click Home→Styles→Conditional Formatting→Icon Sets→ Indicators→3 Flags.

3. Re-size column E so that it is wide enough to display the values.

The visualization is applied (see sidebar).

When the icon set contains three icons, Excel assigns the relative icons to the top third, middle third, and bottom third of the value range.

You will often need to change these arbitrary values.

5   Use the Rules Manager to modify the *Sales by Month* visualization so that three green flags are shown.

The *Sales by Month* visualization may discourage our salesmen because only one month is flagged as green with four months flagged red. We'll adjust the criteria for flag allocation so that three months are shown as green.

1. Select cells E20:E25.

2. Click Home→Styles→Conditional Formatting→Manage Rules.

The *Conditional Formatting Rules Manager* dialog is displayed.

	A	B
3	**Sales By Country**	
4	Country	Total Sales
5	Argentina	762.60
6	Austria	33,462.58
7	Belgium	6,109.48
8	Brazil	20,524.42
9	Canada	21,306.29
10	Denmark	16,658.80
11	Finland	5,525.00
12	France	26,155.54
13	Germany	28,361.38
14	Ireland	6,157.76

	D	E
3	**Sales by Category**	
4	Category	Total Sales
5	Beverages	70,168.10
6	Condiments	24,938.06
7	Confections	31,883.54
8	Dairy Products	49,902.95
9	Grains/Cereals	19,570.36

	D	E
18	**Sales by Month**	
19	Date	Total Sales
20	Oct	37,515.73
21	Nov	45,600.05
22	Dec	45,239.63
23	Jan	61,258.07
24	Feb	38,483.64

Sales Report-1

© 2011 The Smart Method® Ltd

tip

Use the *Show Bar Only* feature to create quick charts

To create a "quick chart" for cells E5:E12:

1. Type the formula **=E5** into cell F5.

2. AutoFill cell F5 down to F12.

3. Create a bar visualization for cells F5:F12 with the *Show Bar Only* option checked.

4. Widen column F to display a "quick chart".

Total Sales	
70,168.10	
24,938.06	
31,883.54	
49,902.95	

	D	E
18	**Sales by Month**	
19	Date	Total Sales
20	Oct	37,515.73
21	Nov	45,600.05
22	Dec	45,239.63
23	Jan	61,258.07
24	Feb	38,483.64
25	Mar	38,547.22
26	**Grand Total**	266,644.33

	A	B
3	**Sales By Country**	
4	Country	Total Sales
5	Argentina	
6	Austria	
7	Belgium	
8	Brazil	
9	Canada	
10	Denmark	

3. Click the *Edit Rule* button.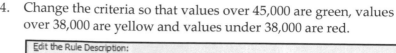

4. Change the criteria so that values over 45,000 are green, values over 38,000 are yellow and values under 38,000 are red.

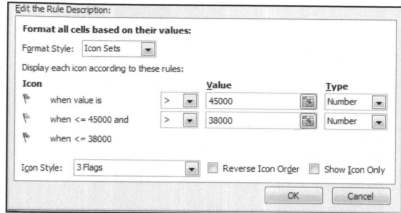

5. Click OK and OK again.

The flags are displayed as required, with three green flags (see sidebar).

6 Use the *Rules Manager* to show the visualizations for *Sales by Country* without the underlying data.

1. Select cells B5:B25.

2. Click Home→Styles→Conditional Formatting→Manage Rules.

The *Conditional Formatting Rules Manager* dialog is displayed.

3. Click the *Edit Rule* button.

4. Check the *Show Bar Only* check box.

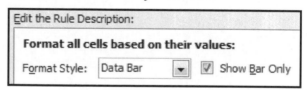

5. Click the OK button on each dialog to close them.

The bars are shown without the values (see sidebar).

7 Use the *Rules Manager* to bring back the values for *Sales by Country*.

Follow the same procedure as in the previous step to uncheck the *Show Bar Only* check box.

8 Save your work as *Sales Report-2*.

Lesson 4-18: Create a formula driven conditional format

While the built-in conditional format options are very powerful, you will occasionally have a conditional format requirement that is not catered for.

For example, I've lost count of the number of times I have been asked if it is possible to highlight an entire row, rather than a single cell within a row, based upon the value in one of the row's cells.

This lesson will show you how to achieve this using a formula-driven conditional format.

1   Open *Sales Summary First Quarter 2008* from your sample files folder.

Our challenge will be to highlight the entire row when the Country column contains the value: *USA*.

2   Apply a conditional format to Column C to change the background color to light Red when the text contains the text: USA.

1.   Select column C and apply a *Text that Contains...* conditional formatting rule selecting *Custom Format* as the fill color:

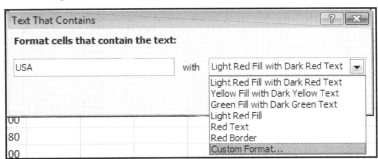

This was covered in: *Lesson 4-15: Use simple conditional formatting.*

2.   Click the *Fill* tab and select a light red color for the conditional fill

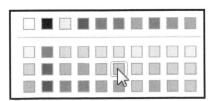

3.   Click the OK Button.

Every instance of *USA* in the worksheet now has the cell in column C highlighted.

	B	C	D
40	Familia Arquibaldo	Brazil	100.00
41	Hungry Coyote Import Store	USA	62.40
42	Hungry Coyote Import Store	USA	40.00
43	Wartian Herkku	Finland	146.00

note

A more expert solution using mixed cell references

In my classroom courses I always teach this lesson as presented here.

I like to keep things simple by solving the problem using a simple formula.

The reason I do this is that many students find mixed cell references challenging (the subject of: *Lesson 3-13: Understand mixed cell references*).

If you completely understood *Lesson 3-13: Understand mixed cell references* you might find it interesting to solve this problem in a more efficient way.

You can apply a single mixed cell reference to all four columns in a single operation:

1.   Select columns A to D.

2.   Click Home→Styles→ Conditional Formatting→ New Rule...

3.   Select: *Use a formula to determine which cells to format.*

4.   Type this formula (note the use of a mixed cell reference) into the *Format values where this formula is true* box:

=$C1="USA"

5.   Click the *Format...* button.

6.   Click the *Fill* tab and select a light red color for the conditional fill.

7.   Click OK and OK again.

Sales Summary First Quarter 2008

3 Apply a formula-driven conditional format to column B so that the same rows are highlighted.

This is a lot more difficult than the simple conditional format applied to column C.

1. Select column B.

2. Click Home→Styles→Conditional Formatting→New Rule…

   The *New Formatting Rule* dialog appears.

3. Select *Use a formula to determine which cells to format* from the *Select a Rule Type* list.

4. Type the formula **=C1="USA"** into the formula text box.

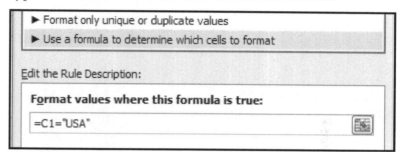

See sidebar for a discussion of this formula.

5. Click the *Format* button, then the *Fill* tab and apply the same light red fill color.

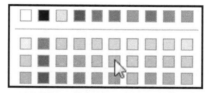

6. Click the OK button once, and then again, to close both dialogs.

Both columns now have a light red fill when the country is USA.

	A	B	C	D
40	14-Jan-08	Familia Arquibaldo	Brazil	100.00
41	15-Jan-08	Hungry Coyote Import Store	USA	62.40
42	15-Jan-08	Hungry Coyote Import Store	USA	40.00
43	16-Jan-08	Wartian Herkku	Finland	146.00

4 Apply the same formula-driven conditional format to columns A and D so that the whole row is highlighted.

	A	B	C	D
40	14-Jan-08	Familia Arquibaldo	Brazil	100.00
41	15-Jan-08	Hungry Coyote Import Store	USA	62.40
42	15-Jan-08	Hungry Coyote Import Store	USA	40.00
43	16-Jan-08	Wartian Herkku	Finland	146.00

5 Save your work as *Sales Summary First Quarter 2008-1*.

tip

Why does the formula relate to cell C1?

At first it seems rather odd that we refer to cell C1 in the conditional formatting formula.

C1 is in the title row so how can this be right?

The answer is to be found in Excel's treatment of absolute and relative cell references (originally explained in: *Lesson 3-12: Understand absolute and relative cell references*).

Excel regards the cell reference to be relative to the first row in the selected range.

Since we selected an entire column, row 1 is the reference row used to adjust the formula for every other row within the column.

In other words, Excel will look at cell C2 when applying row 2 conditional formatting, C3 when applying row 3… and so on.

This is exactly what we want to happen.

Lesson 4-19: Insert a Sparkline into a range of cells

Sparklines are one of the most important new features in Excel 2010. They solve a very common worksheet problem.

In *Lesson 4-17: Bring data alive with visualizations* you discovered how visualizations can illustrate the differences between values in a single column of data (see example in sidebar).

In: *Session Five: Charts and Graphics*, you will discover Excel's ability to create fantastic charts of all descriptions. These are especially useful when your data has two dimensions (several columns per row). You'll create this chart:

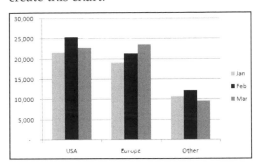

But imagine you had a large number of rows of two dimensional data to compare. This is the case in the sample worksheet for this lesson where there are 36 rows (one for each branch), each having six values (Jan-Jun):

	A	B	C	D	E	F	G	H
4	Country	Branch	Jan	Feb	Mar	Apr	May	Jun
5	USA	Chicago	671,185	359,811	745,471	685,637	- 16,562	711,009
6	USA	Dallas	708,157	276,972	227,227	482,136	377,175	198,273

The worksheet has 216 values and would produce a very confusing chart:

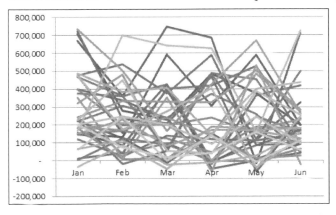

A Sparkline is a chart that can be inserted into a single cell, typically charting the values on its left hand side.

Sparklines provide an elegant way to provide users with a visual depiction of large two dimensional data sets, even when they contain thousands of rows.

	A	B	C	D	E	F	G	H	I
4	Country	Branch	Jan	Feb	Mar	Apr	May	Jun	
5	USA	Chicago	671,185	359,811	745,471	685, Sparklines		711,009	
6	USA	Dallas	708,157	276,972	227,227	482,		198,273	

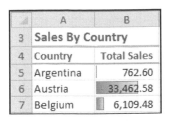

	A	B
3	**Sales By Country**	
4	Country	Total Sales
5	Argentina	762.60
6	Austria	33,462.58
7	Belgium	6,109.48

First Half-Year Profit Report

1 Open *First Half-Year Profit Report* from your sample files folder (if it isn't already open).

2 Create a *Line Sparkline* in cell I5 that charts the data in cells C5:H5.

   1. Click in cell I5.

   2. Click Insert→Sparklines→Line.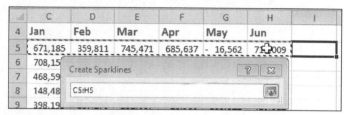

       The *Create Sparklines* dialog appears:

   3. Click in the *Data Range:* box and then select cells C5:H5

	C	D	E	F	G	H	I
4	Jan	Feb	Mar	Apr	May	Jun	
5	671,185	359,811	745,471	685,637 -	16,562	71,009	
6	708,15						
7	468,59	Create Sparklines					
8	148,48	C5:H5					
9	398,19						

   4. Click the OK button.

       A Sparkline appears in cell I5:

	H	I
4	Jun	
5	711,009	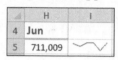

3 AutoFill the Sparkline to cells I6:I40.

You learned how to do this in: *Lesson 2-14: Use AutoFill for text and numeric series*.

You can now see how Sparklines visualize each branch's performance in a way that is beyond the scope of Visualizations and Charts.

	A	B	C	D	E	F	G	H	I
4	Country	Branch	Jan	Feb	Mar	Apr	May	Jun	
5	USA	Chicago	671,185	359,811	745,471	685,637 -	16,562	711,009	
6	USA	Dallas	708,157	276,972	227,227	482,136	377,175	198,273	
7	USA	Houston	468,592	358,841	426,955 -	2,625	86,518	96,686	

4 Use the same technique to place a *Column Sparkline* in cells J5:J40 that charts the same data range (C5:H5).

5 Use the same technique to place a *Win/Loss Sparkline* in cells K5:K40 that charts the same data range (C5:H5).

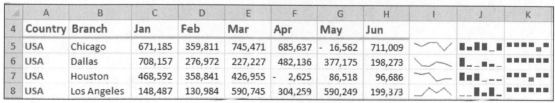

	A	B	C	D	E	F	G	H	I	J	K
4	Country	Branch	Jan	Feb	Mar	Apr	May	Jun			
5	USA	Chicago	671,185	359,811	745,471	685,637 -	16,562	711,009			
6	USA	Dallas	708,157	276,972	227,227	482,136	377,175	198,273			
7	USA	Houston	468,592	358,841	426,955 -	2,625	86,518	96,686			
8	USA	Los Angeles	148,487	130,984	590,745	304,259	590,249	199,373			

The *Column Sparkline* is very similar to the *Line Sparkline* but represents data as a bar chart.

Notice how the *Win/Loss Sparkline* enables you to see at a glance that Chicago and Houston had one loss-making month while Dallas and Los Angeles made a profit every month.

6 Save your work as *First Half Year Profit Report-1*.

important

Win/Loss Sparklines depict zero values with a blank space

In the example data for this lesson all of the branches have either made a profit or a loss.

If you have a data set with zero values the Win/Loss Sparkline will show blank spaces in the chart to illustrate zero values.

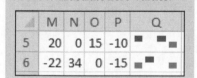

	M	N	O	P	Q
5	20	0	15	-10	
6	-22	34	0	-15	

Lesson 4-20: Apply a common vertical axis and formatting to a Sparkline group

Consider the following column Sparklines:

	A	B	C	D	E	F	G	H	J
4	Country	Branch	Jan	Feb	Mar	Apr	May	Jun	
5	USA	Chicago	671,185	359,811	745,471	685,637 -	16,562	711,009	▪▫▪▪_▪
28	UK	Manchester	180,988	209,763	203,761	2,201	165,328	124,392	▪▪▪_▪▫

If you only looked at the bars (and not the values) you'd guess that Manchester made more profit in the first three months than Chicago.

A glance at the actual profit values shows that Chicago actually made about three times more profit than Manchester.

The Column Sparklines are misleading because, by default, Excel only considers each row's values when setting the Maximum and Minimum values for the bars (also called the *Vertical Axis* values).

In this lesson we'll change this behaviour so that the size of the bars gives a true indication of each branch profit.

1 Open *First Half-Year Profit Report-1* from your sample files folder (if it isn't already open).

2 Delete columns I and K so that only the Column Sparklines remain.

> You learned how to do this in: *Lesson 3-1: Insert and delete rows and columns*. Removing the two other Sparklines will help to focus upon the *Column Sparkline*.

3 Set a common Maximum and Minimum value for all Sparklines.

1. Click on any of the Sparklines in column I.

    Notice that a thin blue line has appeared around all of the Sparklines in column I. This happens because Excel views all of the Sparklines as a *Sparkline Group*. This means that when we use any of the *Sparkline Design Tools* on the Ribbon, the settings will apply to all Sparklines in the group.

2. Click Sparkline Tools→Design→Group→Axis drop-down.

3. Click Vertical Axis Minimum Value Options→ Same for All Sparklines.

4. Click Vertical Axis Maximum Value Options→ Same for All Sparklines.

5. Notice the change in the Chicago and Manchester Sparklines:

	F	G	H	I
4	Apr	May	Jun	
5	685,637 -	16,562	711,009	▪▫▪▪_▪
28	2,201	165,328	124,392	_ _ _ _ _ _

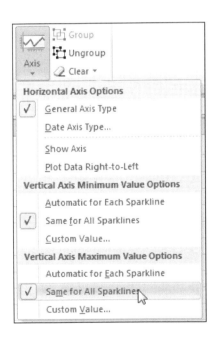

First Half-Year Profit Report-1

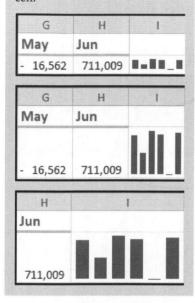
It is now clear, from looking at the bars alone, that in every month (except May) Manchester produced far less profit than Chicago.

4   Explore Sparkline formatting options.

The *Sparkline Tools Design* tab on the Ribbon provides many ways in which you can change the appearance of a group of Sparklines. Try experimenting with them.

1. Use the *Show* and *Marker Color* options.

    The *Show* check boxes allow you to apply a chosen color to any of the following points on a Sparkline.

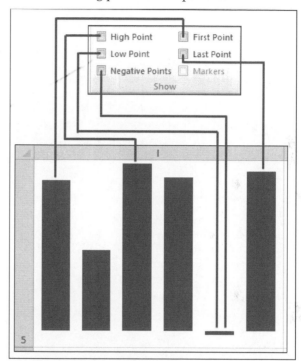

    You can choose a color for each of the points you check from the Style→Marker Color drop down.

2. Choose a new *Sparkline Style* from the *Style* gallery.

    Styles allow you to change the color scheme for your Sparkline. Note that the styles use theme colors and will change if you change the current theme. (You learned about Themes in: *Lesson 4-8: Understand themes*).

3. Change the *Sparkline Type* to *Line* by clicking Type→Line.

4. Add *Markers*.

    When the Sparkline type is *Line* you are able to select the *Markers* option in the *Show* group. Each data point on the Sparkline is then marked with a dot.

5. Clicking Sparkline Tools→Design→Style→Sparkline Color.

6. Change the line color.

7. Change the line thickness by clicking *Weight*.

5   Close *First Year Profit Report-1* without saving.

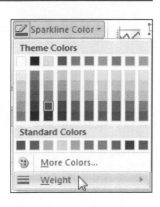

Learn Excel 2010 Essential Skills with The Smart Method

Lesson 4-21: Apply a date axis to a Sparkline group and format a single Sparkline

Sometimes you will encounter data that is attached to dates with uneven time intervals. Here's some of the sample data for this lesson:

	A	B	C	D	E	F	G	H
1	**Number of Rings to Answer Phone Survey**							
2								
3	Country	Branch	01-Mar-11	03-Mar-11	04-Mar-11	07-Mar-11	08-Mar-11	09-Mar-11
4	USA	Chicago	3	1	1	2	3	2
5	USA	Dallas	2	3	1	3	2	1
6	USA	Houston	10	8	11	7	11	5
7	USA	Los Angeles	1	3	2	3	3	1

This company has a policy that the telephone should be answered within three rings. To make sure the staff are hitting this target head office phone each branch occasionally and record the number of rings taken to answer. You can see that Chicago, Dallas and Los Angeles are doing well but Houston is performing well below standard.

Head office don't ring every day – only when they have time to do so. This means that they didn't ring at all on 2nd, 5th and 6th March.

By default a Sparkline will assume that the data is at equal intervals and chart like this:

	C	D	E	F	G	H	I
3	01-Mar-11	03-Mar-11	04-Mar-11	07-Mar-11	08-Mar-11	09-Mar-11	
4	3	1	1	2	3	2	
5	2	3	1	3	2	1	
6	10	8	11	7	11	5	
7	1	3	2	3	3	1	

… but we'd like the Sparklines to show a gap for the missing dates like this:

	E	F	G	H	I
3	04-Mar-11	07-Mar-11	08-Mar-11	09-Mar-11	
4	1	2	3	2	
5	1	3	2	1	
6	11	7	11	5	
7	2	3	3	1	

1 Open *Phone Survey* from your sample files folder.

2 Insert a Column Sparkline in cell I4 to chart data in cells C4:H4 and AutoFill it to the end of the range.

   You learned to do this in: *Lesson 4-19: Insert a Sparkline into a range of cells.*

3 Set the Vertical Axis Maximum and Maximum Values to be the same for all Sparklines.

   You learned to do this in: *Lesson 4-20: Apply a common vertical axis and formatting to a Sparkline group.*

Phone Survey

note

Options for worksheets that contain Hidden and Empty cells

In:

Lesson 5-10: Chart non-contiguous source data by hiding rows and columns

And

Lesson 5-12: Deal with empty data points.

... you will learn the concept of hidden rows and columns, and also learn how to use Excel's *Hidden and Empty Cells* dialog.

You'll then also be able to use these features when you add Sparklines to worksheets that contain empty cells or hidden rows and columns.

Your worksheet should now look like this:

⊿	D	E	F	G	H	I
3	03-Mar-11	04-Mar-11	07-Mar-11	08-Mar-11	09-Mar-11	
4	1	1	2	3	2	_ _ _ _ _
5	3	1	3	2	1	_ _ _ _ _
6	8	11	7	11	5	▪▪▪▪▪
7	3	2	3	3	1	_ _ _ _ _

4   Set the *Sparkline Date Range* to C3:H3.

1. Click any Sparkline in column I to select the Sparkline group.

2. Click:

    Sparkline Tools→Design→Group→Axis→Date Axis Type...

    The *Sparkline Date Range* dialog appears.

3. Select cells C3:H3 with the mouse.

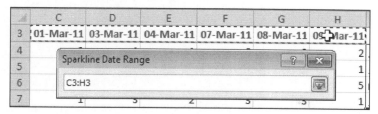

4. Click the OK button.

    The Sparkline is now shown with gaps for the missing dates:

⊿	E	F	G	H	I
3	04-Mar-11	07-Mar-11	08-Mar-11	09-Mar-11	
4	1	2	3	2	_ __ `_ __
5	1	3	2	1	_ __ ___
6	11	7	11	5	▪ ▪▪ ▪▪▪
7	2	3	3	1	_ __ ___

5   Format the Houston Sparkline (in cell I6) so that all bars are Red.

To format a single Sparkline it is necessary to *Ungroup* the Sparklines. When Sparklines are ungrouped it is possible to format them individually.

1. Click in cell I6.

2. Click Sparkline Tools→Design→Group→Ungroup.

3. Click:

    SparklineTools→Design→Style→Sparkline Color→ Red Accent 2

4. The Houston Sparkline is now colored red while all other Sparklines remain black.

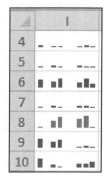

6   Save your work as *Phone Survey-1*.

Lesson 4-22: Use the Format Painter

The format painter is one of the most useful tools in Microsoft Office.

You can use the format painter in PowerPoint, Word and all other Office products.

I find that at least half of the experienced Excel users who attend my classroom courses have never discovered the format painter. I love it when they gasp in amazement at the enormous amount of time and effort they will save in future when using this tool.

In this lesson we're going to take a worksheet that is partially formatted and use the format painter to quickly copy formatting information (as opposed to values) from one cell to another.

1   Open *Sales Report-FP from* your sample files folder.

This worksheet has been partially formatted.

	A	B	C	D	E
1	Sales Report - 6 Months ended March 2008				
2					
3	Sales By Country			Sales by Category	
4	Country	Total Sales		Category	Total Sales
5	Argentina	762.6		Beverages	70168.1
6	Austria	33462.58		Condiments	24938.055
7	Belgium	6109.48		Confections	31883.54
8	Brazil	20524.42		Dairy Products	49902.95
9	Canada	21306.29		Grains/Cereals	19570.36
10	Denmark	16658.8		Meat/Poultry	35767.63
11	Finland	5525		Produce	17109.18
12	France	26155.54		Seafood	17304.51
13	Germany	28361.38		Grand Total	266644.325
14	Ireland	6157.755			

2   Apply the comma style to all of the values in column B.

This was covered in: *Lesson 4-3: Format numbers using built-in number formats.*

Values are now formatted with two decimal places and a thousand comma separator.

	A	B
9	Canada	21,306.29
10	Denmark	16,658.80
11	Finland	5,525.00

3   Click any value in column B and then click:

Home→Clipboard→Format Painter.

The cursor shape changes to a paint brush.

Sales Report-FP

note

Autofill and Paste are also able to match formatting in the same way as the Format Painter

The Format Painter is the fastest and most convenient way to match formatting when you only have to deal with a small range of cells.

Sometimes you'll need to match formatting in very large ranges containing thousands of cells. This would take a long time using the Format Painter but can be quickly achieved using *AutoFill,* or by using *Paste* along with the skills you learned in*: Lesson 2-8: AutoSelect a range of cells.*

AutoFill

AutoFill options were covered in depth in*: Lesson 2-16: Use AutoFill options.*

When you AutoFill using a right-click and drag (or AutoFill and then look at the Smart tag options) you'll notice that there's a *Fill Formatting Only* option.

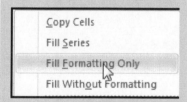

Paste

Copy and Paste were covered in depth in*: Lesson 3-3: Cut, copy and paste.*

When you paste there's also a *Formatting* option in the *Paste Options.*

4 Click and drag across cells E5:E13.

The format of cells E5:E13 changes to match those of the values in column B.

	D	E
4	Category	Total Sales
5	Beverages	70,168.10
6	Condiments	24,938.06

5 Do the same for cells E20:E26.

Repeat exactly the same steps.

1. Click on any value in column B (this is the source).

2. Click Home→Clipboard→Format Painter.

3. Drag across cells E20:E26 (this is the target).

All values in this worksheet are now formatted with the comma style.

6 Use the format painter to copy formatting from cell A3 to cells D3 and D18.

This time we will use the format painter in a slightly different way.

If you double-click the format painter icon  a *sticky format painter* results. This will stay switched on until you once again click the format painter icon to switch it off.

1. Click on cell A3 to make it the active (source) cell.

2. Double-click Home→Clipboard→Format Painter.

       🖌 Format Painter

3. The cursor shape changes to a paint brush.

4. Click cell D3. The format now matches cell A3 but the cursor remains the same.

5. Click cell D18. The format now matches cell A3 but the cursor remains the same.

6. Click Home→Clipboard→Format Painter 🖌 Format Painter to switch off the format painter. The cursor reverts to the normal shape.

7 Copy formatting from cell A4 to cells D4:E4 and D19:E19 using the format painter.

8 Apply the *Total* style to cell B26.

This was covered in*: Lesson 4-9: Use cell styles and change themes.*

9 Copy the total style from cell B26 to cells E13 and E26 using the format painter.

10 Save your work as *Sales Report-FP-1.*

Lesson 4-23: Rotate text

1   Open *Top 20 Films from* your sample files folder.

2   Insert a new column to the left of column A.

This was covered in: *Lesson 3-1: Insert and delete rows and columns.*

3   Cut and paste the contents of cell B1 to cell A1.

This was covered in: *Lesson 3-3: Cut, copy and paste.*

4   Apply the *Title* style to cell A1, the *Heading 2* style to cells A3:E3 and the *Heading 4* style to cell D25.

This was covered in: *Lesson 4-9: Use cell styles and change themes.*

5   Type: **Over 400M** into cell A4, **Over 350M** into cell A12 and **Over 300M** into cell A17.

6   Select cells A4:A11.

3		Title	Year
4	Over 400M	Titanic	1997
5		The Dark Knight	2008
6		Star Wars	1977
7		Shrek 2	2004
8		E.T.: The Extra-Terrestrial	1982
9		Star Wars: Episode I - The Phantom Menace	1999
10		Pirates of the Caribbean: Dead Man's Chest	2006
11		Spider-Man	2002
12	Over 350M	Star Wars: Episode III - Revenge of the Sith	2005

7   Merge the selected cells.

This was covered in: *Lesson 4-6: Merge cells, wrap text and expand/collapse the formula bar.*

8   Rotate the text through ninety degrees.

1. Click Home→Alignment→Orientation.

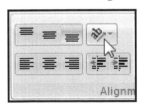

2. Select *Rotate Text Up* from the drop-down list.

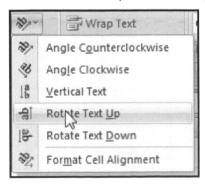

note

Other ways to rotate text

You can also rotate text using the *Format Cells* dialog though you'll nearly always find the Ribbon method faster and more convenient.

The *Format Cells* dialog is slightly more powerful as it allows you to rotate text by any angle.

1. Right-click a cell or range and click *Format Cells* from the shortcut menu.

2. Click the *Alignment* tab.

3. In the *Orientation* pane either type in the number of degrees of rotation or click and drag the red diamond to set it visually.

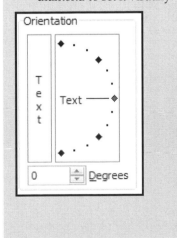

Top 20 Films

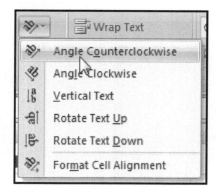

3		Title
4		Titanic
5		The Dark Knight
6		Star Wars
7		Shrek 2
8	Over 400M	E.T.: The Extra-T
9		Star Wars: Episo
10		Pirates of the Ca
11		Spider-Man
12		Star Wars: Episo
13		The Lord of the
14	Over 350M	Spider-Man 2
15		The Passion of t
16		Jurassic Park
17		The Lord of the
18		Finding Nemo
19		Spider-Man 3
20		Forrest Gump
21	Over 300M	The Lion King
22		Shrek the Third
23		Transformers

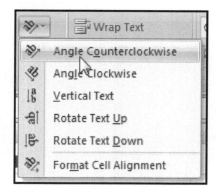

Wrap Text

Angle Counterclockwise

Angle Clockwise

Vertical Text

Rotate Text Up

Rotate Text Down

Format Cell Alignment

9 Merge and rotate the text in cells A12:A16 and A17:A23.

Your worksheet should now look like the sidebar.

10 Select cells A4:A17 and set the horizontal alignment to center and the vertical alignment to middle.

This was covered in: *Lesson 4-5: Horizontally align the contents of cells* and *Lesson 4-7: Vertically align the contents of cells.*

11 Apply the *Heading 4* style to cells A4:A17.

12 AutoFit cells A4:A17 so that they are just wide enough for the text.

This was covered in: *Lesson 2-9: Re-size rows and columns.*

13 Apply the *40% Accent 3* style to cell A4.

This was covered in: *Lesson 4-9: Use cell styles and change themes.*

Note that the cell reference for the old range A4:A11 is now the single cell reference A4.

14 Apply the *40% Accent 6* style to cell A12.

15 Apply the *40% Accent 2* style to cell A17.

16 Widen row 3 so that it is about three times the normal height.

17 Rotate the text in row 3 through 45 degrees.

Select row 3 and click Home→Alignment→Orientation→ Angle Counter Clockwise.

18 Make columns C and E a little wider.

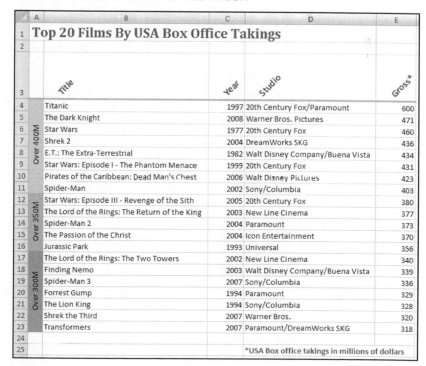

19 Save your work as *Top 20 Films-1*.

Session 4: Exercise

1 Open *House Mortgage* from your sample files folder.

2 Merge and center cells B3:J3.

3 Apply the *Title* style to cell A1, the *Heading 1* style to cell B3, the *Heading 3* style to cells A4:J4 and the *Heading 3* style to cells A10:C10.

4 Apply the *Heading 4* style to cells A5:A8 and cells A11:A15.

5 Apply the *Percentage* style to cells B4:J4.

6 Apply the *Comma* style to cells B5:J8.

7 Apply the *Percentage* style to cells B11:C15 and then increase decimals to one place.

8 Type the word *Average* into cell A16 and use the *Format Painter* to match the formatting to that of the cell above (A15).

9 Horizontally right-align the text in cell A16.

10 Use *AutoSum* to place an *Average* function into cells B16 and C16.

11 Place a thin black border beneath cells A15:C15.

12 Apply a *20% Accent 1* cell style to cells B4:J4 and B10:C10.

13 Change the theme to *Foundry* and adjust the width of column A so that all text is displayed.

14 Save your work as *House Mortgage-1*.

	A	B	C	D	E	F	G	H	I	J
1	**House Mortgage Monthly Payments - 25 year term**									
2										
3						interest rate				
4	House Value	2%	3%	4%	5%	6%	7%	8%	9%	10%
5		50000	211.93	237.11	263.92	292.30	322.15	353.39	385.91	419.60	454.35
6		100000	423.85	474.21	527.84	584.59	644.30	706.78	771.82	839.20	908.70
7		150000	635.78	711.32	791.76	876.89	966.45	1,060.17	1,157.72	1,258.79	1,363.05
8		200000	847.71	948.42	1,055.67	1,169.18	1,288.60	1,413.56	1,543.63	1,678.39	1,817.40
9										
10	Historical Base/Prime Rates	UK	USA							
11	1990	14.8%	7.3%							
12	1995	6.7%	5.5%							
13	2000	6.0%	5.5%							
14	2005	4.7%	2.3%							
15	2008	5.0%	2.0%							
16	Average	7.4%	4.5%							

House Mortgage

If you need help slide the page to the left

Session 4: Exercise answers

These are the four questions that most students find the most difficult to remember:

Q 13	Q 11	Q 10	Q 8
1. Click Page Layout→Themes→Themes→Foundry. 2. Select cells A4:A16. 3. Click Home→Cells→Format→AutoFit Column Width. This was covered in: *Lesson 2-9: Re-size rows and columns.*	1. Select cells A15:C15. 2. Click Home→Font→Borders→Bottom Border. This was covered in: *Lesson 4-11: Add borders and lines.*	1. Select cells B16:C16. 2. Click Home→Editing→AutoSum→Average. 3. Either press the **<Enter>** key or click the AutoSum button again. This was covered in: *Lesson 2-11: Use AutoSum to quickly calculate averages.*	1. Click in cell A15. 2. Click Home→Clipboard→Format Painter. 3. Click in cell A16. This was covered in: *Lesson 4-22: Use the Format Painter.*

If you have difficulty with the other questions, here are the lessons that cover the relevant skills:

1   Refer to: Lesson 1-4: Download the sample files and open/navigate a workbook.

2   Refer to: Lesson 4-6: Merge cells, wrap text and expand/collapse the formula bar.

3   Refer to: Lesson 4-9: Use cell styles and change themes.

4   Refer to: Lesson 4-9: Use cell styles and change themes.

5   Refer to: Lesson 4-3: Format numbers using built-in number formats.

6   Refer to: Lesson 4-3: Format numbers using built-in number formats.

7   Refer to: Lesson 4-3: Format numbers using built-in number formats.

9   Refer to: Lesson 4-5: Horizontally align the contents of cells.

12   Refer to: Lesson 4-9: Use cell styles and change themes.

14   Refer to: Lesson 1-5: Save a workbook.

Session Five: Charts and Graphics

Charts (also called graphs) are one of Excel's most powerful features.

While very numerate readers may be able to reach conclusions by scanning a range of numbers, most will find a chart a lot more intuitive.

PowerPoint presentations that are packed with numbers will send your audience to sleep, while hard-hitting graphical representations of your data will maintain interest and attention.

In this session you'll learn to present your data in a chart. You'll also learn some valuable "tricks of the trade" to present your data in the most effective way.

Charts never lie but they can give the truth scope!

Session Objectives

By the end of this session you will be able to:

- Create a simple chart with two clicks
- Move, re-size, copy and delete a chart
- Change chart layouts
- Format chart element fills and borders
- Format 3-D elements and align text
- Move, re-size, add and delete chart elements
- Change a chart's source data
- Create a chart with numerical axis
- Deal with empty data points
- Add data labels to a chart
- Highlight specific data points with color and annotations
- Add gridlines and scale axis
- Emphasize data by manipulating pie charts
- Create a chart with two vertical axis
- Create a combination chart containing different chart types
- Add a trend line
- Switch chart rows/columns
- Add a gradient fill
- Create your own chart templates

Lesson 5-1: Create a simple chart with two clicks

note

Create a chart with the <F11> key

If you click inside a range and then press the <F11> key Excel will instantly create a new chart on a new worksheet.

1 Open *World Sales from* your sample files folder.

This is a very simple worksheet showing January, February and March sales figures for three regions.

	A	B	C	D
1	Month	USA	Europe	Other
2	Jan	21,600	19,200	10,800
3	Feb	25,400	21,400	12,200
4	Mar	22,800	23,600	9,600

2 Select all of the data and all of the labels.

When Excel creates a chart it must know what each data element means. For this reason you must always select the labels *as well as* the values before you create your chart.

Missing the labels is one of the commonest errors in my classroom courses.

tip

You can create a chart without selecting any data

When you want to chart an entire range (as is the case in this lesson) you don't need to select the data.

If you simply click anywhere within the range and then click Insert→Charts→Column, Excel will assume that you want to chart the entire range and select it for you.

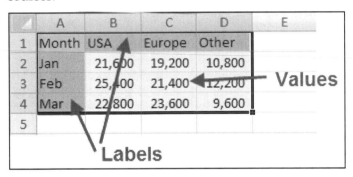

3 Click Insert→Charts→Column and hover the mouse pointer over some of the charts in the gallery.

As you hover the mouse button over each chart type Excel provides a ScreenTip describing the chart.

important

Charts are dynamic

If the data underpinning a chart changes, the chart will instantly change to represent the new data values.

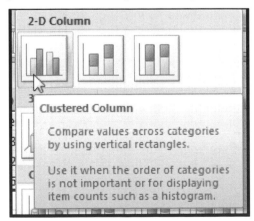

4 Click the left-most 2-D Column chart (the *Clustered Column* chart).

World Sales

note

The chart tools Ribbon group only displays when a chart is activated

Excel allows you to embed multiple chart objects into one worksheet.

The *Chart Tools* Ribbon group (consisting of *Design*, *Layout* and *Format*) will operate on only one chart at a time – the currently activated chart.

If you don't see the *Chart Tools* Ribbon group, click anywhere on the chart to activate it and the group will appear.

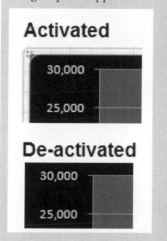

note

Preventing the gallery from obscuring the chart

You can click each option in the *Chart Styles* gallery to apply the style to the chart so that you can see how it looks.

Sometimes the gallery will obscure the chart, making it impossible to see how the new chart style looks. To prevent this happening use the *Next Row* button to view chart styles one row at a time.

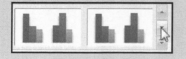

In just two clicks we have created a very presentable chart. Excel uses the default layout and colors from the current workbook's theme.

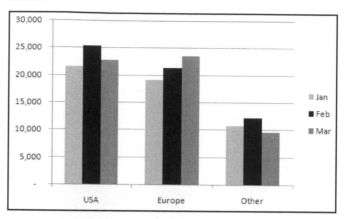

Notice that three new tabs have appeared on the Ribbon below a group called *Chart Tools*.

If you don't see this it is because you haven't activated the chart (see sidebar).

5 Change the chart style.

1. Click Chart Tools→ Design→Chart Styles→ Chart Styles Gallery.

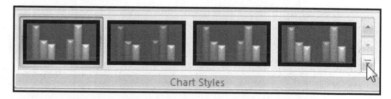

When you click the gallery button you are able to choose a new chart style from 48 pre-defined options. Each chart style uses theme colors so the appearance will change if you later change the workbook's theme.

2. Click a new chart style to change the appearance of your chart.

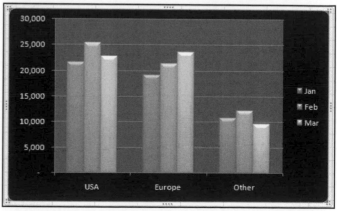

6 Save your work as *World Sales-1*.

Lesson 5-2: Move, re-size, copy and delete a chart

1　Open *World Sales-1* from your sample files folder (if it isn't already open).

2　Move the chart to a different position on screen.

   1.　Hover with the mouse just inside the border of the selected chart until you see the four headed arrow cursor shape.

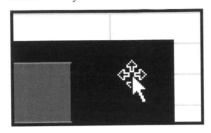

   2.　Click and drag the chart to the required position.

3　Re-size the chart.

   1.　Click just inside the border of the chart to activate it. When the chart is activated you will see a frame and corner handles around it. Excel also displays the *Chart Tools* group of Ribbon tabs.

   2.　Hover over one of the corner or side sizing handles on the edges of the chart until you see the two-headed arrow cursor shape.

   3.　When you see the two-headed arrow cursor shape, click and drag to re-size the chart. If you hold down the **<Shift>** key as you click-and drag one of the corners of the chart, the perspective will remain constant (ie the chart will get proportionately wider as it gets taller).

4　Create a duplicate chart by copy and paste.

   1.　Click just inside the border of the chart to activate it.

   2.　Right-click, on the border of the activated chart (just inside the border works too) and click *Copy* from the shortcut menu.

Right-click anywhere on the worksheet and click *Paste* 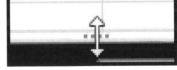 from the shortcut menu to create the duplicate chart.

World Sales-1

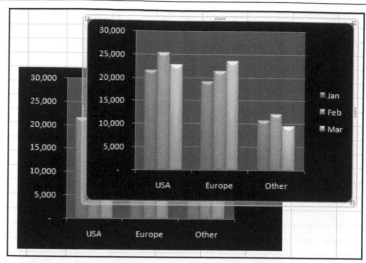

note

Other ways to copy charts

Hold down the **<Ctrl>** key and then click and drag the border of an embedded chart (or a chart sheet tab).

The cursor shape will change to a small plus sign.

You can then drag and drop a copy of the chart to any other location.

Note that even though the new chart is a duplicate, it is not linked to the original chart in any way. You can freely change any part of either chart and it will never affect the other.

You can also use this technique to move a chart to a different worksheet (covered later in this lesson). The chart will still be linked to the data in the original worksheet.

5 Delete one of the charts.

   1. Click just inside the border of either of the charts to activate it.

   2. Press the **<Delete>** key on the keyboard.

6 Move the chart to its own worksheet.

Sometimes it is better to keep charts and data separate by placing a chart in its own chart worksheet. A chart worksheet is a special worksheet without any cells that can only contain a single chart.

note

Advantages of placing charts on chart sheets:

- They are easier to find as you can give each sheet a meaningful name.

- They are easier to view as the chart normally takes up the entire screen. You can re-size a chart on a chart sheet but this isn't often done.

- They are easier to print as you can simply click the sheet tab and print. You can also print an embedded chart in isolation but to do so you must first find and activate the chart.

Advantages of embedding charts within worksheets:

- You are able to print a chart and worksheet data on the same page.

If you have no need to print worksheet data alongside your chart it is better to place your charts on chart sheets.

   1. Right-click just inside the border of the chart to activate it and then click *Move Chart...* from the shortcut menu.

   2. Click the *New Sheet* option button, name the new sheet *Sales Summary Chart* and click the OK button.

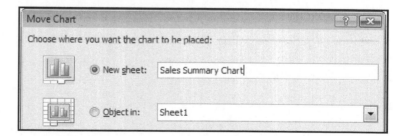

The chart is now displayed within its own dedicated worksheet.

7 Move the chart back to its original location.

   1. Right-click just inside the border of the chart and click *Move Chart...* from the shortcut menu.

   2. Click the *Object in* option button, choose *Sheet1* from the drop down list and click the OK button.

8 Save your work as *World Sales-2*.

Lesson 5-3: Change chart layouts

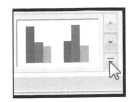

1   Open *World Sales-2* from your sample files folder (if it isn't already open).

2   Click just inside the border of the chart to activate it.

3   Change the chart style back to the default style.

1.   Click Chart Tools→Design→Chart Styles Gallery.

2.   Click the second chart style from the left on the first row (the default style).

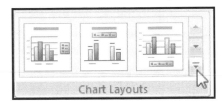

4   Click Chart Tools→Design→Chart Layouts Gallery.

The gallery contains eleven pre-defined chart layouts.

The main differences between the layouts are:

*   Some layouts have a *Chart Title* across the top of the chart.

*   Some layouts have a *Legend* which can be situated at the top, bottom, or right of the screen.

*   Some layouts have *Axis Titles* on the horizontal axis, vertical axis, or both.

*   Some layouts include a *Data Table.*

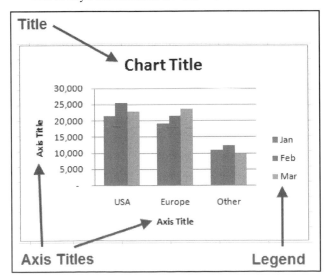

note

More about the horizontal and vertical axis

A chart normally shows category (non-numerical) data along the horizontal axis. The horizontal axis is also sometimes called the X axis.

The vertical axis normally contains numerical data. The Vertical axis is also sometimes called the Y Axis.

The chart used in this lesson has the non-numerical region categories (USA, Europe and Other) along the horizontal (or X) axis and numerical sales data along the vertical (or Y) axis.

World Sales-2

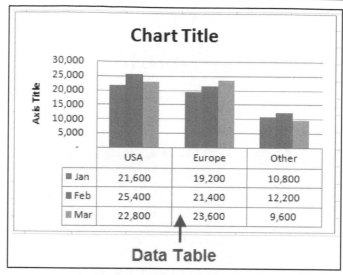

5   Choose *Layout 9*. This layout includes a *Chart Title* element. a *Legend* element and two *Axis Title* elements.

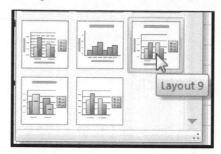

6   Click the *Chart Title* element and type the title: **Sales First Quarter**.

7   Click the *Vertical Axis Title* element and type the title: **Sales.**

8   Click the *Horizontal Axis Title* element and type the title: **Region.**

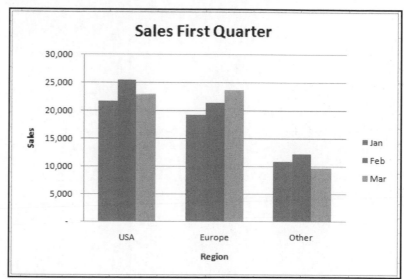

9   Save your work as: *World Sales-3*.

Lesson 5-4: Format chart element fills and borders

Up until now we've selected pre-defined chart layouts from the gallery.

To unleash the real power of Excel charts we need to think of a chart as a collection of graphic elements (sometimes also called objects), each of which can be individually formatted.

Once you have the hang of how to format one graphic element it becomes easy to work with any other element, because the options are broadly the same.

In this lesson we'll learn some of the formatting options for the *Chart Title* element.

1 Open *World Sales-3* from your sample files folder (if it isn't already open).

2 Click the chart to activate it.

3 Click the *Chart Title* element to select it.

A frame appears:

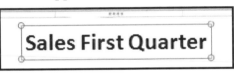

Sales First Quarter

4 Right-Click the *Chart Title* element and click *Format Chart Title* from the shortcut menu.

The *Format Chart Title* dialog appears.

5 Apply a *Blue Accent 1* fill (background color) to the *Chart Title* element.

   1.   Click the *Solid Fill* option.

   2.   Click the *Color* button and choose the *Blue, Accent 1* fill color.

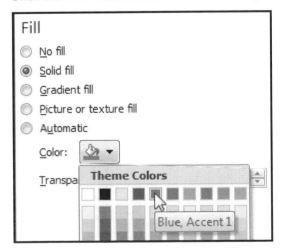

   3.   Drag the slider to the right to set the transparency to about 80%.

note

Chart titles can display the contents of a specific cell

Normally you will simply type the text that you need directly into the *Chart Title* element.

It is also possible to link the *Chart Title* to a worksheet cell so that it displays whatever text is in the specified cell.

Here's how it is done:

1.   Click the *Chart Title* element.

2.   Type **=A1** (or any other cell reference.

   The contents of cell A1 are then displayed in the *Chart Title* element and will change whenever the text in cell A1 changes.

World Sales-3

note

All of the *Chart Format* dialogs are modeless

Modeless dialogs are quite unusual within Windows and Office.

Consider the *Format Cells* dialog (a modal dialog).

Until you've dismissed the *Format Cells* dialog you can't do anything else at all. If you click anywhere on the worksheet or Ribbon you'll just hear a "ding" noise!

In other words, modal dialogs take over the application and stubbornly refuse to let you do anything else until you've dismissed them.

All of the *Chart Format* dialogs (such as the *Format Chart Title* dialog in this lesson) are much better behaved modeless dialogs.

This means that you can go on working and leave the *Format* dialog happily sitting in the background. Even better, as you select different chart elements the *Format* dialog will change to the settings appropriate for the selected element.

This is a huge time saver, especially if you have a large screen that enables you to "park" the dialog out of the way of the worksheet.

Notice that the background color of the *Chart Title* element becomes lighter as you drag to the right, and darker as you drag to the left.

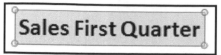

6   Click *Border Color* from the category list on the left of the dialog.

7   Click the *Solid Line* option button.

8   Choose a solid black color.

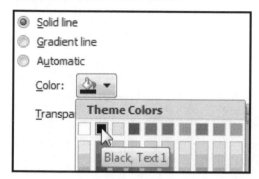

9   Click *Border Styles* from the category list on the left of the dialog.

Change the width to *1 pt*.

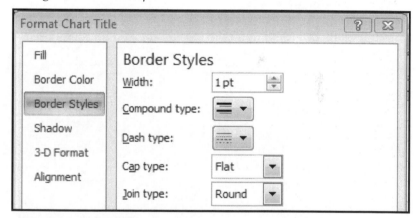

10   Click *Close* to apply a 1 point black border to the *Chart Title* element.

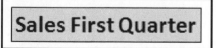

11   Save your work as *World Sales-4*.

Lesson 5-5: Format 3-D elements and add drop shadows

Shadows and 3-D formats were introduced for the first time in Excel 2007. The use of subtle shadows and 3-D formats will add a professional sheen to your work that was only previously possible with high-end graphics applications such as Adobe Photoshop.

1   Open *World Sales-4* from your sample files folder (if it isn't already open) and click just inside the border of the chart to activate it.

2   Click Chart Tools→Layout→Current Selection→ Chart Elements Drop Down →Chart Title.

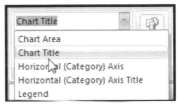

This is an alternative way to select chart elements. The drop-down shows every element in the currently selected chart.

The right-click method is usually faster but there are some chart elements (such as gridlines) that can sometimes be difficult to select with the mouse.

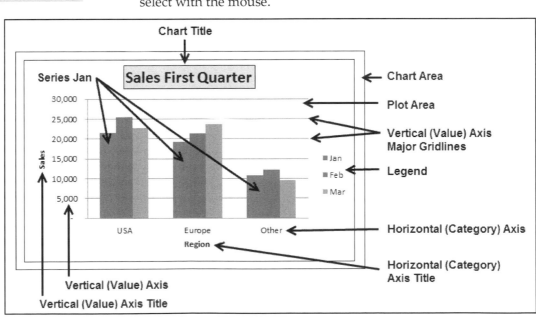

If you do a lot of work with charts it is well worth adding the *Chart Elements Drop-Down* list to the *Quick Access Toolbar* (this was covered in: *Lesson 1-13: Customize the Quick Access Toolbar and preview the printout*).

3   Click Chart Tools→Layout→Current Selection→ Format Selection.

World Sales-4

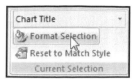

This is an alternative way to bring up the *Format* dialog.

Notice the *Reset to Match Style* option in the *Current Selection* group. This allows you to reset the formatting back to the default when you've messed things up and want to start again!

4   Select *Shadow* from the category list on the left of the *Format Chart Title* dialog.

5   Apply an *Offset Diagonal Bottom Right* shadow to the *Chart Title* element.

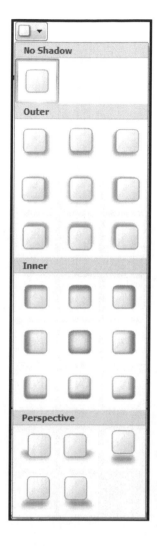

While you can create your own shadows using the *Transparency, Size, Blur, Angle* and *Distance* sliders you'll probably find that the presets will suffice. Presets will also maintain uniformity between different chart elements.

There are plenty of shadows to choose from (see sidebar).

1.   Click the *Shadow Presets* drop-down arrow.

2.   Select the *Offset Diagonal Bottom Right* shadow (the top left shadow in the *Outer* group.

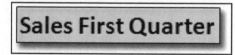

Notice that when you click, the effect is applied to the chart even before you've closed the dialog.

Sales First Quarter

6   Select *3-D Format* from the category list on the left of the dialog.

7   Apply a *Circle* top bevel to the *Chart Title* element.

Just like shadows, you'll probably find what you need in the 3-D presets rather than creating your own custom 3-D effects.

Click the *Top Bevel* preset button to display a Top Bevel gallery and choose a *Circle* top bevel.

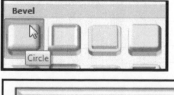

Sales First Quarter

8   Click the *Close* Button.

9   Save your work as *World Sales-5.*

Lesson 5-6: Move, re-size, add and delete chart elements

Several elements such as the *Chart Title, Legend* and *Horizontal/Vertical Axis Titles* can be moved by drag and drop.

In this lesson we'll see how to move these, and how to re-instate them to their pixel-perfect locations if you change your mind.

We'll also remove and add chart elements. Once you've got the hang of this you'll be able to custom design charts for any specific requirement.

1 Open *World Sales-5* from your sample files folder (if it isn't already open) and click the chart to activate it.

2 Click and drag the *Chart Title* element to the left hand side of the chart.

   1. Click the *Chart Title* element to select it.

   2. Hover with the mouse over the border of the *Chart Title* element until you see a four headed arrow.

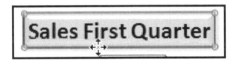

   3. When you see the four headed arrow, click and drag to move the element to the top left corner of the chart.

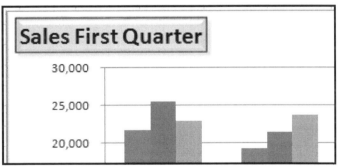

3 Move the *Chart Title* element back so that it is above the chart at dead center.

You couldn't get this pixel-perfect using the mouse.

Click Chart Tools→Layout→Labels→Chart Title→Above Chart.

The *Chart Title* element is restored to dead center.

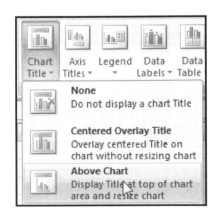

4 Delete the legend.

   1. Click the *Legend* element to select it

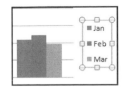

   2. Press the **<Delete>** key.

World Sales-5

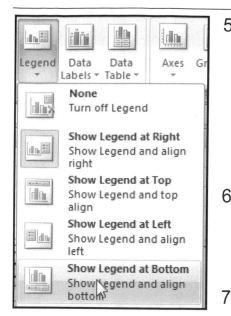

5 Display the legend at the bottom of the screen.

With the chart activated, click Chart Tools→Layout→ Labels→Legend→Show Legend at Bottom.

6 Add a thin black border to the *Legend* element.

This was covered in: *Lesson 5-4: Format chart element fills and borders.*

7 Re-size the *Legend* element so that it spans the entire width of the plot area.

1. Click the *Legend* element to select it. Notice the sizing handles on each corner and edge.

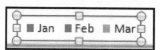

2. Hover over the square sizing handle on the right-hand edge of the element. Notice that the cursor shape changes to a two headed arrow.

3. When you see the two-headed arrow click and drag to re-size the legend so that it is the same width as the plot area. (You'll have to first size the right side and then the left).

8 Increase the size of the font within the *Legend* element.

1. Click the *Legend* element to select it.

2. Click Home→Font→Font Size Drop-down. Hover the mouse cursor over each font size and note that *Live Preview* allows you to see the effect of your choice.

3. Select 14 points for the new text size.

You'll often want to increase text sizes when you create charts for PowerPoint slides.

9 Save your work as *World Sales-6*.

Lesson 5-7: Change a chart's source data

You'll often need to change the data that the chart is depicting.

In this lesson you will change the chart so that it depicts sales for the USA only rather than the USA, Europe and Other territories.

1   Open *World Sales-6* from your sample files folder (if it isn't already open) and click just inside the border of the chart to select it.

2   Right-click in the *Plot Area* of the chart and click *Select Data* from the shortcut menu.

The *Select Data Source* dialog appears.

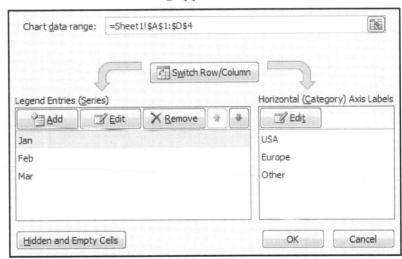

Notice the *Chart data range* shown at the top of the dialog. For the moment this is all that I want you to concentrate upon.

The range is shown as Sheet1!$A$1:$D$4.

This means the absolute range A1:D4 on the *Sheet1* worksheet.

(Absolute cell references were covered in: *Lesson 3-12: Understand absolute and relative cell references*).

3   Change the *Chart data range* so that only USA sales are charted.

The current range is A1:D4.

	A	B	C	D
1	Month	USA	Europe	Other
2	Jan	21,600	19,200	10,800
3	Feb	25,400	21,400	12,200
4	Mar	22,800	23,600	9,600
5				

If we change the range to A1:B4 the other two regions will be removed.

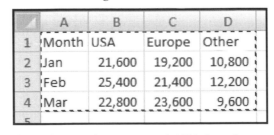

World Sales-6

You could simply type the new reference into the *Chart Data Range* text box but it is less error prone if you visually select the data with the mouse.

Click and drag with the mouse across cells A1:B4.

The data range displays in both the *Select Data Source* dialog and as a marquee on the worksheet.

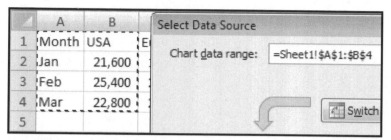

It is very easy to mess up the data range in the text box. If you get an obscure error message simply delete all of the contents of the *Chart data range* text box and re-select.

Notice that, in the background, the chart has changed to reflect the new data range.

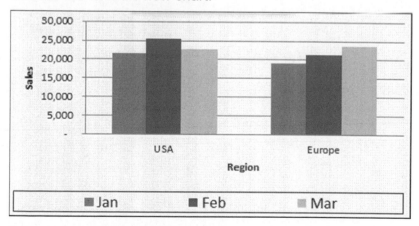

4   Change the *Chart data range* to A1:C4 to chart sales for the USA and Europe.

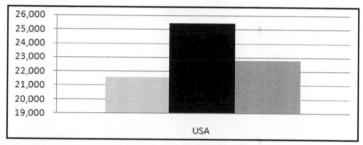

5   Click OK to view the new chart.

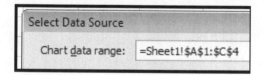

6   Save your work as *World Sales-7*.

Lesson 5-8: Assign non-contiguous source data to a chart

In the previous lesson it was easy to select the source data because it comprised of a single block (we use the word: *contiguous* for this type of range).

In this lesson we'll take things a little further by selecting data that isn't in a single block (ie non-contiguous data) to show sales for the *USA* and *Other* categories.

1   Open *World Sales-7* from your sample files folder (if it isn't already open) and click the chart to activate it.

2   Right-click in the plot area of the chart and click *Select Data* from the shortcut menu.

The *Select Data Source* dialog appears.

3   Select the range A1:B4,D1:D4.

   1.   Select the range A1:B4.

   2.   Hold down the **<Ctrl>** key.

   3.   Select the range D1:D4.

   4.   Click the OK button.

Selecting non-contiguous ranges was covered extensively in: *Lesson 2-7: Select non-contiguous cell ranges and view summary information.*

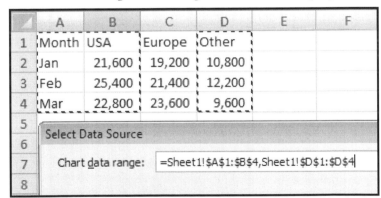

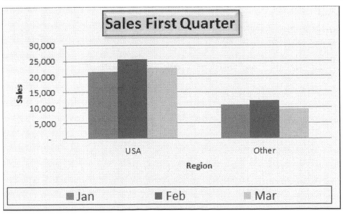

World Sales-7

4   Display totals in column E.

Type the word: **Total** into cell E1 and then use AutoSum to place the total for all regions into cells E2:E4.

AutoSum was covered in: *Lesson 2-3: Use AutoSum to quickly calculate totals.*

	A	B	C	D	E
1	Month	USA	Europe	Other	Total
2	Jan	21,600	19,200	10,800	51,600
3	Feb	25,400	21,400	12,200	59,000
4	Mar	22,800	23,600	9,600	56,000

5   Change the source data so that only totals are charted.

1.   Right-click in the plot area of the chart and click *Select Data* from the shortcut menu.

2.   Select cells A1:A4.

3.   Hold down the **<Ctrl>** key.

4.   Select cells E1:E4.

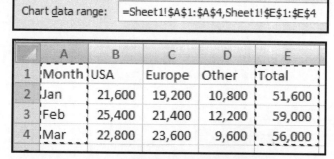

Chart data range: =Sheet1!$A$1:$A$4,Sheet1!$E$1:$E$4

	A	B	C	D	E
1	Month	USA	Europe	Other	Total
2	Jan	21,600	19,200	10,800	51,600
3	Feb	25,400	21,400	12,200	59,000
4	Mar	22,800	23,600	9,600	56,000

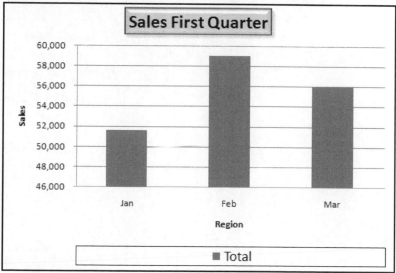

6   Click OK to close the *Select Data Source* dialog.

7   Save your work as *World Sales-8.*

note

An alternative method for selecting source data

The *Select Source Data* dialog is by far the best way to set and modify source data for charts.

An alternative way is to copy a data range, activate the chart, and then click:

Home→Clipboard→Paste→Paste Special...

A *Paste Special* dialog is then displayed that is specifically designed for charts:

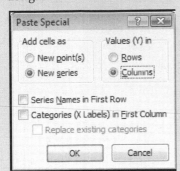

Lesson 5-9: Change source data using the Select Data Source dialog tools

In versions of Excel prior to Excel 2007 it was only possible to define source data using the *Chart data range* text box. The new dialog provides a better way of defining source data and axis labels.

1 Open *World Sales-8* from your sample files folder (if it isn't already open) and click the chart to activate it.

2 Right-click in the plot area of the chart and click *Select Data* from the shortcut menu.

The *Select Data Source* dialog appears:

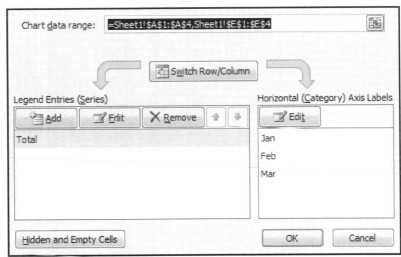

3 Add a *USA* data series.

Click the Add button 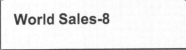 in the *Legend Entries (Series)* pane.

1. Type **USA** for the series name.

2. Delete any text currently appearing in the *Series values* text box.

3. Select the range B2:B4 for the *Series values*.

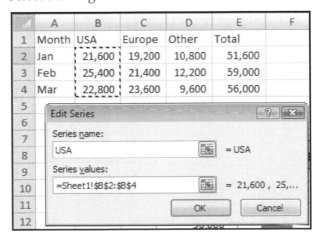

4. Click OK.

The series is added to the dialog.

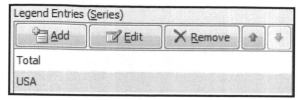

4   Delete the *Total* data series.

1.   Click the *Total* data series in the *Legend Entries (Series)* list to select it.

2.   Click the Remove button.

5   Add the *Europe* and *Other* series.

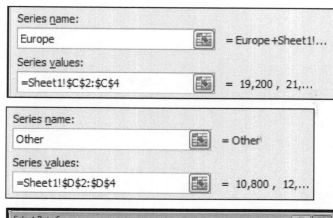

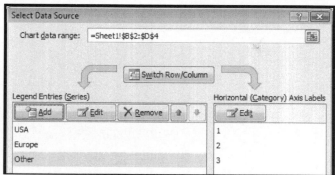

The graph still isn't quite right because *1, 2* and *3* are showing as *Horizontal (Category) Axis Labels* instead of *Jan, Feb and Mar.*

6   Change the *Horizontal (Category) Axis Labels* to Jan/Feb/Mar.

1.   Click the *Edit* button at the top of the *Horizontal (Category) Axis Labels* pane.

2.   Select cells A2:A4 (the cells containing the text: *Jan/Feb/Mar*).

3.   Click OK and OK again to dismiss both dialogs.

7   Save your work as *World Sales-9.*

Lesson 5-10: Chart non-contiguous source data by hiding rows and columns

In this lesson we'll look at an alternative method of charting a non-contiguous range simply by hiding the data elements we don't want to chart.

Excel allows you to hide rows and columns in a worksheet by effectively setting their width to zero. The default behavior of charts is to ignore these hidden rows and columns.

It is also possible to over-ride the default behavior and instruct Excel to chart hidden rows and columns.

1   Open *World Sales-9 from* your sample files folder (if it isn't already open) and click the chart to activate it.

2   Remove the *Europe* series from the chart by hiding column C.

Right-click on the button at the top of column C and then click *Hide* from the shortcut menu.

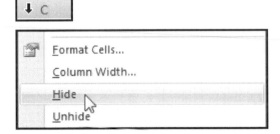

The *European* sales data is no longer shown on the chart.

3   Remove the *February* data from the chart by hiding row 3.

Right-click on the button on the left of row 3 and click *Hide* from the shortcut menu.

February data is no longer shown on the chart.

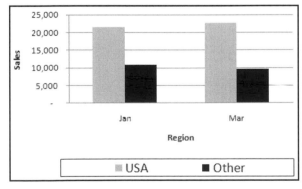

4   Display the hidden data in the chart.

Excel allows you to chart hidden data if you want to.

1.   Right-click in the plot area of the chart and click *Select Data...* from the shortcut menu.

World Sales-9

The *Select Data Source* dialog appears.

2. Click the *Hidden and Empty Cells* button on the bottom left corner of the dialog.

The *Hidden and Empty Cells* dialog appears.

3. Check the *Show data in hidden rows and columns* check box and click the OK button.

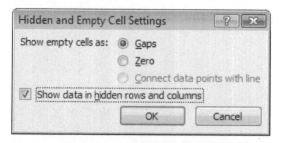

4. Click the OK button to dismiss the dialog.

The previously hidden chart data re-appears.

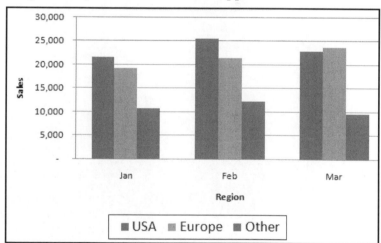

note

The *Hidden and Empty Cell Settings* dialog can also be used with Sparklines

If you select a Sparkline group and click:

Sparkline Tools→Design→ Sparkline→Edit Data→ Hidden & Empty Cells

… you will see the same *Hidden and Empty Cell Settings* dialog that is used in this lesson to deal with hidden rows and columns in charts.

You can use it in exactly the same way to deal with hidden rows and columns in Sparklines.

You learned to create Sparkline groups in: *Lesson 4-19: Insert a Sparkline into a range of cells.*

5 Unhide the hidden rows and columns.

1. Click any cell in the worksheet to de-activate the chart.

2. Click the *Select All* button at the top left corner of the worksheet to select every cell.

3. Click Home→Cells→Format→Hide & Unhide→Unhide Rows.

4. Click Home→Cells→Format→Hide & Unhide→Unhide Columns.

6 Save your work as *World Sales-10*.

Lesson 5-11: Create a chart with numerical axis

Sometimes Excel gets a little confused when it attempts to automatically generate a chart.

Problems usually occur when you need to plot numerical information along the horizontal axis. Excel sees the numerical labels and assumes that they are a series.

In this example we'll use such a worksheet to confuse Excel and then fix things up manually using the *Select Data Source* dialog.

1 Open *Annual Sales Summary* from your sample files folder.

2 Display the range as a clustered column chart.

   1. Click anywhere inside the range.

     Note that it isn't necessary to select the range when you want to chart all of it.

     If you simply click any cell inside the range Excel will automatically select the entire range for the chart's source data.

   2. Click Insert→Charts→Column→Clustered Column.

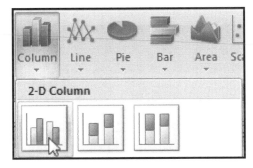

     The range is displayed as a chart but there's a problem. Excel has assumed that the numbers in the *Year* column are a data series.

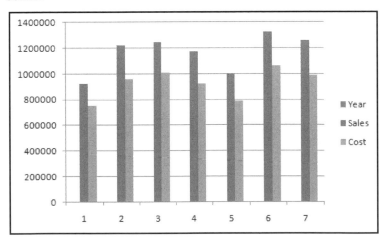

Note that the numbers for the *Date* data are so small in relation to the *Sales* and *Cost* data that you can't even see their bars in the bar chart. The blue bars are there but they are so short that they are invisible.

Annual Sales Summary

3   Right-click just inside the plot area of the chart and click
Select Data… from the shortcut menu.

The *Select Data Source* dialog is displayed.

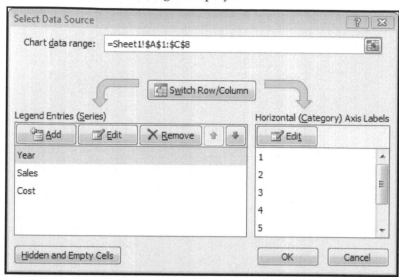

The problem is immediately apparent. Excel has wrongly
identified the year as series data rather than as axis labels.

4   Remove the Year *data series* and add the Year data as
Horizontal (Category) Axis Labels.

1.   Click *Year* in the left hand pane of the dialog and then click the
Remove button. ☒ Remove

2.   Click the Edit button ✏ Edit on the right hand pane (the
pane showing *Horizontal (Category) Axis labels*.

3.   Select cells A2:A8 for the Axis label range (the year data but
not the column header).

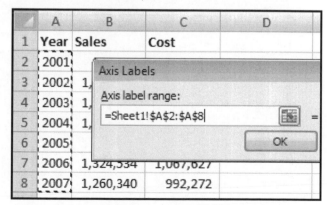

4.   Click the OK button twice to close both dialogs.

5.   The graph now displays correctly.

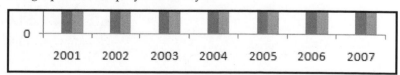

5   Save your work as *Annual Sales Summary-1*.

Lesson 5-12: Deal with empty data points

Sometimes you'll only have partial data for a series.

In the worksheet used for this lesson I'll share a secret with you. I weigh myself every day and keep a chart on my bathroom wall to make sure I'm staying at a healthy weight.

Sometimes I'm away travelling and can't weigh in as usual. When I get back I need to fill in the gaps.

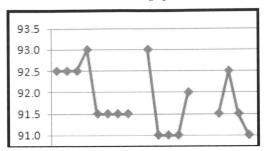

I use a line chart for my weight so the best solution is to simply draw a line connecting the last data point recorded before I went away with the first recorded upon my return.

For a bar chart the best solution would be to show no bars for the missing days. In other words, there would be gaps for each date when there was a missing bar.

1   Open *Weight 2008* from your sample files folder.

This is a simple worksheet showing my weight in kilograms for each date in July 2008. Notice that there are missing days when I was away from home.

2   Display the range as a *Line with Markers* chart.

1.   Click on any of the date values within the range.

2.   Click Insert→Charts→Line→Line with Markers.

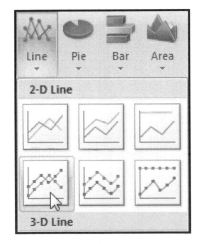

The chart displays but there are gaps for the missing entries.

Weight 2008

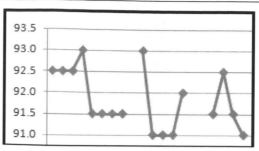

3   Tell Excel to connect the gaps in the chart with a line.

1.   Right-click just inside the plot area of the chart and click *Select Data* from the shortcut menu.

     The *Select Data Source* dialog is displayed.

2.   Click the *Hidden and Empty Cells* button at the bottom left corner of the dialog.

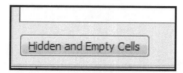

     The *Hidden and Empty Cells* dialog appears.

3.   Click the *Connect data points with line* option button.

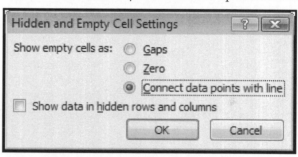

4.   Click the OK button and OK again to dismiss both dialogs

     All data points are now connected with a line.

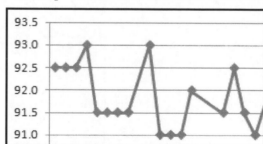

note

The *Hidden and Empty Cell Settings* dialog can also be used with Sparklines

If you select a Sparkline group and click:

Sparkline Tools→Design→ Sparkline→Edit Data→ Hidden & Empty Cells

... you will see the same *Hidden and Empty Cell Settings* dialog that is used in this lesson to deal with empty data points in charts.

You can use it in exactly the same way to deal with empty data points in Sparklines.

You learned to create Sparkline groups in: *Lesson 4-19: Insert a Sparkline into a range of cells.*

4   Save your work as *Weight 2008-1.*

Lesson 5-13: Add data labels to a chart

It is possible to approximate the values that are displayed in a chart by looking at the vertical axis.

Sometimes you will need to convey the precise values that are being charted. There are three ways of doing this:

- Embed the chart in the worksheet containing the source data so that the user can see both the chart and data.

- Add data labels to each point on the chart.

- Add a table to the bottom of the chart.

1 Open *Annual Sales Summary-1* from your sample files folder.

2 Change the source data so that only sales (not costs) for 2004 to 2007 are charted.

This will allow you to test your understanding of the skills learned in: *Lesson 5-8: Assign non-contiguous source data ,*
Lesson 5-9: Change source data using the Select Data Source dialog tools.
and *Lesson 5-11: Create a chart with numerical axis.*

1. In the *Select Data Source* dialog select this range for *the Chart data range:*

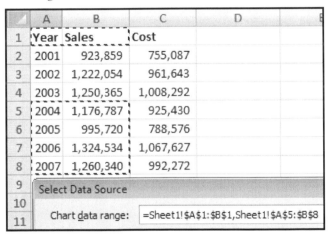

2. In the *Select Data Source* dialog select this data range for the *Horizontal (Category) Axis Labels.*

3. In the *Select Data Source* dialog delete the *Year* item from the *Legend Entries (Series).*

The *Select Data Source* dialog should then look like this:

Annual Sales
Summary-1

tip

Data labels can be moved and formatted just like any other element

When preparing a chart for a PowerPoint presentation the data labels are often too small to be visible at the back of the room.

You may also want to fine-tune the positioning of data labels.

For most formatting options, right-click a data label to select the entire series and then click *Format Data Labels* from the shortcut menu.

If you need to change the font size select the series of data labels and then click:

Home→Font→Font Size

If you need to re-position or format a single data label, click once to select the data label series and then a second time to select the individual label you want to work with.

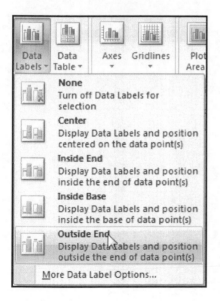

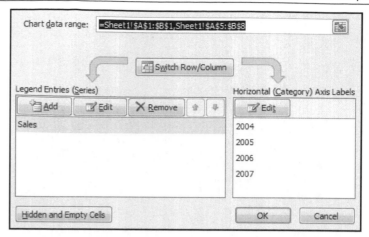

... Resulting in the following chart:

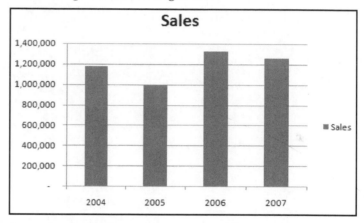

4. Click the OK button to close the dialog.

3 Add data labels to each bar.

Activate the chart and then click Chart Tools→Layout→ Labels→Data Labels→Outside End (see sidebar).

Data labels are now displayed at the center top of each bar.

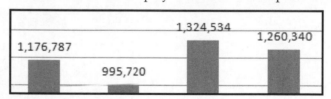

4 Switch off the data labels.

Activate the chart and then click:

Chart Tools→Layout→Labels→Data Labels→None

5 Add a table to the bottom of the chart.

Activate the chart and then click:

Chart Tools→Layout→Labels→Data Table→Show Data Table

A table is displayed below the chart:

	2004	2005	2006	2007
Sales	1,176,787	995,720	1,324,534	1,260,340

6 Save your work as *Annual Sales Summary-2*.

Lesson 5-14: Highlight specific data points with color and annotations

Sometimes you will want to emphasize a specific data point in a series. For example, you may want to color a single column differently to its neighbors to emphasize some special attribute of the data point.

Color alone cannot convey why the data point is special. You will normally want to add a text box to the chart to qualify the reason for its different color.

In this lesson we'll imagine that the company is a hotel, and that 2005 was the centenary year in a competing resort leading to an expectation of decreased sales. To mark this we'll color the 2005 bar red and add an annotation saying *Centenary Year* to the bar.

1 Open *Annual Sales Summary-2 from* your sample files folder (if it isn't already open).

2 Change the color of the 2005 bar to red.

1. Click the 2005 bar once. Notice that the entire data series is selected.

2. Click the 2005 bar once more. This time only the 2005 bar is selected.

3. Click Chart Tools→Format→Shape Styles→Shape Fill→Red.

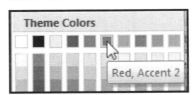

4. The 2005 bar is now colored red. The legend has also changed to give a further visual prompt that the red bar relates to 2005.

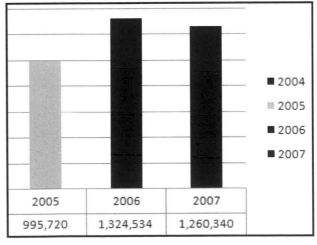

2005	2006	2007
995,720	1,324,534	1,260,340

3 Add a text box above, and to the right of, the red bar containing the text: **Centenary Year**.

1. Click just inside the border of the chart to activate it.

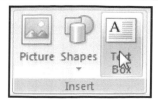

2. Click Chart Tools→Layout→Insert→Text Box.

3. Click on the chart, above and to the right of the red 2005 bar, and type **Centenary,** then press **<Shift>+<Enter>** and then type **Year.** (The **<Shift>+<Enter>** key combination moves you to the next line in a text box).

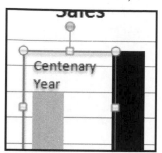

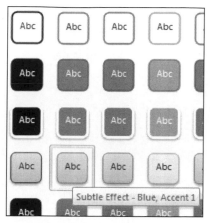

4 Add a border and fill to the text box.

Click the text box to select it and then click:

Drawing Tools→Format→Shape Styles→
Visual Style Gallery Drop-Down→Subtle Effect – Blue,-Accent 1

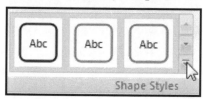

This effect is the second on row four (see sidebar).

5 Re-size the text box.

Click the text box once to select and then drag the sizing handles to re-size so that the text fills the box.

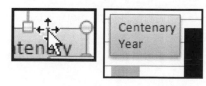

6 Move the text box.

Click the text box once to select and then hover over any part of the border that is not a sizing handle. You will see the four-headed arrow cursor shape (see sidebar). When you see the four-headed arrow, click and drag to move the text box to an ideal position.

7 Add an arrow pointing from the text box to the red 2005 bar.

1. Click the chart to activate it. (Make sure that you click just inside the border of the chart and not on the text box. The *Chart Tools* tab will not be displayed when the text box is selected).

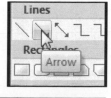

2. Click Chart Tools→Layout→Insert→Shapes→Arrow (see sidebar).

3. Click and drag to draw an arrow pointing from the text box to the red bar.

4. With the arrow selected, click Drawing Tools→Format→ Shape Styles→Gallery drop-down.

5. Choose an attractive style for the arrow.

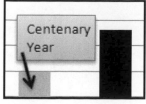

8 Save your work as *Annual Sales Summary-3.*

Lesson 5-15: Add gridlines and scale axes

As mentioned in this session's introduction, charts never lie but they can give the truth scope!

In this session we'll manipulate the vertical axis of a sales chart to give two entirely different views of a company's sales. Each chart emphasizes one of the following true statements.

- It is true that sales are increasing every month.

- It is true that sales are almost completely flat.

You'll see how we can manipulate a column chart to visually convey each of these "truths" to an audience. After this session you'll never look at a chart again without paying close attention to the vertical axis!

1   Open *Sales First Quarter* from your sample files folder.

	A	B
1	Month	Sales
2	Jan	80,010
3	Feb	80,040
4	Mar	80,080

This worksheet shows sales that are almost completely flat. Sales increased by 0.04% in February and by 0.05% in March.

A twentieth of a percent increase isn't anything at all.

2   Create a chart that illustrates flat sales.

Imagine you are the sales director of the company and need to have a pep talk with your salespeople. You want to show them a chart that demonstrates the lack of sales growth in order to motivate them to do better in April!

1. Click inside the data range.

2. Click Insert→Charts→Column→Clustered Column.

The following chart is automatically generated:

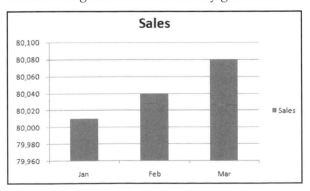

This isn't the chart you want at all. Sales look rather good!

The reason that the chart isn't as honest as it should be is because the vertical axis begins at 79,960. We're looking at the tips of bars that are very long.

Sales First Quarter

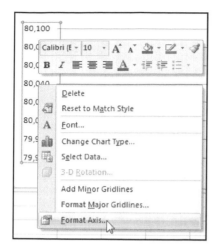

To fix things up we need a more honest vertical axis, one that begins at zero.

3. Right-click the vertical axis (you may have to do this twice) and select *Format Axis...* from the shortcut menu.

4. Change the *Minimum* value to zero.

5. Click the *Close* button. The chart now depicts a more honest representation of flat growth.

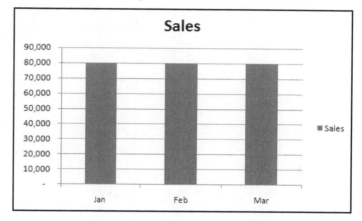

6. Right-click the vertical axis and select *Format Axis...* from the shortcut menu.

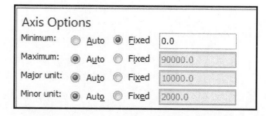

Notice how Excel has automatically managed the other settings. *Major units* for gridlines (the interval between numbers on the vertical axis) have now changed to 10,000.

7. Change the *Minor unit* gridline value to 5000 (without the comma as Excel has a problem with commas in this dialog). We will enable the display of minor gridlines in a moment and will expect to see one minor gridline between each major gridline.

8. Click the *Close* button.

3 Enable minor gridlines.

Select the chart and then click:

Chart Tools→Layout→Axes→Gridlines→
Primary Horizontal Gridlines→Major & Minor Gridlines

Minor gridlines are now displayed on the chart (see sidebar).

4 Save your work as *Sales First Quarter-1*.

---

tip

Use gridlines sparingly

Too many gridlines can make a chart difficult to read. This lesson's chart looks cluttered with minor gridlines and might even look cleaner without any gridlines at all.

When you do use gridlines always choose a light color to focus attention upon foreground elements.

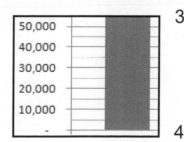

Lesson 5-16: Emphasize data by manipulating pie charts

In the last session we saw how a column chart could visually re-enforce different characteristics of the same data.

Pie charts also offer several techniques to present data in a way that will best convey your objectives. Designers of pie charts often use the presentational methods described in this lesson to make one value in a series seem bigger or smaller in relation to its neighbors.

1　Open *Competitor Analysis* from your sample files folder (if it isn't already open).

	A	B	C
1	Splendid Supplies Competitor Analysis		
2			
3	Competitor	Annual Sales (Millions)	Market Share
4	Cheapo discount stores	22.2	28%
5	Budget supplies	16.3	21%
6	Lo Cost warehouse	24.5	31%
7	Splendid Supplies	16.2	20%

This worksheet has been compiled by Splendid Supplies to monitor the activity of their three competitors. Splendid aren't doing so well, in fact, they have the lowest market share of the four.

There's a big investor meeting coming up and Splendid would like to make their market share seem a little more impressive!

2　Create a 3-D pie chart for the range A3:B7.

1. Select the range A3:B7.

2. Click Insert→Charts→Pie→Pie In 3-D (see sidebar).

A pie chart is displayed illustrating the market share of the four companies.

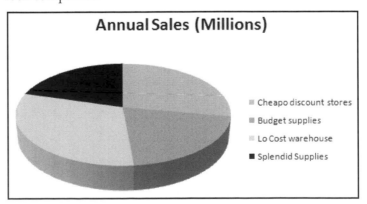

Splendid Supplies don't look very impressive on this chart. Let's use our first presentational technique to make things seem a little better.

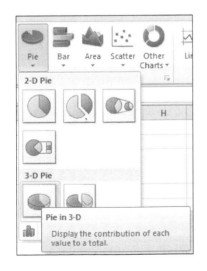

Competitor Analysis

3 Rotate the pie chart so that Splendid Supplies sales are at the front.

Because of the perspective of a 3-D pie, the slice at the front always seems the biggest (especially if you keep the perspective angle high).

1. Click just inside the chart border to activate the chart.

2. Click Chart Tools→Layout→Background→3-D Rotation.

The *Format Chart Area* dialog is displayed with the *3-D Rotation* category selected.

3. Use the *Rotation X* spin buttons to bring the Splendid Supplies slice to the front (about 220 degrees).

4. Change the *Perspective* to 35 degrees.

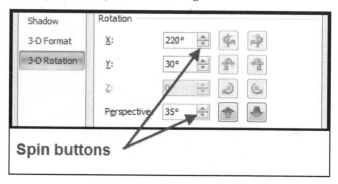

You'd never guess now that Splendid Supplies have the lowest market share.

4 Pull the Splendid Supplies slice slightly out of the pie.

A very common pie chart presentational technique is to pull the slice that you want to emphasize away from the pie chart. This slice then appears to be larger in relation to the other slices.

1. Click just inside the chart border to activate the chart.

2. Click one of the slices on the chart once to select the entire pie.

3. Click the Splendid Supplies slice once to select it.

4. Click and drag the slice slightly out of the pie.

Splendid Supplies now appears to be doing even better.

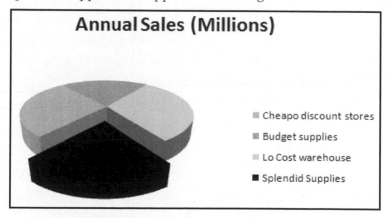

5 Save your work as *Competitor Analysis-1*.

Lesson 5-17: Create a chart with two vertical axis

Sometimes you'll have two data series that are very different in magnitude but you still want to show them on the same chart.

The examples used in this lesson are *UK Average House Prices* and *Bank Base Rates*. Analysts have noticed that when interest rates come down, house prices go up. To test this theory we will create a chart showing UK bank base rates against average house prices for the twelve years to 2008.

During the twelve year period house prices ranged from 68,788 to 199,021 while base rates fluctuated between 3.5% and 6.75%. We need two different vertical axes to make this chart work.

1   Open *UK House Prices* from your sample files folder.

2   Create a default *Line with Markers* chart from the range.

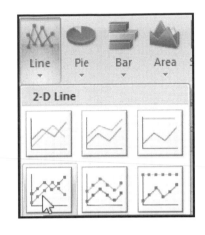

Click anywhere within the data and then click:

Insert→Charts→Line→Line with Markers

The default chart is displayed.

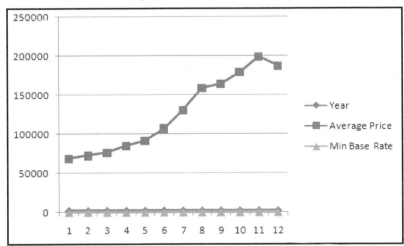

3   Remove *Year* from the *Legend* and show the years 1997 to 2008 along the *Horizontal Axis*.

We covered this in: *Lesson 5-11: Create a chart with numerical axis.*

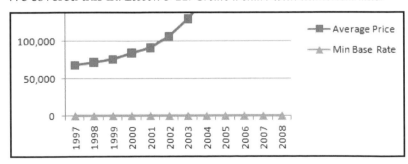

4   Select the *Min Base Rate* series.

Because the *Min Base Rate* series is in almost the same place as the horizontal axis this can be difficult with the mouse (though it is possible).

UK House Prices

You may find it easier to select the chart and then click:

Chart Tools→Layout→Current Selection→
Chart Elements drop down→Series "Min Base Rate"

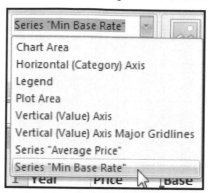

5   Move the *Min Base Rate* series to a secondary axis.

    1.   With the *Min Base Rate* series selected click:

        Chart Tools→Layout→Current Selection→Format Selection

        The *Format Data Series* dialog is displayed.

    2.   Click the *Secondary Axis* option button and then click *Close.*

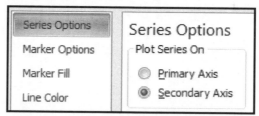

    The chart is displayed with two vertical axes and Excel even auto-scales the new axis for you.

note

The secondary axis always appears on top of the primary axis

You can see in the example chart that when the *Min Base Rate* series (the green line) crosses the *Average Price* series (the red line), the green line is on top.

There's no way to change the stacking order of the two lines.

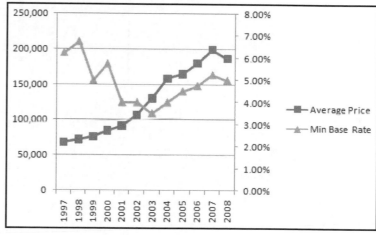

6   Save your work as UK House Prices-1.

Lesson 5-18: Create a combination chart containing different chart types

Excel allows you to allocate a different chart type to each data series. This opens up many interesting possibilities such as superimposing a *Line* chart on top of a *Column* chart.

In this lesson we'll re-cast the UK House Prices chart as a combination Column/Line chart with columns for house prices and a line for base rates.

1 Open *UK House Prices-1* from your sample files folder (if it isn't already open).

2 Select the *Average Price* data series.

   This was covered in: *Lesson 5-17: Create a chart with two vertical axis.*

3 Click Chart Tools→Design→Type→ Change Chart Type→Column→Clustered Column, and then click the OK button.

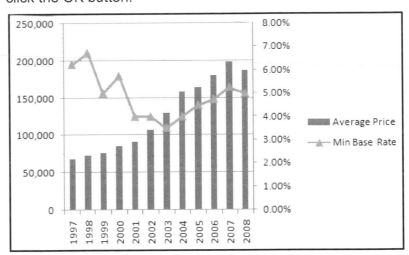

4 Adjust the *Min Base Rate* axis to move the series line as high as possible on the chart.

   The chart looks a little untidy as the line crosses the bars. Let's try to avoid this happening by adjusting the *Min Base Rate* series axis.

   1. Right-click the *Min Base Rate* vertical axis and then select *Format Axis…* from the shortcut menu.

   2. Click the Fixed option button next to *Maximum.*

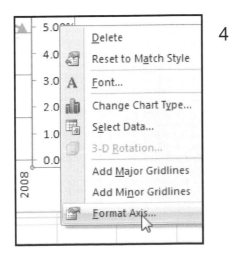

UK House Prices-1

   3. Type **0.0675** into the text box followed by the **<Enter>** key.

   This will ensure that the line touches the top of the chart because the maximum base rate was 6.75%.

This is very nearly the chart we need:

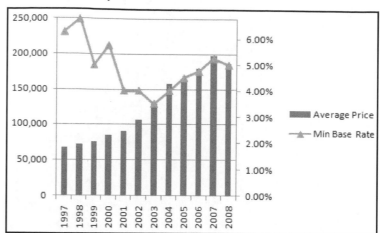

We can't do anything more to the *Min Base Rate* series to lift it higher.

The answer will be to adjust the *Average Price* series bars so that they are not as long.

5   Adjust the *Average Price* axis to reduce the height of the bars.

The bars will shrink in size if we change the minimum value to 50,000 but retain the maximum value of 250,000. They would shrink even more if we also adjusted the maximum value to a figure above 250,000.

1.   Right Click the *Average Price* vertical axis and click *Format Axis...* from the shortcut menu.

2.   Click the *Fixed* option button next to *Maximum* to prevent Excel from automatically adjusting the maximum value to a lower number.

3.   Click the *Fixed* option button next to *Minimum*.

4.   Type **50000** (without a comma) into the *Minimum* text box followed by the **<Enter>** key. For some reason Excel won't recognize the number if you include a comma.

The chart now displays as intended.

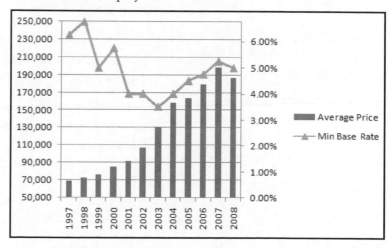

6   Save your work as *UK House Prices-2.*

Lesson 5-19: Add a trend line

It is impossible to demonstrate empirically that a cause produces an effect. Just because the sun has risen every day since the beginning of the Earth does not mean that it will rise again tomorrow. However; it is impossible to go about one's life without assuming such connections, and the best that we can do is to maintain an open mind and never presume that we know any laws of causality for certain.

David Hume (1711-1776),
Scottish philosopher, economist, and historian.
From "An Enquiry Concerning Human Understanding".

Trend analysis applies the science of mathematics to the art of fortune telling.

If a value has been increasing for a long time, trend analysis would suggest that it will go on increasing. Some would say that the reverse is true, but Excel remains healthily optimistic that we can predict the future from the past!

Excel provides several different types of trend analysis. We're going to use a linear trend line and a two-period moving average to decide whether it is a good idea to buy a house this year!

1   Open *UK House Prices-2* from your sample files folder (if it isn't already open).

2   Remove the *Min Base Rate* data series.

> This was covered in: *Lesson 5-9: Change source data using the Select Data Source dialog tools.*

3   Change the chart type from *Clustered Column* to *Line with Markers.*

> Activate the chart and then click:
>
> Chart Tools→Design→Type→Change Chart Type→
> Line with Markers

4   Add a linear trend line to forecast where property prices will be in the year 2012.

1.   Click the chart to activate it.

2.   Click Chart Tools→Layout→Analysis→Trendline→
     More Trendline Options…

     The *Format Trendline* dialog is displayed.

3.   As 2012 is 4 periods after 2008 enter 4 in the *Forecast Forward* text box and then click the *Close* button.

Forecast		
Forward:	4.0	periods
Backward:	0.0	periods

UK House Prices-2

Excel confidently predicts that that the house you buy for 187K this year will bring you back a cool quarter of a million in four years time (though David Hume would advise you not to bet on it).

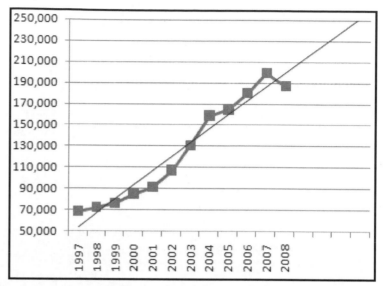

5   Remove the trend line.

Activate the chart and click:

Chart Tools→Layout→Analysis→Trendline→None.

6   Add a two period moving average.

Moving averages are one of the most loved instruments of speculators who predict the future values of shares, currencies and commodities based entirely upon charts. The theory is that when the moving average crosses the price line it is time to get out.

1.   Activate the chart.

2.   Click Chart Tools→Layout→Analysis→Trendline→ Two Period Moving Average.

This time the analysis shows that, for the first time in ten years, it is time to sell up because the price has crossed the moving average!

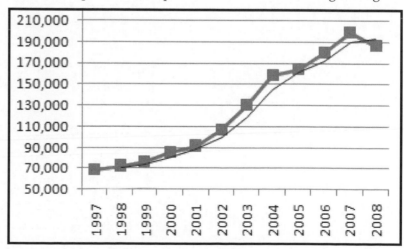

7   Save your work as *UK House Prices-3*.

Lesson 5-20: Switch chart rows/columns and add a gradient fill.

When a chart plots several data series it is possible to show the chart in two different ways. Transposing the rows and columns allows you to choose between these views.

When you prepare a chart for a PowerPoint presentation, or for inclusion in a high quality color publication, you want the chart to look professional and interesting. A *Gradient* background fill will put the finishing touch to your chart so that it looks like it was produced by a professional graphic artist.

1   Open *World Sales* from your sample files folder.

2   Create a Clustered Column chart from the entire range.

Click anywhere in the range and then click:

Insert→Charts→Column→2-D Column→Clustered Column.

The chart is created:

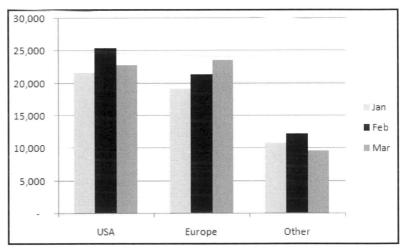

Notice that the regions (*USA, Europe* and *Other*) are situated along the horizontal axis and the months (*Jan, Feb* and *Mar*) are listed in the legend.

3   Switch Rows/Columns to transpose the *Legend* and *Regions*.

Activate the chart and then click:

Chart Tools→Design→Data→Switch Row/Column

The regions are now listed in the legend and the months are shown along the horizontal axis.

World Sales

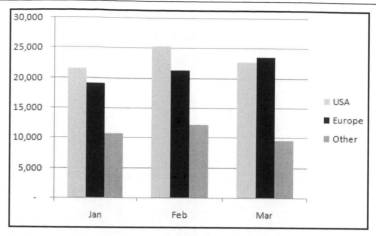

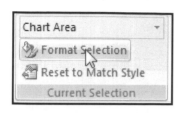

4   Add a gradient fill to the chart background.

1.   Select the *Chart Area* element and then click:

Chart Tools→Format→Current Selection→Format Selection

(You could also have done this more quickly by right-clicking the *Chart Area* and selecting *Format Chart Area...* from the shortcut menu).

2.   Click the *Gradient Fill* option button.

3.   Choose one of the preset colors (I chose *Parchment*). As you click each fill color, notice that Live Preview displays your fill on the chart.

4.   Explore the *Type/Direction/Angle/Transparency* and other settings until you are happy with the fill.

5.   Click the *Close* button.

5   Set the *Plot Area* background to *No fill*.

The chart doesn't look so good with a white plot area.

1.   Select the *Plot Area* element and then click:

Chart Tools→Format→Current Selection→Format Selection

2.   Click the *No fill* option. This makes the *Plot Area* transparent.

The chart now looks very professional with a gradient fill across the entire chart area.

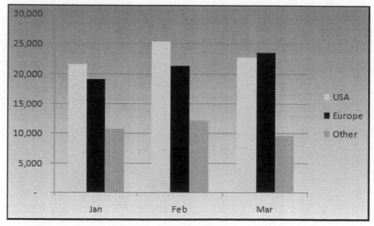

6   Save your work as *Gradient Fill*.

Lesson 5-21: Create your own chart templates

If you use charts a lot you may find yourself applying the same fonts, fills, layouts and other attributes over and over again. If you find this happening it is time to create a chart template.

Templates can be used just like the built-in gallery charts. You can use templates to create a unique, personal, or corporate chart style that will enable you to produce consistently styled work.

In this lesson we'll develop a useful chart template with larger fonts to enable them to be more readable when incorporated into a PowerPoint presentation. We can then use this template in future for any chart that is destined to be used in a presentation.

1   Open *Gradient Fill* from your sample files folder (if it isn't already open).

2   Add a *Chart Title* element to the chart.

Activate the chart and then click Chart Tools→Design→ Chart Layouts Gallery→Layout 1.

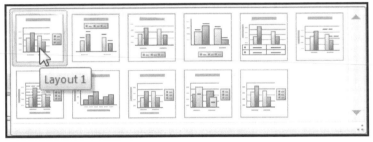

3   Increase the font size of the *Chart Title* element to 28 Points.

Select the *Chart Title* element and then click Home→Font→Font Size Drop-Down to set the font to 28 points.

4   Increase the font size of the *Vertical (Value) Axis*, *Horizontal (Category) Axis* and *Legend* elements to 14 points.

Select each element in turn and set the font in the same way as in the previous step.

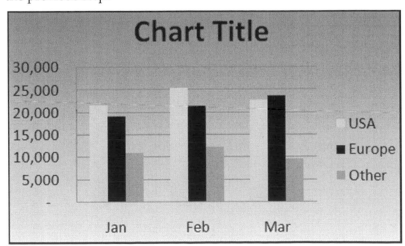

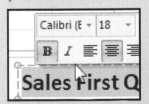

The chart now has labels that will be readable by viewers at the back of the room when projected onto a screen.

5   Save the chart design as a template.

1.   Select the chart and then click:

Chart Tools→Design→Type→Save As Template

2.   Type **PowerPoint Clustered Column with Title and Gradient Fill** as the File Name.

3.   Click the *Save* button.

6   Delete the chart.

Click once, just inside the border of the chart, to select it and then press the **<Delete>** key.

7   Create a new chart from the template.

1.   Click anywhere inside the data range A1:D4.

2.   Click Insert→Charts→Dialog Launcher.

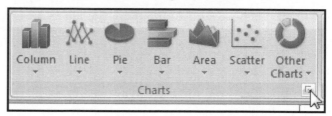

The *Insert Chart* dialog is displayed.

3.   Click the *Templates* category on the left of the dialog and hover the mouse cursor over the single icon displayed on the right hand side of the dialog. Notice that the tip text displays the name of the template you have just saved.

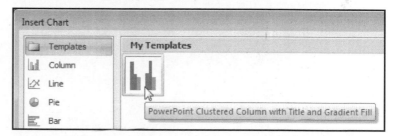

4.   Either double-click the template icon, or click it once to select and then click the OK button. A chart is displayed with all of the attributes of your template.

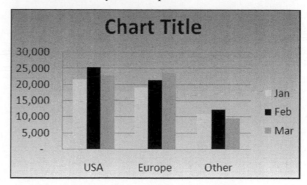

8   Save your work as *PowerPoint Template*.

Session 5: Exercise

1   Open the *Exercise 5* file from your sample files folder.

2   Create a *2-D Clustered Column* chart showing all data in the range.

      The chart will look strange at first because Excel isn't capable of automatically charting this data.

3   Switch rows and columns so that the European country names are shown in the *Legend*.

4   Use the *Select Data Source* dialog to remove the *Year* series and place the years along the *Horizontal (Category) Axis*.

5   Change the scale of the vertical axis so that it has a *Minimum* value of 15 and a *Maximum* value of 50.

6   Format the *Legend* so that a solid line black border appears around it.

7   Use the *Select Data Source* dialog to only show sales for the UK, Spain and Italy.

8   Increase the font size of the legend to 12 points.

9   Add a *Chart Title* by changing the layout of the chart to *Layout 1*.

10   Change the *Chart Title* text to: *European Sales*.

11   Add a gradient fill to the *Chart Area* element using the *Daybreak* preset colors.

12   Format the *Plot Area* element so that it has no fill.

13   Save your work as *Exercise 5-1*.

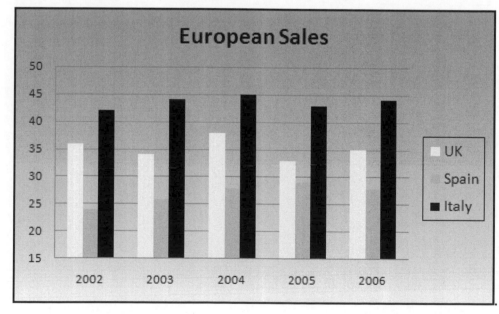

Exercise 5

If you need help slide the page to the left

Session 5: Exercise answers

These are the four questions that most students find the most difficult to remember:

Q 11	Q 7	Q 5	Q 4
1. Right-click just inside the border of the chart and click *Format Chart Area...* from the shortcut menu.	1. Right-click just inside the border of the chart and click *Select Data...* from the shortcut menu.	1. Click the vertical axis to select it.	1. Right-click just inside the border of the chart and click *Select Data...* from the shortcut menu.
2. Click the *Gradient Fill* option button.	2. Click the *France* item in the *Legend Entries (Series)* list and then click the *Remove* button.	2. Right-click the vertical axis and click *Format Axis...* from the shortcut menu.	2. Click the *Year* item in the *Legend Entries (Series)* list and then click the *Remove* button.
3. Choose the *Daybreak* preset color from the colors gallery.	3. Click the *Germany* item in the *Legend Entries (Series)* list and then click the *Remove* button.	3. Click the *Fixed* option buttons for the *Maximum* and *Minimum* values.	3. Click the *Edit* button on top of the *Horizontal (Category) Axis Labels* list.
5. Click the *Close* button.	4. Click the OK button.	4. Type the value **15** in the *Minimum* value text box and make sure that **50** is shown in the *Maximum* value text box.	4. Select cells A4:A8.
This was covered in: *Lesson 5-20: Switch chart rows/columns and add a gradient fill.*	This was covered in: *Lesson 5-9: Change source data using the Select Data Source dialog tools.*	5. Click the *Close* button.	5. Click the OK button on each dialog.
		This was covered in: *Lesson 5-15: Add gridlines and scale axes.*	This was covered in: *Lesson 5-11: Create a chart with numerical axis.*

If you have difficulty with the other questions, here are the lessons that cover the relevant skills:

1   Refer to: *Lesson 1-4: Download the sample files and* **open/navigate a workbook.**

2   Refer to: *Lesson 5-1: Create a simple chart with two clicks.*

3   **Activate the chart and then click Chart Tools→Design→Data→Switch Row/Column.**

6   Refer to: *Lesson 5-4: Format chart element fills and borders.*

8   Refer to: *Lesson 5-21: Create your own chart templates.*

9   Refer to: *Lesson 5-3: Change chart layouts.*

10   Refer to: *Lesson 5-3: Change chart layouts.*

12   Refer to: *Lesson 5-20: Switch chart rows/columns and add a gradient fill.*

13   Refer to: *Lesson 1-5: Save a workbook.*

Session Six: Working With Multiple Worksheets and Workbooks

> There are no big problems; there are just a lot of little problems.
>
> *Henry Ford (1863-1947)*
> *American industrialist and pioneer of assembly-line production*

Henry Ford knew that big problems are really just a lot of little problems bundled together.

Often you will find that a worksheet is getting over-complicated and difficult to work with. This session will give you the skills needed to quickly break one, very complex, worksheet into many smaller, and easier to manage, worksheets.

This session will also show you how to view different parts of large worksheets at the same time and how to create cross-worksheet formulas that summarize data from several different worksheets.

Session Objectives

By the end of this session you will be able to:

- View the same workbook in different windows
- View two windows side by side and perform synchronous scrolling
- Duplicate worksheets within a workbook
- Move and copy worksheets from one workbook to another
- Hide and unhide a worksheet
- Create cross-worksheet formulas
- Understand worksheet groups
- Use find and replace

Lesson 6-1: View the same workbook in different windows

Excel allows you to view the same worksheet in two separate worksheet windows. This is useful when you need to compare different areas of the same worksheet.

1   Close any Excel workbooks that are currently open.

2   Open *Sales First Quarter 2008* from your sample files folder.

This workbook has only one worksheet containing 242 rows of data.

3   Open a new window to see February 2008 and January 2008 sales at the same time.

Click: View→Window→New Window.

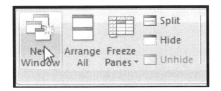

Nothing seems to have happened except that the Title bar now reads: *Sales First Quarter 2008:2*

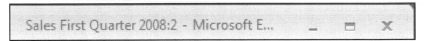

Two views of the same workbook are now open at the same time but you can only view one at a time which isn't very useful.

4   View both windows at the same time.

Click View→Window→Arrange All.

The *Arrange Windows* dialog appears:

5   Select the *Horizontal* option and then click the OK button.

Both worksheets are displayed in the worksheet window, one below the other. You are able to freely scroll to any position in either window.

Sales First Quarter 2008

In the screen grab below I've scrolled the bottom window down to see February sales:

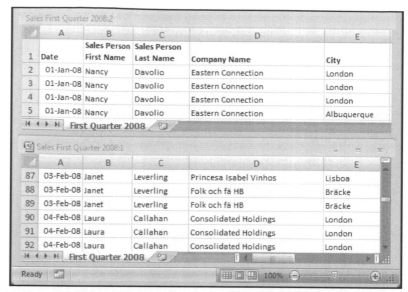

It's important to realize that we are not looking at two different worksheets, but two different views of the same worksheet.

If you change a value in one of the views, you'll immediately see the changed value in the other.

You will now appreciate the importance of closing any open workbooks in step 1. If you had several workbooks open, you would now be viewing all of them in multiple windows.

6 Close the *Sales First Quarter 2008:2* view and maximize the *Sales First Quarter 2008:1* worksheet.

1. Click in the *Sales First Quarter 2008:2* window. Notice how the title bar changes color to indicate that this is now the active window.

2. Click the *Close* button in the top right hand corner of the worksheet.

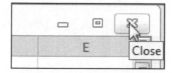

3. Click the *Maximize* button in the top right-hand corner of the *Sales First Quarter 2008* worksheet.

Lesson 6-2: View two windows side by side and perform synchronous scrolling

When only two workbooks are open, the *Arrange All* method covered in the previous lesson will work just fine.

It is more likely that you will have many workbooks (or views of the same workbook) open and will want to see two specific workbooks on screen at the same time.

You may sometimes be given a workbook that somebody else has changed and need to identify what has been altered. We'll use Excel's synchronous scrolling feature to make this task easier.

1   Close any Excel workbooks that are currently open.

2   Open *Exercise 6* from your sample files folder.

3   Open *Sales First Quarter 2008 Revised* from your sample files folder.

4   Open *Sales First Quarter 2008* from your sample files folder.

Only the last workbook opened: *Sales First Quarter 2008* is visible on screen:

5   Click View→Window→View Side By Side.

The *Compare Side By Side* dialog is displayed:

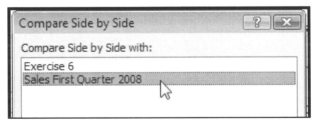

6   Select *Sales First Quarter 2008 Revised* as the workbook you want to view with the current workbook and then click the **<OK>** button.

The workbooks should display one above the other.

Sales First Quarter 2008

Sales First Quarter 2008 Revised

Exercise 6

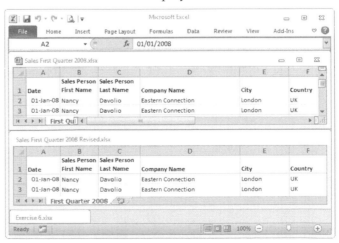

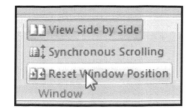

If you don't see this, click:

View→Window→Reset Window Position

This is often needed when the workbooks are not maximized within the Excel application window.

You also need to do this after re-sizing the Excel application window. (The Excel application and workbook windows were covered in depth in: *Lesson 1-3: Understand the Application and Workbook windows*).

7 Unlock the windows so that they no longer scroll together.

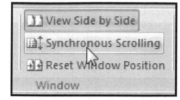

1. Click View→Window→Synchronous Scrolling to switch synchronous scrolling off. You are now able to freely scroll each window independently.

2. Scroll each window to the top (so that row 1 is at the top of each window).

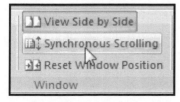

3. Click View→Window→Synchronous Scrolling to switch synchronous scrolling back on so that both windows automatically scroll together.

8 Identify differences between the two workbooks.

1. Scroll one of the windows and notice that both windows now scroll together.

2. Scroll down so that you can see row 77. Notice that row 78 has gone out of synchronization because one of the 29-Jan-08 sales to Hungry Owl has been deleted from the *Revised* workbook.

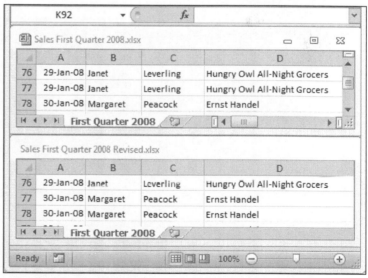

9 Re-synchronize the windows.

1. Click View→Window→Synchronous Scrolling to switch Synchronous Scrolling off.

2. Scroll so that the first transaction on 30th Jan 2008 is on the first row in both windows.

3. Click View→Window→Synchronous Scrolling to switch Synchronous Scrolling back on.

10 Close all open workbooks without saving.

Lesson 6-3: Duplicate worksheets within a workbook

In this lesson we're going to disassemble a large worksheet and make it into three smaller worksheets.

You'll often find that data is easier to work with if you divide it into logically separated sections.

1 Open *Sales First Quarter 2008* from your sample files folder.

This workbook shows all sales completed in January, February and March 2008. Our task will be to split them into separate months.

2 Create a new worksheet and name it *January*.

This skill was covered in *Lesson 1-8: View, move, add, rename, delete and navigate* worksheet tabs.

3 Select every cell in the *First Quarter 2008* worksheet.

1. Click the *First Quarter 2008* worksheet tab.

There's a special button at the top left corner of every worksheet called the *Select All* button.

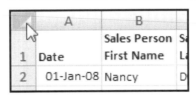

2. Click the *Select All* button to select every cell in the worksheet.

4 Copy all selected cells.

The easiest way to do this is to right-click within the selected range and then select *Copy* from the shortcut menu.

5 Paste the copied cells into the *January* worksheet beginning at cell A1.

Click the *January* tab, right-click in cell A1 and select *Paste* from the shortcut menu.

6 Create another copy of the worksheet using *Move or Copy*.

Excel provides a simpler way to duplicate a worksheet.

1. Right-click the First Quarter 2008 worksheet tab and choose *Move or Copy…* from the shortcut menu.

The *Move or Copy* dialog appears.

2. Select *(move to end)* in the *Before sheet* list.

3. Check the *Create a copy* check box.

Sales First Quarter 2008

4. Click the *OK* button.

Notice that Excel has named the new worksheet: *First Quarter 2008 (2)*.

7 Change the name of the new worksheet to *February*.

This skill was covered in *Lesson 1-8: View, move, add, rename, delete and navigate* worksheet tabs.

8 Create another copy of the worksheet using *drag and drop*.

There's an even quicker way to create a duplicate worksheet.

1. Click once on the *First Quarter 2008* tab to select it.

2. Hold down the **<Ctrl>** key.

3. Click and hold the mouse button on the *First Quarter 2008* tab.

The cursor changes shape to a page with a plus sign:

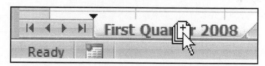

4. Drag to the right until you see a black insertion arrow to the right of the *February* tab.

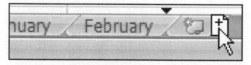

When you release the mouse button another copy of the worksheet is created.

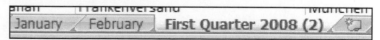

9 Change the name of the new worksheet to *March*.

10 Remove rows from the January, February and March workbooks so that only the named month's transactions remain.

This was covered in: *Lesson 3-1: Insert and delete rows and columns*.

11 Save your work as *Sales First Quarter 2008-1*.

Lesson 6-4: Move and copy worksheets from one workbook to another

In *Lesson 6-3: Duplicate worksheets within a workbook* we worked with a single workbook.

It is also possible to move and copy worksheets between different workbooks using a similar technique.

1   Close any workbooks that are currently open.

2   Open *Sales First Quarter 2008-1* from your sample files folder (if it isn't already open).

3   Open *First Quarter Sales and Bonus* from your sample files folder.

4   Click View→Window→ Arrange All to arrange the windows *Horizontally* in the Excel window.

> This was covered in: *Lesson 2-2: Create a new workbook and view two workbooks at the same time.*

The two workbooks are now shown together.

First Quarter Sales and Bonus

Sales First Quarter 2008-1

5   Rename *Sheet1* in the *First Quarter Sales and Bonus* workbook to *Bonus*.

> This was covered in: *Lesson 1-8: View, move, add, rename, delete and navigate* worksheet tabs.

6   Hold down the **<Ctrl>** key and drag and drop the *Bonus* sheet from the *First Quarter Sales and Bonus* workbook to the *Sales First Quarter 2008-1* workbook.

A copy of the *Bonus* worksheet is created in the *Sales First Quarter 2008-1* workbook.

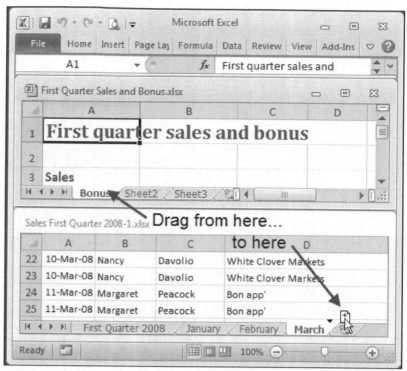

7   Drag and drop the *Sheet3* worksheet from the *First Quarter Sales and Bonus* workbook to the *Sales First Quarter 2008-1* workbook.

You will have to click the *First Quarter Sales and Bonus* workbook once to activate it before you can drag and drop the sheet tab.

This time, because you didn't hold the **<Ctrl>** key down, the worksheet is moved rather than copied.

8   Change the name of the moved worksheet to *Summary*.

This skill was covered in: *Lesson 1-8: View, move, add, rename, delete and navigate* worksheet tabs.

9   If necessary, move the worksheet tabs in the *Sales First Quarter 2008-1* workbook so that they appear in the following order:

This skill was covered in: *Lesson 1-8: View, move, add, rename, delete and navigate* worksheet tabs.

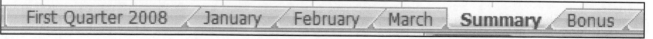

10 Maximize the *Sales First Quarter 2008-1* workbook window.

This was covered in: *Lesson 1-3: Understand the Application and Workbook windows.*

11 Save your work as *Sales First Quarter 2008-2.*

Lesson 6-5: Hide and unhide a worksheet

Sometimes you'll want to prevent users from viewing and changing one or more worksheets.

In this case you will want to *Hide* the worksheet.

A hidden worksheet becomes invisible to the user but is still there. You can bring back hidden worksheets by *Unhiding* them.

1 Open *Sales First Quarter 2008-2* from your sample files folder (if it isn't already open).

In this workbook you may not want viewers to see the *First Quarter 2008* worksheet as the information is already contained in the *January/February/March* worksheets.

You might also want to hide the *Bonus* worksheet as it contains confidential information.

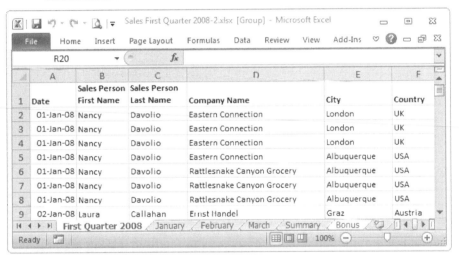

2 Select the *First Quarter 2008* and *Bonus* worksheets.

1. Click on the *First Quarter 2008* worksheet tab.

2. Hold down the **<Ctrl>** key.

3. Click on the *Bonus* worksheet tab.

   Both worksheet tabs should now appear slightly lighter than the others:

First Quarter 2008 / January / February / March / Summary / Bonus /

3 Hide the *First Quarter 2008* and *Bonus* worksheets.

The easiest way to do this is to right click either of the selected tabs and then click *Hide* from the shortcut menu.

The worksheets vanish.

January / February / March / Summary /

It's also possible to do this from the Ribbon less efficiently (see facing page sidebar).

Sales First Quarter 2008-2

note

Hiding and unhiding a worksheet using the Ribbon

The right-click method is far faster than using the Ribbon but here's how it can be done:

To *Hide* a worksheet

Click:

Home→Cells→Format→ Hide & Unhide→Hide Sheet

To *Unhide* a worksheet

Click:

Home→Cells→Format→ Hide & Unhide→Unhide Sheet

Then select the sheet you want to hide/unhide from the dialog and click the OK button.

important

Don't rely on hidden worksheets for security

There is no password associated with hiding and unhiding a worksheet. A knowledgeable user can easily unhide any hidden worksheets.

It is possible to password-protect the structure before distributing a workbook. When this is done it isn't possible to unhide and view the hidden worksheet unless you know the password.

This topic is fully covered in the *Expert Skills* book in this series in which a whole session is dedicated to security.

4   Unhide the *Bonus* worksheet.

Excel will never allow you to hide all worksheets so this method will always work.

1.   Right-click on any of the visible worksheet tabs.

2.   Click *Unhide* from the shortcut menu.

The *Unhide* dialog is displayed:

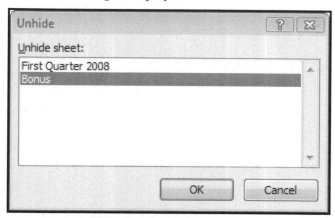

3.   Click *Bonus* and then click the OK button

You can also unhide the worksheets less efficiently using the Ribbon (see sidebar).

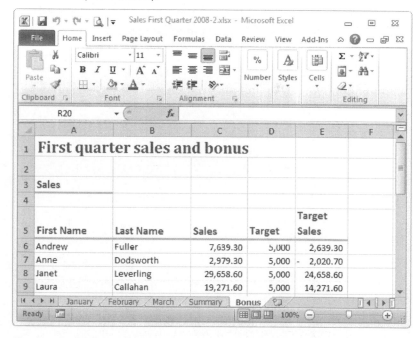

5   Save your work as *Sales First Quarter 2008-3*.

Lesson 6-6: Create cross worksheet formulas

You'll often want to summarize information from multiple worksheets within a workbook.

This can be done by simply prefixing the cell reference with the worksheet name followed by an exclamation mark.

1   Open *Sales First Quarter 2008-3* from your sample files folder (if it isn't already open).

2   Select the *January* tab and scroll to the bottom of the range.

3   Type the word **Total:** into the first empty cell in column G (cell G87).

4   Right-Align cell G87.

   This was covered in: *Lesson 4-5: Horizontally align the contents of cells.*

5   Bold-face all of row 87.

   This was covered in: *Lesson 1-14: Use the Mini Toolbar, Key Tips and keyboard shortcuts.*

6   Use AutoSum to add totals to columns H and J.

   This was covered in: *Lesson 2-3: Use AutoSum to quickly calculate totals.*

	G	H	I	J
85	Gumbär Gummibärchen	10	24.90	249.00
86	Tourtière	40	5.90	236.00
87	Total:	2,401		66,692.80

7   Add similar totals to the *February* and *March* worksheets.

8   Select the *Summary* tab.

9   Type the text: **First Quarter Summary** into cell A1 and apply the *Title* cell style.

   This was covered in: *Lesson 4-9: Use cell styles and change themes.*

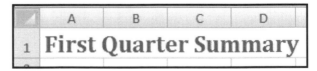

10 Type **Month**, **Units** and **Price** into cells A3, B3 and C3.

11 Type **Jan** into cell A4 and then AutoFill down two cells to add Feb and Mar.

   This was covered in: *Lesson 2-14: Use AutoFill for text and numeric series.*

12 Apply the *Heading 2* style to cells A3:C3.

Sales First Quarter 2008-3

13   Apply the *Heading 4* style to cells A4:A6.

	A	B	C	D
1	**First Quarter Summary**			
2				
3	**Month**	**Units**	**Price**	
4	**Jan**			
5	**Feb**			
6	**Mar**			

14   Add a formula to cell B4 to display the total units sold in January.

1. Click cell B4.

2. Press the equals key on your keyboard (**=**) to begin a formula.

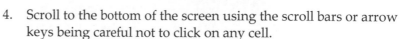

3. Click on the *January* tab.

4. Scroll to the bottom of the screen using the scroll bars or arrow keys being careful not to click on any cell.

5. Click on cell H87 (the cell with the total units in it).

6. Press the **<Enter>** key on the keyboard.

The total is shown on the summary sheet.

3	**Month**	**Units**	**Price**
4	Jan	2401	

15   Use the same technique to add summary totals to **Units** and **Price** for all three months.

3	**Month**	**Units**	**Price**
4	Jan	2401	66,692.80
5	Feb	2132	41,207.20
6	Mar	1770	39,979.90

16   Note the formulas that Excel has created.

Click cell B4 and then look at the formula bar at the top of the screen. Note that the formula is:

f_x	=January!H87

	A	B	C
3	**Month**	**Units**	**Price**
4	Jan	2401	66,692.80

The formula is simply the worksheet name, followed by an exclamation mark, followed by the cell reference.

Note the important sidebar information regarding worksheet names that contain spaces.

17   Save your work as *Sales First Quarter 2008-4*.

---

important

You must use quotation marks if a worksheet name contains spaces

The example worksheet names used in this session do not contain any spaces.

If you had a worksheet called *January Sales* you would have to construct your formula like this:

='January Sales'!K22

Because worksheet names with spaces are more difficult to work with, many Excel users prefer to name their sheets without spaces by capitalizing the first letter of every word.

Example:

JanuarySales
EuropeIncludingSouthAfrica

Lesson 6-7: Understand worksheet groups

A very interesting (and little known) feature of Excel is its ability to group worksheets into a three-dimensional array of worksheet cells.

When worksheets are grouped, it is possible to perform a single operation upon all of the worksheets in the group. This can be very useful when you need to:

- Print out all of the worksheets in the group.

- Enter data into the same cell for all worksheets in the group.

- Apply formatting to the same cell or range for all worksheets in the group.

1   Open *Widget Supplies Price List* from your sample files folder.

The formatting of this workbook leaves a lot to be desired. It consists of three worksheets all showing similar information but lacking any style.

	A	B	C	D	E	F	G
1	Price List						
2	Prices Effe	20th March 2008					
3	When calculating prices the following exchange rates will be used						
4							
5		USD	GBP	EUR	JPY		
6	USD	1	1.8383	1.4708	0.00911		
7							
8	Descriptic	Dollars	Pounds	Euros	Yen		
9	Standard \	3.75	2.039928	2.549633	411.6356		
10	Premium	5.5	2.991895	3.739462	603.7322		
11	De-luxe g	7.95	4.324648	5.405222	872.6674		

We're going to use the magic of grouping to format all three worksheets at the same time.

2   Select all three worksheets to create a worksheet group.

1.   Click the *Widgets* worksheet tab.

2.   Hold down the **<Shift>** key and click the *Sprockets* worksheet tab.

All three tabs now have a white background to show that they are selected.

Something else has also happened. The bar at the top of the screen now indicates that the worksheets form a worksheet group.

Widget Supplies Price List [Group] - Microsoft Excel

note

Selecting non-contiguous worksheets

Non-contiguous simply means *not next to each other*.

When the worksheet tabs aren't next to each other, hold down the **<Ctrl>** key and click each in turn. If you make a mistake you can **<Ctrl>+<Click>** a second time to de-select one tab.

You can be even cleverer and use a combination of **<Shift>+<Click>** and **<Ctrl>+<Click>** when some of the tabs are next to each other and others are not.

Widget Supplies Price List

3   Apply formatting to the *Sprockets* worksheet to make it look attractive.

When you have grouped every worksheet in a workbook, you have a little problem. You can't switch between worksheets and still keep the group selected. As soon as you click a selected sheet the other two are de-selected.

To work-around this we'll have to insert a new blank worksheet. The sheet's only purpose is to allow you to switch between sheets in the selected group.

1. Add a worksheet called *Dummy*.

2. Select the *Widgets, Grommets* and *Sprockets* group as before.

3. Click on the *Sprockets* tab. The group remains selected and the *Sprockets* worksheet is now active.

4. Apply the comma style to the range B9:E11. This was covered in: *Lesson 4-3: Format numbers using built-in number formats*.

5. Adjust the widths of all columns so that they fully display their contents. *This was covered in: Lesson 2-9: Re-size rows and columns.*

6. Apply the *Title* style to cell A1, the *Heading 4* style to cells A2, A6 and A9:A11 and the *Heading 3* style to cells B5:E5 and A8:E8. This was covered in: *Lesson 4-9: Use cell styles and change themes.*

7. Adjust the height of rows 2, 3 and 4 to tidy the top part of the price list.

8. Click on each of the other two tabs to ensure that columns are also wide enough for their content. Adjust if needed.

	A	B	C	D	E
1	**Price List**				
2	Prices Effective:		20th March 2008		
3	When calculating prices the following exchange rates will be used				
5		USD	GBP	EUR	JPY
6	USD	1	1.8383	1.4708	0.00911
7					
8	Description	Dollars	Pounds	Euros	Yen
9	Standard widget	3.75	2.04	2.55	411.64
10	Premium widget	5.50	2.99	3.74	603.73
11	De-luxe gold plated widget	7.95	4.32	5.41	872.67

4   With the group still selected, change some exchange rates and the *Prices Effective* date.

I saved the best bit for last. You can now update the exchange rates for all three price lists at the same time. This would be regularly needed as exchange rates fluctuate. When a group of worksheets are selected, any change made to one worksheet is also made to all of the others.

5   Save your work as *Widget Supplies Price List-1*.

Lesson 6-8: Use find and replace

note

Other ways to display the *Find and Replace* dialog

Find

Use the <Ctrl>+<F> keyboard shortcut.

Replace

Use the <Ctrl>+<H> keyboard shortcut.

note

Searching only part of a worksheet

If you only select a single cell, *Find and Replace* will search the entire worksheet.

If you select a range of cells, *Find and Replace* will only search within that range.

Sales First Quarter 2008-4

Excel's find and replace tool is amazingly powerful. There are several bells and whistles that can massively shorten many common tasks.

This lesson will explore all of the features and suggest useful ways in which they can be used to solve real-world problems.

1   Open *Sales First Quarter 2008-4* from your sample files folder (if it isn't already open).

2   Use *Find and Replace* to change the text *Davolio* to *O'Reilly* throughout the workbook.

Nancy Davolio has married Sean O'Reilly and she is very proud of her new name. She's made a special request for you to change her name in the workbook too!

1.   Click Home→Editing→Find & Select→Replace. The *Find and Replace* dialog is displayed.

2.   Type **Davolio** in the *Find what:* text box and **O'Reilly** in the *Replace with:* text box.

3.   Click the *Options>>* button.   Options >>

We don't want to only look in the current worksheet but in all of the worksheets in this workbook so select the *Within: Workbook* option.

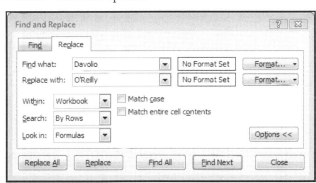

4.   Click the *Find Next* button. The first instance of *Davolio* is found on the worksheet.

5.   Click the *Replace* button to replace just this one instance. The cursor moves to the next instance found.

6.   Click *Replace All* to replace all remaining instances of *Davolio* with *O'Reilly*. Excel prompts that it has made 28 replacements.

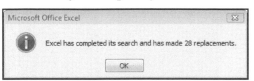

7.   Check out the worksheets. Notice that Nancy's surname has now changed in every worksheet.

8.   Click the *OK* and *Close* buttons to close both dialogs.

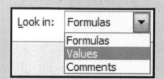
3   Apply the *Good* style to cell G21 on the *January* worksheet.

Click cell G21 to select and then click:

Home→Styles→Cell Styles→Good

The *Good* cell style has a light green background and a dark green foreground.

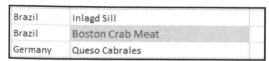

4   Apply the same style to every other mention of *Boston Crab Meat* in the workbook.

1. With cell G21 still visible on the workbook click:

   Home→Editing→Find & Select→Replace…

2. Type **Boston Crab Meat** in the *Find what:* text box.

3. Click the *Format* button alongside *Replace with:* and select *Choose format from Cell…* from the drop-down menu.

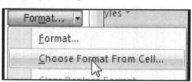

(It is really important that you click the lower of the two *Format* buttons. If you get it wrong click Format→Clear Find Format to start again).

The cursor shape changes to an eye-dropper. Click on cell G21.

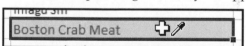

The same format now appears in the *Replace with:* format text box on the *Find and Replace* dialog

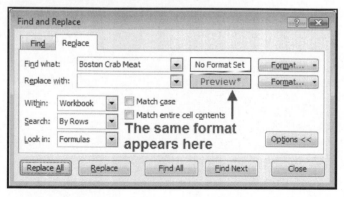

4. Click *Replace All* to re-format all instances of *Boston Crab Meat* to the *Good* cell style. Excel advises that it has changed the format of seven cells.

5. Click the *OK* and *Close* buttons to close both dialogs.

6. Check out all of the worksheets and notice that every cell containing the text *Boston Crab Meat* has now turned green.

5   Save your work as *Sales First Quarter 2008-5.*

Session 6: Exercise

1   Close any workbooks that are open.

2   Open *Exercise 6* from your sample files folder.

This spreadsheet shows sales to the USA and UK during the first quarter of 2008.

3   View two copies of the worksheet in the same window and scroll one of the windows so that the first USA sale is visible in the first row.

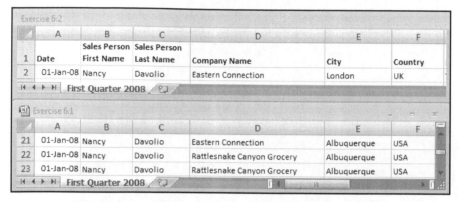

4   Close the *Exercise 6:2* window and maximize the *Exercise 6:1* window.

5   Make two duplicate copies of the *First Quarter 2008* worksheet and name them *USA* and *UK*.

6   Delete all of the non USA rows from the USA worksheet and all of the non UK rows from the UK worksheet.

7   Hide the *First Quarter 2008* worksheet tab.

8   Use AutoSum to create a total at the bottom of Columns H and J (Quantity and Total) for both the *USA* and *UK* worksheets.

9   Add a new worksheet and name it *Summary*.

10 Create a summary sheet as illustrated below using cross-worksheet formulas to calculate the totals.

	A	B	C	D	E
1	**USA and UK Sales Summary**				
2					
3	**Country**	**Units**	**Sales**		
4	USA	913	26,572.20		
5	UK	379	7,299.40		
6	Total	1292	33,871.60		

11 Save your work as *Exercise 6-End*.

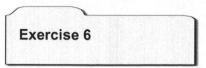

Exercise 6

If you need help slide the page to the left

Session 6: Exercise answers

These are the four questions that most students find the most difficult to remember:

Q 9	Q 6	Q 4	Q 3
In the example the following styles were used: A1 Title A3:C3 Heading 2 A4:A5 Heading 4 A6:C6 Total 1. Click cell B4 and type an equals sign into it (=). 2. Click the *USA* tab. 3. Use the scroll bars to make the total cell (cell H27) visible being careful not to click in the cell area. 4. Click cell H27 and then press the **<Enter>** key. This was covered in: *Lesson 6-6: Create cross worksheet formulas.*	1. Right-click the *First Quarter 2008* worksheet tab. 2. Click *Hide* on the shortcut menu. This was covered in: *Lesson 6-5: Hide and unhide a worksheet.*	1. Click on the *First Quarter 2008* worksheet tab to select it. 2. Hold down the **<Ctrl>** key. 3. Click and drag the *First Quarter 2008* worksheet tab to the right. 4. Double-click the duplicated worksheet's tab and type the tab's new name. This was covered in: *Lesson 6-3: Duplicate worksheets within a workbook.*	1. Click: View→Window→ New Window 2. Click: View→Window→ Arrange All 3. Click the *Horizontal* option in the *Arrange Windows* dialog. 4. Click the OK button. 5. Scroll one of the windows to the first USA sale (Row 21). This was covered in: *Lesson 6-1: View the same workbook in different windows.*

If you have difficulty with the other questions, here are the lessons that cover the relevant skills:

1   **Refer to: Lesson 1-2: Maximize, minimize, re-size, move and close the Excel window.**

2   **Refer to: Lesson 1-4: Download the sample files and open/navigate a workbook.**

5   **Refer to: Lesson 3-1: Insert and delete rows and columns.**

7   **Refer to: Lesson 2-3: Use AutoSum to quickly calculate totals.**

8   **Refer to: Lesson 1-8: View, move, add, rename, delete and navigate worksheet tabs.**

10   **Refer to: Lesson 1-5: Save a workbook.**

Session Seven: Printing Your Work

> The greatest misfortune that ever befell man was the invention of printing.
>
> *Benjamin Disraeli, British Prime Minister and Novelist (1804-1881).*

As we move towards the paperless office printing will become less important.

In the last year or so, screen and rendering technology have improved to the extent that I now prefer to read on-screen rather than from paper.

Perhaps we are not far from the time when all communication will be done electronically, but we're not quite there yet.

Excel has a range of tools that will allow you to present your work as polished and professional printed reports. This session will give you all of the skills you need to control every aspect of printing your work on paper.

Session Objectives

By the end of this session you will be able to:

- Print Preview and change paper orientation
- Use Page Layout view to adjust margins
- Use Page Setup to set margins more precisely and center the worksheet
- Set paper size and scale
- Insert, delete and preview page breaks
- Adjust page breaks using Page Break Preview
- Add auto-headers and auto-footers and set starting page number
- Add custom headers and footers
- Specify different headers and footers for the first, odd and even pages
- Print only part of a worksheet
- Add row and column data labels and grid lines to printed output
- Print several selected worksheets and change the page order
- Suppress error messages in printouts

Lesson 7-1: Print Preview and change paper orientation

tip

Add a print preview button to the Quick Access toolbar

I use the *Backstage Print View* such a lot that I like display it with a single click (instead of two). To do this I always add the *Print Preview and Print* button to the Quick Access Toolbar.

I recommend that this button is a "must have" for the Quick Access Toolbar.

You'll find out how to add the button in:
Lesson 1-13: Customize the Quick Access Toolbar and preview the printout.

The above lesson also includes a screen grab of my own heavily modified Quick Access Toolbar and may give you more ideas for buttons you'd like to add.

1   Open *Sales Report* from your sample files folder.

Make sure that you open the Session 7 *Sales Report* file as there's also a sample file of the same name in an earlier session.

2   *Print Preview* the worksheet to see how it will look on paper.

1.   Click File➔Print.

The *Backstage View* appears showing a preview of the printed page in the right-hand pane.

2.   Click the *Next Page* and *Previous Page* buttons to page through the document.

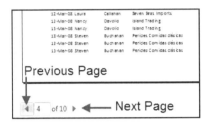

Notice that the paper isn't wide enough to show all of the columns. Excel tries to help out by printing the left-most columns across the first five or six pages followed by the right-most columns on the next five or six pages.

Sales Report for First Quarter 2008

Date	Sales Person First Name	Sales Person last Name	Company Name	City	Country
01-Jan-08	Nancy	Davolio	Eastern Connection	London	UK
01-Jan-08	Nancy	Davolio	Eastern Connection	London	UK
01-Jan-08	Nancy	Davolio	Eastern Connection	London	UK

Product Name	Qty	Unit Price	Total
Thüringer Rostbratwurst	21	99.00	2,079.00
Steeleye Stout	35	14.40	504.00
Maxilaku	30	16.00	480.00

You would have to take the two pages, cut them with scissors, and tape them together in order to see all of the rows and columns.

3   Change the paper orientation to *Landscape* in order to print more columns on each sheet of paper.

Click the drop-down arrow next to *Portrait Orientation* in the center pane of the *Backstage View* and then click on *Landscape Orientation*.

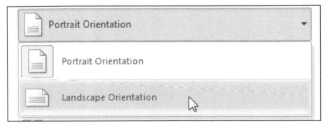

Sales Report

In *Landscape* orientation the paper is printed as if it had been put into the printer sideways.

The printout is very nearly there now. But we still have a problem with the last column which prints out all on its own.

Sales Report for First Quarter 2008

Date	Sales Person First Name	Sales Person Last Name	Company Name	City	Country	Product Name	Qty	Unit Price
01-Jan-08	Nancy	Davolio	Eastern Connection	London	UK	Thüringer Rostbratwurst	21	99.00
01-Jan-08	Nancy	Davolio	Eastern Connection	London	UK	Steeleye Stout	35	14.40
01-Jan-08	Nancy	Davolio	Eastern Connection	London	UK	Maxilaku	30	16.00

Total
2,079.00
504.00
480.00

We'll discover a solution to this problem later in: *Lesson 7-2: Use Page Layout view to adjust margins.*

4 Print a copy of the worksheet.

If you'd like to save the forests (and save the cost of sixteen sheets of paper) you may wish to skip this step.

Click the *Print* button.

Even if you didn't actually print the worksheet, I'm sure you will believe that the print out would not have been very good. You'd be back to the scissors and tape if you wanted the pages to show that missing last column.

The printout will be in *Landscape* orientation because you've told Excel to do that.

5 Save your work as *Sales Report-1*.

important

If you are in North America or Canada you may see a slightly different printout

If you are in North America or Canada your printer will probably contain Letter size paper.

The sample file has been set up for A4 size paper.

You'll still be able to complete all lessons in this session, but you may find that screen grabs and any hard copy printed is slightly different to that shown in the book.

International differences in paper sizes will be discussed in depth in the sidebar "A4 and Letter Paper Size" in: *Lesson 7-4: Set paper size and scale.*

Lesson 7-2: Use Page Layout view to adjust margins

Page Layout view was added to Excel for the first time in the 2007 release.

It's a bit like Print Preview as you can see just how your page prints. The big difference is that, unlike Print Preview, you can edit a worksheet in this view. You can also set up many page layout features including margins, headers, footers and page numbering.

We'll be exploring all of this view's features in coming lessons. This lesson will focus upon changing the page margins (the blank areas at the top, bottom, left and right of the printout).

1   Open *Sales Report-1* from your sample files folder (if it isn't already open).

2   Display Page Layout view.

The fastest way to do this is to click the *Page Layout* button on the status bar at the bottom right of the screen.

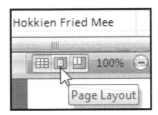

You can also do this from the Ribbon by clicking:

View→Workbook Views→Page Layout

Page layout shows almost exactly how the worksheet will print.

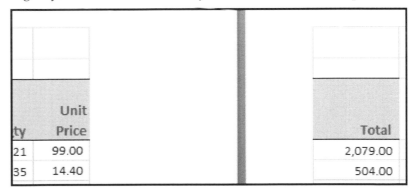

The missing Total problem is immediately obvious.

3   Make sure the rulers are on display.

Unless you've turned them off, you'll see a ruler at the top and left of the page that contains the active cell.

Click cell A1, to make it the active cell, and look for the rulers.

Sales Report-1

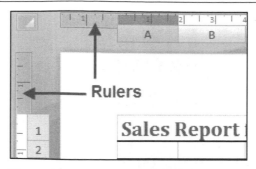

Rulers

If you don't see the rulers switch them on by clicking:

View→Show/Hide→Ruler

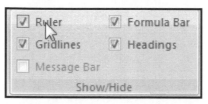

4   Adjust the left and right margins using the rulers.

1.   Hover the mouse cursor over the ruler at the point directly above the left-hand side of the column A header.

The cursor shape changes to a double headed arrow and the current left-hand margin size is displayed. (See sidebar if the margin doesn't display in centimeters)

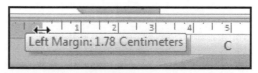

2.   When you see the double-headed arrow, click and drag to the left to reduce the margin to about one centimeter. You'll probably find it impossible to set exactly 1.0 centimeters with this method and will have to settle for 1.01.

3.   Repeat the same operation to adjust the right hand margin to about one centimeter.

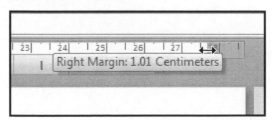

All of the columns now fit onto one page. Notice that even though the margins are equal, the right hand margin seems too wide. We'll learn how to make the margins even in: *Lesson 7-3: Use Page Setup to set margins more precisely and center the worksheet.*

5   Save your work as *Sales Report-2.*

---

note

Changing ruler units to inches, centimeters or millimeters

1.   Click:

File→Options→ Advanced→ Display→Ruler Units

2.   Select *Inches, Centimeters* or *Millimeters* from the *Ruler Units* drop-down list.

note

Can I change the default margin settings?

You can set the default margins, and any other Excel default setting, by changing the default template.

1.   Create a template consisting of a blank worksheet with the margins set to the required value.

(Creating templates was covered in: *Lesson 3-14: Create a template*).

2.   Save the template to the Excel startup folder with the name Book.

More information is provided in the sidebar "Can I Change the Default Theme?" in: *Lesson 4-8: Understand themes.*

Lesson 7-3: Use Page Setup to set margins more precisely and center the worksheet

In the last lesson you adjusted the margins using the rulers, and that's often the best way. It is quick and easy and you can immediately see the results of the change on the printed output.

Sometimes you will want the pages in your report to have precise margins. This would be the case when you were going to insert the report into another report (perhaps prepared in Word) and you need the margins to be consistent throughout the publication.

Another common requirement is the need to center the report on the printed page.

1   Open *Sales Report-2* from your sample files folder (if it isn't already open).

2   Display Page Layout view (if you aren't already in it).

This was covered in: *Lesson 7-2: Use Page Layout view to adjust margins.*

3   Click Page Layout→Page Setup→Margins.

A rich menu appears showing three standard margin setups along with the last custom margins applied.

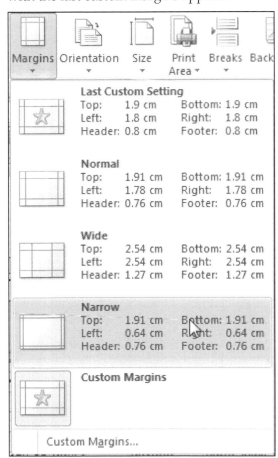

Sales Report-2

4   Click the *Narrow* option to apply left and right margins of 0.64cm.

Notice that all of the margins have now changed to the *Narrow* specification.

5   Set a custom left and right margin of exactly one centimeter.

Let's imagine that this report will be bound within another that uses margins of one centimeter.

Since there's no suitable preset we'll have to apply the margins manually using the *Custom Margins* options.

1. Click:

   Page Layout→Page Setup→Margins→Custom Margins…

   The *Page Setup* dialog appears with the *Margins* tab selected.

2. Type directly into the text boxes, or use the spin buttons, to set the left and right margins to exactly one centimeter.

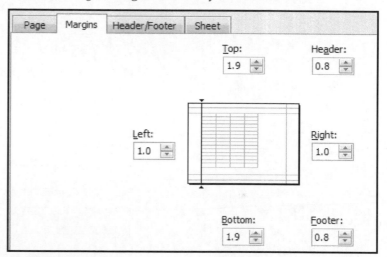

3. Click the OK button.

6   Horizontally center the printout on the page.

The page would look better centered.

1. Bring up the *Print Layout* dialog again by clicking:

   Page Layout→Page Setup→Margins→Custom Margins…

2. Check the *Center on page Horizontally* check box.

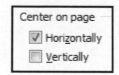

3. Click the OK button.

   The page is now perfectly centered, both on the screen and on any hard copy printed.

7   Save your work as *Sales Report-3.*

Lesson 7-4: Set paper size and scale

Let's imagine that *Landscape* mode isn't an option for you.

You need *Portrait* mode and you simply must get all of the columns on each page.

There's only two ways you can achieve this.

1. Buy some bigger paper. As long as your printer can accept it you will have a larger area upon which to print.

2. Print everything in a smaller font.

The second option often works well (as long as you have good eyesight).

You'll be relieved to know that you don't have to manually re-format every font on the page. You can automatically scale the existing fonts to fit.

1   Open *Sales Report-3* from your sample files folder (if it isn't already open).

2   Display *Page Layout* view (if you aren't already in it).

This was covered in: *Lesson 7-2: Use Page Layout view to adjust margins.*

3   Change the paper orientation back to *Portrait*.

Click Page Layout→Page Setup→Orientation→Portrait.

Notice that the columns no longer fit upon one sheet of paper.

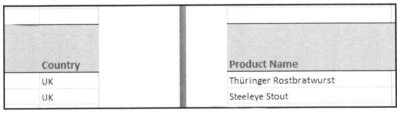

4   Change the paper size to A3.

You will not see an A3 printer option if there are no printer drivers installed on your machine that support A3 (see sidebar).

Click Page Layout→Page Setup→Size→A3.

In the USA and Canada the nearest equivalent of A3 is ANSI B 17X11 (see sidebar on the facing page for more on this). For the purposes of this lesson you should still set the size to A3 if you are able to.

That works fine. All columns now fit across one sheet of A3 paper.

But what if you don't have an A3 printer, or if the report has to fit on a sheet of A4 (or Letter sized) paper?

5   Change the paper size to A4 (or Letter sized).

Everywhere in the world except the USA and Canada the normal business paper size is A4.

Sales Report-3

trivia

A4 and Letter paper size

A long time ago everybody used different sizes of paper until the Germans produced a DIN standard (Din 476) in 1922.

So good and great was their DIN standard (that defined the familiar A0, A1, A2, A3, A4... A8 sizes) that it was gradually adopted by every country in the world except the United States and Canada. It is also the official United Nations document format.

As Din 476 was now a world standard, it was ratified in 1975 as ISO 216.

The genius behind the guiding principle of ISO 216 was the German scientist George Lichtenburg (1742-1799). George noticed that if a sheet of paper with an aspect ratio of the square root of two was folded in half, each half would also have the same aspect ratio.

The wonderful thing about this system is that paper merchants only need stock one size of paper (A0) to be able to cut A1, A2, A3, A4...A8 without any waste. It also means that a document designed in any A size will perfectly scale to all other sizes in the series.

A0 has an area of 1 square metre. Fold it in half and you have A1. Fold that in half for A2, then in half again for A3 and so on.

The USA and Canada are the only major countries that use a different system.

In 1995 the American National Standards institute defined a series of paper sizes based upon 8.5"X11" *Letter sized* paper. Unlike the ISO standard, the arbitrary size means that the series has alternating aspect ratios for other derivative sizes.

The ANSI A size (8.5X11) is the nearest to ISO A4 and the ANSI B size (17X11) is nearest to A3.

In the USA and Canada the slightly narrower and longer Letter size (or ANSI A) is the most common.

6   Make the report fit on a sheet of A4 (or Letter size) paper by scaling the print.

Click the Page Layout→Scale to Fit→Scale spin button. Each time you reduce the percentage the worksheet shrinks until it fits the page at about 70%.

Bear in mind that even though it fits the page, it may not be very easy to read at such a small type size.

Another method of achieving the same result would have been to set the Width to one page.

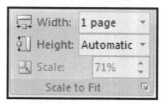

The advantage of this approach is that the content will perfectly fit between the page margins. This will look better and will avoid the need to center the printout on the page.

7   Save your work as *Sales Report-4.*

Lesson 7-5: Insert, delete and preview page breaks

note

If you don't see the dotted line page breaks, somebody has switched them off

By default, page breaks are shown as dotted lines in Normal view.

Like so many features in Excel, Microsoft has given users the ability to switch this feature off, though I can't imagine why anybody would want to.

If you don't see the dotted lines then somebody has done just that on your machine.

To bring the dotted lines back click:

File→Options→ Advanced→ Display Options for This Worksheet→Show Page Breaks

This check box needs to be checked in order to display page breaks in Normal view.

After you've either printed a worksheet (or entered *Print Preview* view and then returned to *Normal* view), you will see thin dotted lines indicating where the page will break.

Sometimes you need to take control of page breaks. This lesson shows you how.

1 Open *Sales Analysis Chart* from your sample file folder.

2 Display Normal View (if you aren't already in it).

Click the *Normal View* button at the bottom right of the screen.

Note that no page breaks are shown. This is because the worksheet has never been printed or previewed.

3 Use the Backstage Print view to Print Preview the worksheet.

Click File→Print.

The *Print Preview* reveals that the printout will cut the pie chart in half:

09-Oct-07 Germany	Dairy Products	1,112.00	USA
10-Oct-07 Spain	Condiments	422.40	Venezuela
10-Oct-07 Spain	Grains/Cereals	249.60	Grand Total
10-Oct-07 Spain	Beverages	310.00	
11-Oct-07 Sweden	Beverages	304.00	
11-Oct-07 Sweden	Dairy Products	672.00	
11-Oct-07 Sweden	Seafood	579.00	

We need to solve this problem by inserting a vertical page break.

4 Return to Normal view and note that page breaks are shown as dotted lines.

Click the *Home* tab on the Ribbon to return to Normal view and note the vertical dotted lines showing the vertical and horizontal page breaks.

If you don't see any dotted lines somebody may have disabled them. See the sidebar for instructions on how to switch them back on.

	A	B	C	D	E	F	G
50	22-Oct-07 Ireland	Dairy Products	200.00				
51	22-Oct-07 Ireland	Dairy Products	122.88				

It is immediately clear where the problem lies. The vertical break needs to occur at the left of column E to solve the problem.

5 Insert a page break to the left of column E.

1. Click cell E1. It is important to choose row 1 otherwise both a horizontal and vertical page break would be inserted.

2. Click Page Layout→Page Setup→Breaks→Insert Page Break.

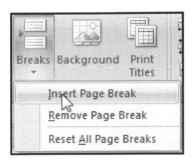

Sales Analysis Charts

The dotted line moves to the left of the active cell to show the new position of the vertical page break.

	D	E	F	G
1				
2	Sales		Sales By Country	
3	154.00		Country	Total Sales
4	86.40		Argentina ⬤	762.60

6   Click File→Print to Print Preview the worksheet (or view the page in Page Layout view) to confirm that the worksheet will now print correctly.

7   Click the Home tab on the Ribbon to return to Normal view.

8   Insert a horizontal page break above row 78.

Row 78 displays the first sale for November 2007.

75	31-Oct-07 Germany	Beverages	216.00
76			37,515.73
77			
78	01-Nov-07 USA	Condiments	616.00

For presentational reasons you want each month to begin on a new page so need to insert a page break above row 78.

1.   Click in cell A78. It's important to click in column A otherwise both a horizontal and vertical page break would be inserted to the left of, and above the active cell.

2.   Click Page Layout→Page Setup→Breaks→Insert Page Break.

A dotted line appears above the active cell (row 78) to show the position of the new horizontal page break.

	A	B	C	D
76				37,515.73
77				
78	01-Nov-07 USA		Condiments	616.00

9   Click File→Print to Print Preview the worksheet (or view the page in Page Layout view) to confirm that the worksheet will now print correctly.

The page now breaks at row 77 and a new page begins for row 78.

10   Remove the horizontal page break above row 78.

Click anywhere in row 78 except cell E78. If you were to select cell E78 you would remove both the horizontal and vertical page breaks.

Click Page Layout→Page Setup→Breaks→Remove Page Break.

The dotted line disappears indicating that the page will no longer break before row 78.

11   Save your work as *Sales Analysis Chart-1*.

Lesson 7-6: Adjust page breaks using Page Break Preview

In the last lesson we learned how to adjust page breaks in Normal view. Many users also like to adjust page breaks in Page Layout view.

Microsoft recommends that you don't use either. There's a purpose-built view just to handle page breaks called Page Break Preview view.

I tie my tongue in knots during my classes just trying to say *Page Break Preview view*!

This view allows you to move page breaks (something you can't do with the other views) and to identify which breaks are manually inserted and which are automatic breaks (created by Excel).

1 Open *Sales Analysis Chart-1* from your sample file folder (if it isn't already open).

2 Display *Page Break Preview* view.

Click the *Page Break Preview* button at the bottom right of the screen.

You can also select this view from the Ribbon by clicking:

View→Workbook Views→Page Break Preview

If it is the first time you've used this view, a dialog will appear.

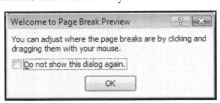

Check the box before you click OK and it won't bother you next time.

Page Break Preview allows you to see which breaks are manual and which are automatic. Breaks shown as solid lines were manually inserted. Breaks shown as dotted lines were automatically inserted by Excel.

Areas that will not print are also easy to see in this view as they are shaded gray.

	A	B	C	D	E
49	22-Oct-07	Ireland	Beverages	85.12	
50	22-Oct-07	Ireland	Dairy Products	200.00	
51	22-Oct-07	Ireland	Dairy Products	122.88	
52	22-Oct-07	Ireland	Produce	1,628.16	

Notice that your manually inserted vertical break (to the left of column E) is shown as a solid line while Excel's automatic page break (after row 50) is shown as a dotted line.

Page Break Preview

Sales Analysis
Charts-1

tip

In Page Break Preview you can enter page breaks using a right-click

It is usually quicker to add page breaks by using the shortcut menu – the menu that appears when you right-click a cell.

1. Right-click the cell that you want the page break to appear above, or to the left of.

2. Click *Insert Page Break* from the shortcut menu.

3 Move the automatic break from between rows 101 and 102 to between rows 77 and 78.

1. Move the mouse cursor over the dotted blue line between rows 101 and 102 until you see the double-headed arrow cursor shape.

2. When you see the double-headed arrow, click and drag to move the page break up the page so that the line is between rows 77 and 78.

Notice that the page break is now shown as a solid blue line.

4 Automatically scale the sheet so that all of November's sales fit on one sheet.

An interesting feature of Page Break Preview is its ability to scale a page to fit the paper. We did this manually in: *Lesson 7-4: Set paper size and scale*. The process is far more intuitive in this view.

1. Scroll to row 128. Notice that there is an automatic page break between rows 128 and 129.

2. Drag this page break to a new position between rows 145 and 146.

Excel hasn't inserted another automatic break anywhere in Page 3 even though Page 3 is now a lot longer than it was before. The only way Excel can possibly print Page 3 is by automatically scaling it down to fit the page.

3. Click File→Print to Print Preview the worksheet and notice that the fonts for the entire report have been reduced. Excel cannot scale a single page in isolation; it scales all pages to keep the font size of all report pages consistent.

4. Click the *Home* tab on the Ribbon to return to *Page Break Preview* view.

Excel's automatic scaling system means that it is easy to lose track of what is happening. Sometimes you want to set everything back the way it used to be and start again.

5 Remove all manually applied page breaks.

Click Page Layout→Page Setup→Breaks→Reset All Page Breaks.

All solid lines disappear and Excel's automatic page breaks reappear.

6 Save your work as *Sales Analysis Chart-2*.

Lesson 7-7: Add auto-headers and auto-footers and set the starting page number

Headers and footers are displayed at the top and bottom of each printed page.

If you are printing a long report it is very useful to add page numbers. Other items commonly added to page headers and footers include:

- A title.

- The date and time that the report was printed.

- The report author's name.

- The name of the Excel file that was used to generate the report.

- The full path to the Excel file.

- A company logo.

- Copyright notices.

- A distribution list or the security level of the document (for example you may want to include the word: *Confidential*).

1 Open *Sales Report-4* from your sample files folder.

2 Display Page Layout view (if you aren't already in it).

This was covered in: *Lesson 7-2: Use Page Layout view to adjust margins*.

3 Click in the Page Header area at the top of the screen.

The page header area contains the text: *Click to add header*.

> Click to add header

When you click in this area a new tab appears on the Ribbon.

We will use this tab to access Excel's Auto Header and Footer feature.

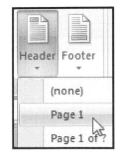

4 Add an Auto-header that will display page numbers at the top of each page in the format: *Page 1*.

When you click in the header area you are able to access the *Header & Footer Tools Design* tab.

1. Click:

   Header & Footer Tools→Design→Header & Footer→Header

2. Choose the option *Page 1* (see sidebar). Page numbers are now shown at the top of each page.

Sales Report-4

Page 1

5   Add an Auto-footer to show the filename at the bottom of the page.

   1.   Click in the *Click to add footer* area at the bottom of the page.

   Click to add footer

   2.   Click:

   Header & Footer Tools→Design→Header & Footer→Footer

   3.   Choose the Sales *Report-4* item from the drop down list (see sidebar).

   The filename is now shown at the bottom of every page in the report.

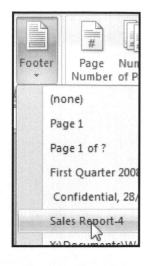

	Montréal	Canada	Steeleye
	Montréal	Canada	Côte de
	Sales Report-4		

6   Change the page numbering so that numbering begins at page ten.

   It is very common to print an Excel report and then collate it into another report (perhaps produced using Word). If the pages were to be inserted after page nine we would want Excel to begin numbering at page ten.

   1.   Click Page Layout→Page Setup→Dialog Launcher.

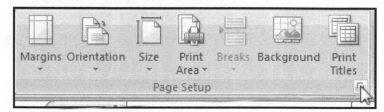

   2.   Click the *Page* tab and type the number 10 into the *First page number* text box.

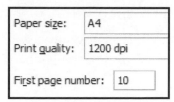

   Click the OK button. Page numbering now begins at Page 10.

   Page 10

7   Save your work as *Sales Report-5.*

Lesson 7-8: Add custom headers and footers

Auto-headers and footers provide a quick and convenient method when your needs are simple. Custom headers allow you to combine your own text with report fields (such as page numbers). You are also able to add text to three different sections in the header and footer areas (Left, Right and Center).

1 Open *Sales Report-5* from your sample files folder (if it isn't already open).

2 Display *Page Layout* view (if you aren't already in it).

This was covered in: *Lesson 7-2: Use Page Layout view to adjust margins*.

3 Click on the Page Header area.

Notice that when you click the Page Header area the contents change from *Page 10* to *Page &[Page]*.

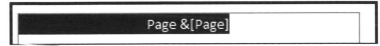

Page &[Page]

The Ampersand (&) is called an *Escape Character*. It tells Excel that whatever text follows is a field rather than literal text. The field &[Page] tells Excel to insert the current page number.

4 Change the page header to: *The Gourmet Food Company*.

Click in the center of the header area (where you currently see the page number) and type **The Gourmet Food Company**.

5 Place the date and time on the left-hand part of the page header.

There's no Auto-header for date and time. In this case you'll have to create your own custom header field.

1. Click in the **left-hand** section of the header area.

Header

The Gou

2. Type the text **Printed on:** followed by a space.

3. Click Header & Footer Tools→Design→ Header & Footer Elements→Current Date.

Current Date   Current Time

4. Type a space followed by **at:** and then another space.

5. Click Header & Footer Tools→Design→ Header & Footer Elements→Current Time

The left-hand section of the header bar now contains the following text:

Header

Printed on: &[Date] at: &[Time]

Sales Report-5

note

Adding a graphical header

Sometimes you will need a page header that requires more sophisticated formatting than Excel is capable of. The solution is to create the header as a graphic using a program such as Adobe Photoshop.

When the graphic has been prepared click:

Header & Footer→Design→ Header & Footer Elements→ Picture

You are then able to insert the graphic into the header.

When a graphic appears in the header a new *Format Picture* button appears in *the Header & Footer Elements* group.

When you click away from the Header section the date and time are displayed. The date is displayed in a format dictated by the locale of your operating system. In this example it is the date: 31st Aug 2008 displayed in UK format (day/month/year):

> Printed on: 31/08/2008 at: 14:30

6   Place the page number on the right-hand side of the page header.

This time there is an Auto Header to suit but you can't use it. Auto headers may only be used in the center section of the header. We'll have to make our own using the Header & Footer Elements just as we did for the date and time.

1.   Click in the right hand part of the page header and type **Page:** followed by a space (the last space won't appear on screen but don't worry, it is there).

2.   Click Header & Footer Tools→Design→ Header & Footer Elements→Page Number.

3.   The right hand section of the header bar now contains the following text:

> Page: &[Page]

When you click away from the Header section, the current page number is displayed:

> Page: 10

| Printed on: 31/08/2008 at 14:52 | The Gourmet Food Company | Page: 10 |

7   Apply an attractive format to the page header section.

1.   Click the left-hand section of the header. The text is automatically selected.

> Header
> Printed on: &[Date] at &[Time]

note

Good design practice

It is always a good idea to restrict your font choice to one of the two provided by the current theme.

The reasons for this are discussed in *Lesson 4-10: Add color and gradient effects to cells* (sidebar).

2.   Click Home→Font→Font and set the font face to *Cambria 10 Point Bold*. Note that, following good design practice, this is one of the two theme fonts (see sidebar).

3.   Click Home→Font→Font Color and set the color to the *Dark Blue, Text 2* theme color.

4.   Apply the same format to the right-hand section of the header.

5.   Format the center section of the header as *Cambria 28 point, Dark Blue, Text 2*.

| Printed on: 31/08/2008 at 15:06 | **The Gourmet Food Company** | Page: 10 |

8   Save your work as *Sales Report-6.*

Lesson 7-9: Specify different headers and footers for the first, odd and even pages

If you look at the pages in this book you'll notice that there's a different header and footer for odd and even pages. The first page of each session is also different.

If the sample worksheet needed to be inserted into a publication similar to this one, you'd need to specify three different headers and footers, one for odd pages, one for even pages, and one for the first page.

1   *Open Sales Report-6 from your sample files folder (if it isn't already open.*

2   Display normal view (if you aren't already in it).

    Click the normal view button at the bottom right of the screen.

3   Insert five blank rows above row 1.

    This was covered in: *Lesson 3-1: Insert and delete rows and columns.*

4   Insert a manual page break above row 6.

    This was covered in: *Lesson 7-5: Insert, delete and preview page breaks.*

    A dotted line appears above row 6.

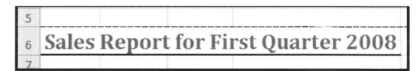

5   Merge and center cells A2:J2 and enter the text: **Sales Report Jan-Mar 2008**.

    This was covered in: *Lesson 4-6: Merge cells, wrap text and expand/collapse the formula bar.*

6   Apply the *Title* style to the newly added text.

    This was covered in: *Lesson 4-9: Use cell styles and change themes.*

7   Merge and center cells A3:J3 and enter the text *Private & Confidential*.

8   Apply the *Heading 4* style to the newly added text.

9   Apply a fill color of *Blue, Accent1, Lighter 80%* to cells A2:A3.

10   Resize Row 1 so that it is three or four centimeters deep.

11   Print Preview the worksheet.

Sales Report-6

We've created a cover sheet for the report. It doesn't look bad but the header and footer are spoiling things. We need to suppress the header and footer from the cover sheet.

12 Remove the header and footer from the first (cover) page.

    1. Change to *Page Layout* view.

    2. Click in the *Header* area of the first page.

    3. Click Header & Footer Tools→Design→ Options→Different First Page.

       The header and footer information vanishes from the cover page.

13 Set a different odd and even page header and footer.

    1. Click in the Header area.

    2. Click Header & Footer Tools→Design→ Options→Different Odd & Even Pages.

       The header and footer information vanishes from odd pages but remains on even pages.

14 Remove all header and footer information.

We're going to replace the existing page header and footer so delete the contents of all header and footer sections.

15 Add odd and even page footers so that the page number appears on the right of all odd pages and on the left of all even pages.

If you look at the footer of this book, you will see that the page numbers are arranged in this manner.

    1. Click in the footer area of one of the pages.

       Notice that when you click in the footer area, Excel indicates which footer you are editing (odd or even).

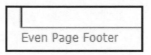

    2. Insert a page number into the odd and even page footer area.

If you're wondering why Excel thinks that even pages are odd, and odd pages are even, see the sidebar for an explanation.

While a cover page is useful in all reports, the different odd and even page headers will only improve the presentation of reports that will be printed on both sides of the paper and then bound.

16 Save your work as *Sales Report-7.*

Important

Page numbering confusion

We have set this workbook to begin its page numbering at page 10 (an even page).

As far as Excel is concerned the "real" starting page number is page one (an odd page).

This can cause a little confusion as you will find:

> Even Page Header

... at the top of the second page in this report even though it has a page number of eleven and is thus an odd page.

Excel uses the "real" page numbers when it labels the page header and footer areas.

note

Print areas do not have to be contiguous

You may want to print several different sections from your worksheet.`

Simply select the non-contiguous (non-adjacent) ranges (covered in: *Lesson 2-7: Select non-contiguous cell ranges and view summary information*) and then use either of the techniques discussed in this lesson to print the selected cells.

trivia

Origins of the term: "One-off"

Many years ago, I studied engineering and spent part of my time discovering the joys of lathes, milling machines, grinders and all of the other paraphernalia found in machine shops.

Sometimes I would wander around the factory where the lathe operators would sit next to their machines – usually reading a book.

They would have a specification drawing next to them with something like "600 Off" written on it. This would mean that they would make 600 parts to the defined specification.

A One-off would be quite unusual as it would be expensive to set-up the lathe to produce just one part.

The term "one-off" is now commonly used in the UK to describe something that happens, or is made, only once.

Sales Report-7

Lesson 7-10: Print only part of a worksheet

Sometimes you will want to only print a range of cells from a worksheet.

Excel provides two ways to do this. The first method is applicable when the requirement is a one-off. In other words, the next time you print, the entire worksheet will be printed in the usual way.

The second method involves setting a print area. If you save the worksheet, the defined print area will then persist (until you clear the print area).

In this lesson we'll explore both methods.

1   Open *Sales Report-7* from your sample files folder (if it isn't already open.

2   Display Normal view (if you aren't already in it).

Click the *Normal* view button at the bottom right of the screen.

We're going to imagine that we need to print a listing for all of January's sales.

3   Select all of the transactions for January 2008 (cells A8:J93).

4   Print only the selected cells.

1.   Click: File→Print.

The *Backstage Print* view is displayed showing many print settings along with a print preview..

Notice the first option in the *Settings* list currently shows:

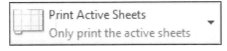

2.   Click the drop-down arrow and select *Print Selection* from the drop-down list:

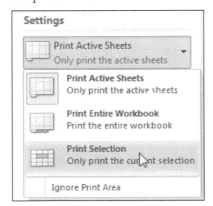

Notice that only January transactions (cells A8:J93) are now displayed in the right-hand *Print Preview* window.

If you were to click the *Print* button at this stage only January sales would be printed.

5 Save, Close and re-open the workbook and then enter *Backstage Print* view.

1. Save and close *Sales Report-7*.

2. Re-open *Sales Report-7*.

3. Click File→Print to return to *Backstage Print* view.

Notice that the print settings have reverted to *Print Active Sheets*.

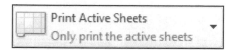

In other words, the instruction to only print the selected cells is lost when the workbook is closed.

But consider the case of a worksheet where you will only ever want to print a selected range. In this case we'd like the print settings to be saved with the workbook.

6 Set the print area to cells (A8:J93).

1. Click the *Home* tab on the Ribbon to return to the worksheet.

2. Select cells A8:J93.

3. Click Page Layout→Page Setup→Print Area→Set Print Area.

When you set the print area it remains active even if you close and re-open a workbook.

4. Click File→Print to return to *Backstage Print* view.

Notice that only January sales are shown in the preview in the right pane of the window.

7 Save Close and re-open the workbook and then enter *Backstage Print* view.

1. Save and close *Sales Report-7*.

2. Re-open *Sales Report-7*.

3. Click File→Print to return to *Backstage Print* view.

Notice that only January sales are still shown in the preview in the right pane of the window.

8 Clear the print area.

Click:

Page Layout→Page Setup→Print Area→Clear Print Area

9 Print preview to prove that the full worksheet will be printed in future.

Click File→Print to enter *Backstage Print* view.

Notice that all sales are now shown in the preview in the right pane of the window.

10 Save *Sales-Report 7*.

Lesson 7-11: Add row and column data labels and grid lines to printed output

1   Open *Sales Report-7* from your sample files folder (if it isn't already open).

2   View the worksheet in *Page Layout* view.

There's a slight problem with this worksheet. The first page is easy to understand as it has a column header row to indicate which data is in each column (such as Date, City and Company Name):

Sales Report for First Quarter 2008				
	Sales Person First Name	Sales Person Last Name		
Date			Company Name	City
01-Jan-08	Nancy	Davolio	Eastern Connection	London
01-Jan-08	Nancy	Davolio	Eastern Connection	London

The second page isn't so easy to understand because the column header row is missing:

The Gourmet Food Company			
23-Jan-08	Robert	King	Mère Paillarde
23-Jan-08	Robert	King	Mère Paillarde
24-Jan-08	Michael	Suyama	La maison d'Asie

3   Add column headings to each printed page.

1. Click Page Layout→Page Setup→Print Titles.

The *Page Setup* dialog is displayed with the *Sheet* tab selected.

2. Click inside the *Rows to repeat at top* text box.

3. Select all of Row 8 by clicking anywhere in row 8.

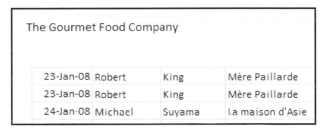

The row reference appears in the dialog.

Note that you could enter these manually if you wanted to. For example, to print rows 6 to 8 on each page you would enter **6:8** (or **$6:$8**)

4. Click the OK button

Notice that the column headings now appear for every page in the printout.

Sales Report-7

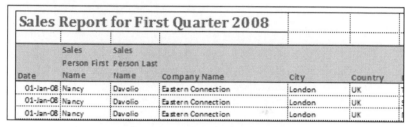

		Sales Person First Name	Sales Person Last Name		
	Date			Company Name	City
75	23-Jan-08	Robert	King	Mère Paillarde	Montréal
76	23-Jan-08	Robert	King	Mère Paillarde	Montréal

4   Add gridlines to the printout.

Sometimes it is difficult for the eye to track across printed lines. For this type of report it is useful to print gridlines onto the printed page in a similar way to the ones displayed on the worksheet.

Click Page Layout→Sheet Options→Gridlines→Print.

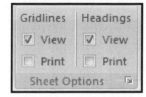

5   Print Preview the worksheet.

Click File→Print to enter Backstage Print view.

The Print Preview in the right-hand pane shows that gridlines will be printed upon each page:

Sales Report for First Quarter 2008

Date	Sales Person First Name	Sales Person Last Name	Company Name	City	Country
01-Jan-08	Nancy	Davolio	Eastern Connection	London	UK
01-Jan-08	Nancy	Davolio	Eastern Connection	London	UK
01-Jan-08	Nancy	Davolio	Eastern Connection	London	UK

6   Add row and column headings to the printout.

You may want to send a printed worksheet to a colleague and then discuss it on the telephone. It would be useful to be able to ask "what do you think of the value in cell H11?" This isn't possible because row and column headings are not shown on the printed page.

Click Page Layout→Sheet Options→Headings→Print.

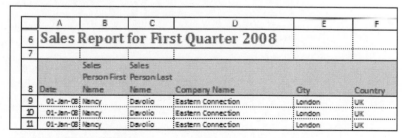

7   Print Preview the worksheet.

Click File→Print to enter Backstage Print view.

The Print Preview in the right-hand pane shows that row and column headings will be printed upon each page:

	A	B	C	D	E	F
6	**Sales Report for First Quarter 2008**					
7						
8	Date	Sales Person First Name	Sales Person Last Name	Company Name	City	Country
9	01-Jan-08	Nancy	Davolio	Eastern Connection	London	UK
10	01-Jan-08	Nancy	Davolio	Eastern Connection	London	UK
11	01-Jan-08	Nancy	Davolio	Eastern Connection	London	UK

8   Remove the gridlines and column headings from the printout.

Clear the check boxes that were ticked in the previous steps.

9   Save your work as *Sales Report-8*.

Lesson 7-12: Print several selected worksheets and change the page order.

1   Open *Palace Hotel Bar Activity* from your sample files folder.

2   Print Preview the worksheet.

Click File→Print to enter Print Backstage view.

Notice that the worksheet prints first downward (listing all activity between 11:00 AM and 4:00 PM for all days.

When it reaches the bottom of the list it moves across to print all activity between 5:00 PM and 10:00 PM and so on.

3   Change the view to *Page Break Preview*.

1. Click the *Home* tab on the ribbon to exit Backstage Print view.

2. Click the *Page Break Preview* button at the bottom right of the screen.

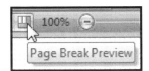

In this view it is easy to see the page order by looking at the watermarks on each page (the watermark is the transparent large gray text saying Page 1, Page 2 etc).

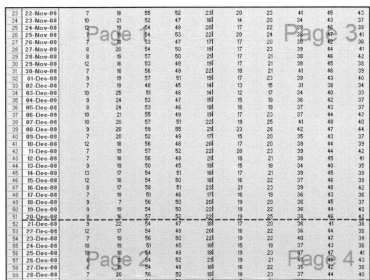

But what if you don't want to print in this order? Perhaps you would like to first print all activity for all times. In other words, you want the above display to make the existing Page 3 into
Page 2.

4   Change the print order to *Over, then down*.

1. Click Page Layout→Page Setup→Dialog Launcher.

2. Click the *Sheet* tab.

3. Click the *Over, then down* option button.

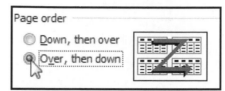

4. Click the OK button.

It can be seen from the page break preview that the order has now changed.

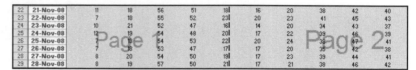

5   Print sales for Jul-Aug and Nov-Dec in one printout.

You can print several worksheets at the same time and they needn't be adjacent.

1. Click the *Jul-Aug* tab.

2. Hold down the **<Ctrl>** key and click the *Nov-Dec* tab.

Both tabs are now colored white

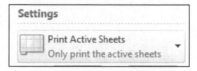

3. Click File→Print.

The Backstage Print view is displayed.

4. Note that when more than one sheet is selected, the first item in the *Settings* list has the *Print Active Sheets* option selected.

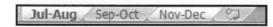

5. Click the *Next Page* button at the bottom left of the print preview to confirm that the contents of the *Jul-Aug* and *Nov-Dec* worksheets would have been printed.

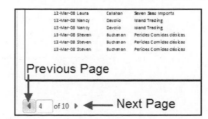

6   Save your work as *Palace Hotel Bar Activity-1*.

Lesson 7-13: Suppress error messages in printouts

Excel has several built-in error messages such as the divide by zero error:

#DIV/0!

Sometimes you're quite happy to have these errors appear in a worksheet. For example, divide by zero errors could be quite normal when there is incomplete data.

Even though the errors are fine in the worksheet, you may not want them to appear in your printed output.

1 Open *Average Revenue per Sale* from your sample files folder.

	A	B	C	D	E
1	**Average Revenue Per Sale**				
2					
3	**First Name**	**Last Name**	**Sales**	**Units**	**Average Revenue per Sale**
4	Andrew	Fuller	7,639.30	15	509.29
5	Anne	Dodsworth	-	-	#DIV/0!
6	Janet	Leverling	29,658.60	60	494.31
7	Laura	Callahan	19,271.60	40	481.79
8	Margaret	Peacock	44,795.20	90	497.72
9	Michael	Suyama	4,109.80	8	513.73
10	Nancy	Davolio	-	-	#DIV/0!
11	Robert	King	21,461.60	43	499.11
12	Steven	Buchanan	2,634.40	5	526.88
13			Total:	129,570.50	261.00	

This is an example of a worksheet with errors. In actual fact, you are simply waiting for Anne Dodsworth and Nancy Davolio to send you their sales figures so they aren't really errors.

Divide by zero errors occur because it is impossible to divide any number by zero (that's not quite correct, you can, but the result is infinity).

We'd like to print out this interim report but replace the ugly #DIV/0 errors with a blank space on the printed page..

2 Replace errors with a blank space in printed output.

1. Click Page Layout→Page Setup→Dialog launcher.

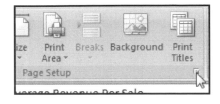

Average Revenue per Sale

The *Page Setup* dialog appears.

2. Click the *Sheet* tab.

3. Click the *Cell errors as* dropdown list and then click <blank>.

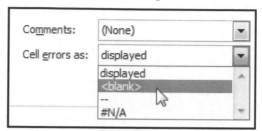

4. Click the OK button.

3   Print Preview the worksheet.

Click File→Print to open Backstage Print view.

The errors are no longer printed. Blank spaces are substituted.

Average Revenue Per Sale

First Name	Last Name	Sales	Units	Average Revenue per Sale
Andrew	Fuller	7,639.30	15	509.29
Anne	Dodsworth	-	-	
Janet	Leverling	29,658.60	60	494.31
Laura	Callahan	19,271.60	40	481.79
Margaret	Peacock	44,795.20	90	497.72
Michael	Suyama	4,109.80	8	513.73
Nancy	Davolio	-	-	
Robert	King	21,461.60	43	499.11
Steven	Buchanan	2,634.40	5	526.88
	Total:	**129,570.50**	**261.00**	

4   Save your work as *Average Revenue per Sale-1.*

Session 7: Exercise

1 Open *Exercise 7* from your sample files folder.

2 Change to *Page Layout* view.

3 Change the left margin to about 1.0 cm using the click and drag method.

4 Click Page Layout→Page Setup→Margins and use the *Custom Margins...* option to set top and bottom margins to 2.0 cm and the right margin to 1.0 cm.

5 Horizontally center the printout on the page.

6 Change the page orientation to landscape.

7 Change the view to *Page Break Preview*.

8 Insert a horizontal page break between rows 27 and 28.

9 Move the page break so that it now occurs between row 24 and 25.

10 Change to *Page Layout* view.

11 Add an auto-header to match the following:

> Page 1 of 3

12 Make the data labels in row 1 repeat on every page.

13 Set the print area to A1:J12 and then Print Preview to prove that only these cells would be printed.

14 Clear the print area.

15 Add gridlines to the printout.

				Page 2 of 3		
Date	Sales Person First Name	Sales Person Last Name	Company Name	City	Country	
08-Jan-08	Laura	Callahan	Folies gourmandes	Lille	France	
08-Jan-08	Laura	Callahan	Folies gourmandes	Lille	France	

16 Save your work as *Exercise 7-End*.

Exercise 7

If you need help slide the page to the left

Session 7: Exercise answers

These are the questions that most students find difficult to remember:

Q 13	Q 12	Q 8	Q 5
1. Select cells A1:J12. 2. Click: Page Layout→ Page Setup→ Print Area→ Set Print Area This was covered in: *Lesson 7-10: Print only part of a worksheet.*	1. Click: Page Layout→ Page Setup→Print Titles 3. Click in the *Rows to repeat at top* text box. 4. Either click in row 1 with the mouse or type 1:1 into the box. This was covered in: *Lesson 7-11: Add row and column data labels and grid lines to printed output.*	1. Click in cell A27. 2. Click: Page Layout→ Page Setup→ Breaks→ Insert Page Break This was covered in: *Lesson 7-5: Insert, delete and preview page breaks.*	1. Click Page Layout→ Page Setup→ Dialog launcher 2. Click the Margins tab. 3. Check the *Center on page horizontally* check box. This was covered in: *Lesson 7-3: Use Page Setup to set margins more precisely and center the worksheet.*

If you have difficulty with the other questions, here are the lessons that cover the relevant skills:

1   Lesson 1-4: Download the sample files and open/navigate a workbook.

2,3   Lesson 7-2: Use Page Layout view to adjust margins.

4   Lesson 7-3: Use Page Setup to set margins more precisely and center the worksheet.

6   Lesson 7-1: Print Preview and change paper orientation.

7   Lesson 7-6: Adjust page breaks using Page Break Preview.

9   Lesson 7-6: Adjust page breaks using Page Break Preview.

10   Lesson 7-2: Use Page Layout view to adjust margins.

11   Lesson 7-7: Add auto-headers and auto-footers and set the starting page number.

14   Lesson 7-10: Print only part of a worksheet.

15   Lesson 7-11: Add row and column data labels and grid lines to printed output.

16   Lesson 1-5: Save a workbook.

Index

H

hashes
 indication that columns are too narrow by, 150
help system, 56
 <F1> key, accessing with, 57
 formula AutoComplete, accessing from within, 89
 help button, accessing with, 56
 Ribbon, accessing directly from, 57
hide rows and columns, 220
hide values, using three semicolon custom format, 157
hiding and unhiding worksheets, 258

I

Intelliprint, 283

J

justify, horizontal alignment option, 159

K

key tips, 50
keyboard shortcuts
 AutoSelect a range, 79
 AutoSum, 68
 bold, 51
 close, 27
 copy, 112
 create a mixed cell reference, 133
 cut, 113
 cycle through worksheets, 39
 fill down, 111
 find, 264
 insert a comment into a cell, 124
 insert column, 108
 insert row, 108
 italic, 51
 make a relative reference absolute, 131
 move to cell A1, 138
 paste, 112
 redo, 122
 replace, 264
 Ribbon, show/hide, 45
 save, 32
 select every cell in a worksheet, 80
 spell check, 142
 underline, 51
 undo, 122
 workbook, create new, 66

L

landscape orientation, 272
letter size paper, 279
lines, adding beneath cells, 170

M

macro enabled workbook format, 34
marching ants, 68
marquee, 68
MAX function, creating using AutoSum, 85
maximize button, 26
menus
 rich, 47
 shortcut (contextual), 51
 standard, 46
merge and center button, 160
merge, cells, 160
mini toolbar
 shortcut (contextual) menu, 51
 using when entering text, 50
minimize button, 26
mixed cell references, 132
moving
 the Excel window, 26
multiplication operator (*), 87

N

name box, 30
normal view, 52
number sign (#), 80
numbers
 changing number of decimal points displayed, 116
 using built-in styles with, 154

O

operating system
 checking version of, 16
 Windows 7, use of, 16
 Windows Vista, use of, 16
 Windows XP, use of, 16

P

page break preview view, 52
page layout view, 52, **274**
paper sizes explained, 279
paste, 112
paste special, 117
paste values, 117

Q

R

Become an Excel Expert with our Expert Skills book

The next book in the series builds upon all of the foundation skills you've learned.

There's a whole lot more to Excel, and you'll learn it all with this book. Security, advanced functions and formulas, tables, macros, pivot tables, what-if analysis... and so much more.

Search for it at **Amazon.com** or **Amazon.co.uk.**

You can also find links to book resellers stocking this title at the **ExcelCentral.com** web site (click *Books* on the top menu bar).

ExcelCentral.com

For many years I have dreamed of creating an online learning resource that would provide the same experience as my classroom courses.

My books cover the same material as my classroom courses, but it is clear that some learners need more than can be delivered via printed media. In 2013 we began the design of an Excel Internet resource that aims to bring my classroom courses onto your desktop.

The site is available at: **www.ExcelCentral.com**

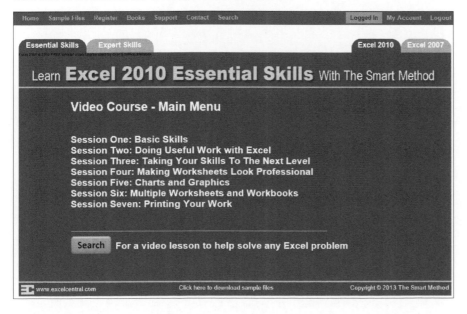

On the site I have recorded a video walk-through for each and every lesson in this book. The videos have also been indexed by keyword to provide a unique interactive Excel reference resource.

Lessons can be viewed without cost by using our *FreeView* facility.

Enhanced features can also be unlocked for a small annual subscription charge.

Printed in Great Britain
by Amazon.co.uk, Ltd.,
Marston Gate.